ROUTLEDGE LIBRARY EDITIONS:
ECONOMETRICS

Volume 14

A STRUCTURAL MODEL OF THE U.S. GOVERNMENT SECURITIES MARKET

A STRUCTURAL MODEL OF THE U.S. GOVERNMENT SECURITIES MARKET

V. VANCE ROLEY

Routledge
Taylor & Francis Group
LONDON AND NEW YORK

First published in 1979 by Garland

This edition first published in 2018
by Routledge
4 Park Square, Milton Park, Abingdon, Oxon OX14 4RN
605 Third Avenue, New York, NY 10017

Routledge is an imprint of the Taylor & Francis Group, an informa business

British Library Cataloguing in Publication Data
A catalogue record for this book is available from the British Library

ISBN: 978-0-8153-9640-6 (Set)
ISBN: 978-1-351-14012-6 (Set) (ebk)
ISBN: 978-0-8153-5021-7 (Volume 14) (hbk)
ISBN: 978-1-351-14048-5 (Volume 14) (ebk)

Publisher's Note
The publisher has gone to great lengths to ensure the quality of this reprint but points out that some imperfections in the original copies may be apparent.

Disclaimer
The publisher has made every effort to trace copyright holders and would welcome correspondence from those they have been unable to trace.

A Structural Model of the U.S. Government Securities Market

V. Vance Roley

GP

Garland Publishing, Inc.
New York & London, 1979

Library of Congress Cataloging in Publication Data

Roley, V. Vance, 1951-
A structural model of the U.S. Government securities market.

(Outstanding dissertations in economics)
Originally presented as the author's thesis, Harvard, 1977.
Bibliography: p.
1. Securities—United States—Mathematical models.
2. Bonds—United States—Mathematical models.
I. Title. II. Series.
HG4936.R58 1979 332.6'323 78-75048
ISBN 0-8240-4127-5

All volumes in this series are printed on acid-free, 250-year-life paper.

Printed in the United States of America.

A STRUCTURAL MODEL OF THE U.S. GOVERNMENT SECURITIES MARKET

A thesis presented

by

Vernon Vance Roley

to

The Department of Economics

in partial fulfillment of the requirements

for the degree of

Doctor of Philosophy

in the subject of

Economics

Harvard University

Cambridge, Massachusetts

September, 1977

TABLE OF CONTENTS

LIST OF TABLES

LIST OF FIGURES

PREFACE

My primary debts are to my thesis advisors, Benjamin M. Friedman and John Lintner. Their comments and suggestions significantly improved the presentation and content of the thesis. In addition, the experience gained during the last two years, while serving as research assistant to Professor Friedman, has been very beneficial to this research project.

The financial support of the National Bureau of Economic Research is also gratefully acknowledged. In particular, the computer time and facilities that were provided resulted in the completion of this research project in a reasonable amount of time. The financial support for the secretarial services of L. J. A. Getchell was also important for the completion of a preliminary draft of the thesis.

Finally, the final form of the thesis has benefitted from the typing of Mrs. L. Vance Roley. The time and effort spent by her on the thesis is greatly appreciated.

CHAPTER I

INTRODUCTION

A. Motivating Issues and Objectives of the Study

The market for long-term financial assets is a primary link between financial and nonfinancial economic activity. The substitutions between different types and maturities of financial assets, and the resultant effects on the nonfinancial economy, are key issues both theoretically and empirically. Nevertheless, there is an absence of an empirical model with strong theoretical underpinnings to analyze present and future financial market activity. While a plethora of forecasts are in evidence for nonfinancial economic activity over both the long- and short-run, most financial forecasts are usually either judgmental or rely on reduced form methodology which can not analyze the underlying financial structure. Clearly, a first step in investigating the interrelations between the financial and nonfinancial economy is to carefully specify the underlying structure of the key financial markets that directly and indirectly influence nonfinancial economic activity.

The formulation of a disaggregated structural model of the U.S. Government securities market provides a foundation in which to analyze one important area of financial market activity. A framework for analyzing "crowding out" effects must necessarily include the U.S. Government securities market. The U.S. Government securities market is also important in any discussion concerning a possible future shortage of financial capital. In addition, certain structural shifts concerning reform and behavioral changes of individual investor groups have implications that become apparent in a disaggregated structural model.

This study focuses primarily on the development of a structural model of the U.S. Government securities market; i.e., the specification and estimation of the demands for disaggregated maturity classes of U.S. Government securities by the individual investor groups participating in the market. A particularly important issue addressed, in this respect, involves the extent of the substitution relationship among different maturity classes of U.S. Government securities. In the model of the U.S. Government securities market, this may be inferred from the effects of relative asset supplies on the jointly determined yields on different maturity classes of U.S. Government securities, and from a comparison within investor groups of the individual asset demand equations. This issue should be resolved before issues concerning the interrelationship of the financial and nonfinancial sectors of the economy are considered.

This study also bases the specifications of the asset demands on an explicit portfolio selection theory. As a result, specific behavioral implications based on the properties of the asset demand equations are introduced. These results may be applied to any similar financial modeling problem.

B. Investors in the U.S. Government Securities Market

The categories of investors participating in the U.S. Government securities market are given, with respect to total Treasury securities outstanding as of yearend 1975, in Table 1.1. The ten investor categories marked with asterisks are those with endogenous asset demands in the model of the U.S. Government securities market. These ten investor groups hold ninety-five percent of the outstanding Treasury securities net of Federal Reserve System and foreign holdings.[1]

Apart from commercial banks, households, and state and local government general funds, the individual investor groups typically do not hold large amounts of U.S. Government securities. This is apparent either in comparison to the total amount of securities outstanding, or in comparison to other asset holdings in their respective portfolios. However, as the summary of net purchases of U.S. Government securities in Table 1.2 indicates, the absolute values of net purchases of U.S. Government securities (ΔUS) are important in comparison to absolute values of net acquisitions of financial assets (ΔW). This results from these securities serving as principle liquid assets in the portfolios of the investor

---

[1]The modeling of foreign purchases of U.S. Government securities involves areas well outside the scope of the study. Therefore, foreign purchases are taken as exogenous.

The supply of U.S. Government securities is determined by fiscal policy and the government budget constraint; and monetary policy determines the Federal Reserve System's total holdings. This results in the net amount of U.S. Government securities to be purchased by private investors. For a discussion of fiscal policy and the government budget constraint, see Carl F. Christ, "A Simple Macroeconomic Model with a Government Budget Constraint", Journal of Political Economy, LXXVI (January/February, 1968), 53-67; and William L. Silber, "Fiscal Policy in IS-LM Analysis: A Correction", Journal of Money, Credit and Banking, II (November, 1970), 461-472.

TABLE 1.1

U.S. GOVERNMENT SECURITIES OUTSTANDING AS OF YEAREND 1975

Securities Held By:	Total Amount	Percentage
Federal Reserve System	87.9	23.5
*Commercial Banks	84.6	22.6
Foreign	66.5	17.8
*Households	49.0	13.1
*State and Local Government General Funds	30.6	8.2
*Nonfinancial Corporate Businesses	14.3	3.8
*Private Pension Funds	7.9	2.1
*Savings and Loan Associations	5.4	1.4
Credit Unions	5.0	1.3
*Life Insurance Companies	4.7	1.3
*Mutual Savings Banks	4.7	1.3
*Other Insurance Companies	4.7	1.3
Sponsored Credit Agencies	3.4	1.0
*State and Local Government Retirement Funds	2.2	0.6
Security Brokers and Dealers	2.1	0.6
Investment Companies	1.1	0.3
Total	374.1	100.0

Notes to Table:
Source: Flow of Funds Accounts 1946-1975
Amounts are in billions of dollars.
Groups marked by asterisk are endogenous in the U.S. Government securities market model.
Detail may not add to total because of rounding.
Agency issues and non-negotiable savings bonds are excluded.

TABLE 1.2

SUMMARY OF NET PURCHASES OF U.S. GOVERNMENT SECURITIES

Investor Category	Average ΔW	Maximum ΔW	Average ΔUS	Maximum ΔUS	Average $\frac{\Delta US}{\Delta W}$ (%)	Maximum $\frac{\Delta US}{\Delta W}$ (%)
Commercial Banks	9.5	27.8	1.9	11.2	43.9	624.5
Households	19.2	43.7	1.7	6.3	9.1	35.5
Life Insurance Companies	2.7	5.7	0.1	0.8	3.3	14.6
Mutual Savings Banks	1.3	3.3	0.1	0.7	12.1	94.8
Nonfinancial Corporate Businesses	5.6	19.1	0.9	6.2	45.7	387.7
Other Insurance Companies	0.8	2.0	0.1	0.6	16.9	73.6
Private Pension Funds	1.7	4.1	0.2	1.6	7.7	61.4
Savings and Loan Associations	4.3	11.6	0.4	2.3	11.1	116.1
State and Local Government General Funds	1.7	5.7	0.6	2.4	62.9	814.5
State and Local Government Retirement Funds	1.3	2.9	0.2	0.5	14.7	56.1

Notes to Table:
Source: Flow of Funds Accounts 1946-1975
Amounts are in billions of dollars and refer to absolute values of quarterly flows for 1960:I-1975:IV.
Agency issues and non-negotiable savings bonds are excluded.

groups. That is, U.S. Government securities are comparatively liquid to other financial assets of similar maturities due to a highly developed secondary market and their risk characteristics. Thus, for these investor groups, U.S. Government securities are important in the short-run portfolio selection problem.

In the empirical investigation, the U.S. Government securities data are disaggregated into four weighted maturity classes.[2] The weighted maturity classes are defined in terms of four "definite" areas and three "borderline" areas. The "definite" areas include the following maturities:

(1) within 1 year (short-term),

(2) 2-4 years (short-intermediate-term),

(3) 6-8 years (long-intermediate-term),

(4) over 12 years (long-term).

U.S. Government securities with maturities in the borderline areas are allocated to the definite classifications according to a weighting scheme.[3] The primary advantage of this procedure is that it avoids the otherwise perverse effects that occur when large debt issues cross fixed maturity boundaries. For the investor groups with endogenous demands in the model, these data are presented for holdings as of yearend 1975 in Table 1.3.

Demand equations for two maturity classes of U.S. Government secur-

---

[2]See Stephen P. Taylor and John Wood, "Federal Debt by Weighted Maturity Classes for Use in Flow-of-Funds Accounts," Mimeo, Board of Governors of the Federal Reserve System, 1963.

[3]For explicit details concerning this weighting scheme, see V.C.1.

TABLE 1.3

U.S. GOVERNMENT SECURITIES OUTSTANDING BY MATURITY CLASS AS OF YEAREND 1975

Securities Held By:	Short-Term		Short-Intermediate-Term		Long-Intermediate-Term		Long-Term	
	Amount	%	Amount	%	Amount	%	Amount	%
Commercial Banks	47.8	38.1	30.7	60.0	4.9	30.6	1.1	7.6
Households	33.8	26.9	5.5	10.6	4.1	25.5	5.6	37.7
Life Insurance Companies	1.3	1.0	0.9	1.8	1.0	6.4	1.5	10.1
Mutual Savings Banks	1.9	1.5	1.7	3.4	0.6	3.8	0.5	3.4
Nonfinancial Corporate Businesses	11.8	9.4	2.0	3.9	0.3	1.6	0.2	1.2
Other Insurance Companies	1.5	1.2	1.5	3.0	1.0	6.1	0.7	4.4
Private Pension Funds	3.1	2.4	1.8	3.5	1.6	10.0	1.4	9.3
Savings and Loan Associations	2.3	1.8	2.4	4.7	0.4	2.3	0.2	1.6
State and Local Government General Funds	21.6	17.2	4.6	9.0	1.8	11.0	2.6	17.5
State and Local Government Retirement Funds	0.5	0.4	0.2	0.4	0.4	2.7	1.1	7.2
Total	125.6	100.0	51.5	100.0	16.1	100.0	14.9	100.0

Notes to Table:

Source: Board of Governors of the Federal Reserve System, "Federal Debt by Weighted Maturity Classes for use in Flow-of-Funds Accounts," unpublished.

Amounts are in billions of dollars.

Detail may not add to total because of rounding.

Data are for endogenous investor groups in the U.S. Government Securities Market Model, with agency issues and non-negotiable savings bonds excluded.

ities are estimated for each of the ten investor categories.[4] These correspond to the short-intermediate-term and long-term classifications. The two remaining maturity classifications, i.e., short-term and long-intermediate-term, will be considered in future research. The two maturity classes selected for the empirical study serve to illustrate the determinants of market yields and asset demands for two unambiguously disjoint maturity classes of U.S. Government securities.

---

[4]The one exception to this procedure involves nonfinancial corporate businesses, where only the demand for the shorter of the two maturity classes is estimated.

C. Organization of the Study

This study proceeds to specify, estimate, and simulate a structural model of the U.S. Government securities market. The specification of the model is developed in chapters II, III, and IV; and the empirical results are presented in chapter V. The main features and conclusions of this study are summarized in chapter VI.

In chapter II, the approximations utilized in the modeling of seven investor groups, i.e., the categories of investors exclusive of depository financial intermediaries, are discussed. The expected utility maximization model is used to represent the portfolio selection behavior of these investor groups, and its applicability to each investor group is discussed therein. In addition, specific expected utility models that reduce to mean-variance analysis are reviewed. The corresponding sets of asset demands are derived from these specific models, and the properties inherent in each are compared.

The analysis of chapter III further develops the mean-variance expected utility maximization model, and considers the implications of certain properties inherent in several of the resulting systems of asset demand equations. These properties include possible row and column sum constraints, and symmetry constraints, on the coefficient matrix that premultiplies the vector of expected holding-period yields. These properties are related to risk aversion; and a hypothesis concerning risk aversion is developed for empirical investigation. The effects of persistent and uncertain price inflation are also related to the properties of the coefficient matrix. However, the effects of price inflation on portfolio selection are dependent on the manner in which expectations concerning asset holding-period yields are formed.

The portfolio selection of depository financial intermediaries is investigated in chapter IV. These investor groups include commercial banks, mutual savings banks, and savings and loan associations. The dependence between both sides of the balance sheet may be especially important for these investor groups. Hence, the portfolio selection model is further developed in chapter IV since the modeling of the other categories of investors abstracted from the liability side of the balance sheet. The resultant model includes many of the special features that influence the short-run portfolio behavior of depository financial intermediaries.

The empirical results for the structural model of the U.S. Government securities market are presented in chapter V. Preliminary to the empirical results, various adjustment models are introduced, based on transactions costs, that translate desired portfolio holdings into actual asset demands. The resultant specifications are then estimated; and several hypotheses concerning the substitutability between the two maturity classes,and the structure of the estimated coefficient matrix, are examined.

The simulation results for the joint determination of the disaggregated endogenous asset demands and the two endogenous interest rates are also included in chapter V. In addition, the market-clearing framework that is utilized for the simulation results is contrasted to alternative approaches.

Finally, the main conclusions resulting from this study are summarized in chapter VI. In addition, areas for future research are indicated.

CHAPTER II

MICROECONOMIC FOUNDATIONS OF ASSET DEMAND EQUATIONS

A. Introduction

This chapter applies a theory of portfolio selection to seven of the ten categories of investors considered in this study.[1] The resultant framework is modified only slightly, however, in its application to the remaining investor groups.

Section II.B includes a review and comparison of three theories of portfolio selection. These consist of the expected utility maximization model, safety-first analysis, and the maximization of the market value of equity given by the Sharpe-Lintner capital asset pricing model. The effects of persistent and uncertain price inflation are also related to these models.

Expected utility is further considered in section II.C. In particular, models are considered that reduce to terms involving the mean and variance of the argument of utility function. This simplification appears

---

[1]i.e., households, life insurance companies, nonfinancial corporate businesses, other insurance companies, private pension funds, state and local government general funds, and state and local government retirement funds. Commercial banks, mutual savings banks, and savings and loan associations are excluded because of the special characteristics inherent in their portfolio selection problem. The portfolio selection theory for the depository financial intermediaries is included in chapter IV. All of the above investor groups correspond to those in Board of Governors of the Federal Reserve System, Flow of Funds Accounts, 1946-1975 (Washington, 1976).

to be necessary in order to form tractable specifications of asset demands for empirical implementation.

In section II.D, multiperiod models of portfolio selection are contrasted to one-period models. In the absence of myopic portfolio selection behavior, multiperiod models do not allow tractable specifications of asset demands.

Asset demands are derived, in section II.E, that are based on the particular specifications of expected utility models that are reviewed in section II.C. The utility functions that are considered include quadratic, negative exponential, and logarithmic utilities. Assumptions concerning the probability distributions of asset holding-period yields are considered jointly with these models.

B. Portfolio Selection Under Uncertainty

Uncertain outcomes and risks are the essence of the portfolio selection problem. The source of uncertainty is confined not only to holding-period yields, but also may include the level of stochastic liabilities. For example, commercial banks (which are not included explicitly in the analysis of this chapter) are confronted with stochastic deposit flows, and this leads to liquidity considerations in conjunction with their portfolio selection problem.

The sources of risk and uncertainty are easily revealed with respect to the holding-period yield on a portfolio.[2] The most obvious is the risk of default. Current financial conditions clearly indicate the effect of this type of risk on certain categories of debt. The risk of default is also very important in the analysis of financial intermediaries (e.g., a commercial bank's loans).

Two additional sources of uncertainty, i.e., income uncertainty and capital uncertainty,[3] depend directly on the duration of the planned holding-period. If an investor intends to liquidate his portfolio at the end of one year, then income uncertainty arises if his investment strategy is, for example, to make a series of investments in default-free three-month securities. The investor then faces an uncertain return beyond the initial three-month period. If, however, this investor

---

[2]For a succinct discussion of this matter, see David H. Pyle, "On the Theory of Financial Intermediation," Journal of Finance, XXVI (June, 1971), 737-746. A historical perspective is given in Axel Leijonhufvud, On Keynesian Economics and the Economics of Keynes (New York: Oxford University Press, 1968), pp. 286-292.

[3]See Leijonhufvud, op. cit.

were to invest in a default-free security maturing in one year, then the return is certain with respect to his nominal return after one year.

Similarly, if this same investor were to purchase a two-year default-free security, then he would be faced with capital uncertainty; i.e., the uncertainty regarding a possible capital gain or loss on the security. Therefore, even though an investor may purchase virtually default-free securities (e.g., U.S. Government securities), the chosen duration of the holding-period makes all assets risky that do not exactly match this duration.[4]

The final source of risk deals with the erosion of the real return of an asset because of price inflation. The recent history and fore-casted persistence of price inflation make this an important consideration in the portfolio selection problem, and accordingly, the effects of price inflation are investigated in conjunction with the portfolio selection models included in this chapter.

The remainder of this section considers several alternative frame-works that have been suggested for the portfolio selection problem under uncertainty. Related areas of investigation such as the choice of assets and liabilities that are taken as endogenous in the portfolio selection problem, the effects of price inflation, and initial considerations con-cerning risk aversion are also examined.

1. The Objective Function

---

[4]The investor could eradicate uncertainty altogether, in nominal terms, if he chose a portfolio that consisted entirely of cash. However, this portfolio is usually dominated by portfolios that have positive expected returns.

The choice of the objective function is taken to mean not only the choice of the functional form, but also the choice of the best representation of an investor's preferences and objectives. That is, it must be decided if the optimization problem may be represented by describing preferences in a utility function, or whether some other framework is desirable, such as a safety-first criterion or the maximization of the market value of an investor's equity.[5]

In the case of households, a utility function provides a natural choice-theoretic framework. Many of the initial presentations of utility functions, in the case of asset selection under uncertainty, could be rationalized in terms of the portfolio selection of an individual. For example, Tobin's[6] problem was the selection of a portfolio after the individual's consumption decision was made. Also, the multiperiod consumption-investment problem of an individual readily adapts to a utility maximization framework.[7]

Nevertheless, it is conceivable that the use of a utility function in the portfolio selection problems of financial institutions, and other investor groups, may not afford the best representations of their particular portfolio selection problems. Thus, the two previously mentioned alternatives, i.e., safety-first and the maximization of the market value

---

[5]This latter alternative may, of course, be directly applied only to a subset of the investor groups in this study.

[6]James Tobin, "Liquidity Preference as Behavior Toward Risk," Review of Economic Studies, XXV (February, 1958), 65-86.

[7]e.g., Eugene F. Fama, "Multiperiod Consumption-Investment Decisions," American Economic Review, LX (March, 1970), 163-174.

of the investor's equity, will be examined in order to indicate any advantages they may have in comparison to expected utility maximization.

The objective function may be utilized not only in conjunction with its role in the selection of the composition of a portfolio, but also in broader issues concerning the existence and scale of a financial firm. Hart and Jaffee,[8] for example, have determined the scale of a depository financial intermediary in an expected utility maximization framework. Others[9] have presented conditions for the existence of financial intermediation conditional on the optimization framework hypothesized. Thus, these issues are considered in the context of the selection of an objective function in the discussion that follows.

2. Preferences and Objectives Represented by a Utility Function

The asset demand equations that are ultimately used in the empirical estimation in this study are based on expected utility maximization. This approach has several attributes that make it especially appealing to the portfolio selection problem considered herein; the predominant factors being its flexible approach to allow for a wide range of application, and the explicit, although general, treatment of risk aversion.

The multifarious set of investor groups, to which the portfolio selection model is applied, necessitates a general model of this kind.

---

[8]Oliver D. Hart and Dwight M. Jaffee, "On the Application of Portfolio Theory to Depository Financial Intermediaries," Review of Economic Studies, XLI (January, 1974), 129-147.

[9]e.g., Pyle, "On the Theory of Financial Intermediation," op.cit.; and John J. Pringle, "The Imperfect-Markets Model of Commercial Bank Financial Management," Journal of Financial and Quantitative Analysis, IX (January, 1974), 69-87.

Thus, expected utility maximization is taken as an approximation to the decision problems facing each investor group. This framework is flexible enough, however, to incorporate many of the investor groups' special characteristics.

As is shown below in this chapter, the set of asset demand equations, that result from the optimization problem, can be constructed in a manner that is consistent with previous financial modeling approaches. These include the Brainard-Tobin[10] model, and Friedman's[11] corporate bond market model. The asset demand equations, in these models, are linear homogeneous in wealth prior to their respective portfolio adjustment processes.[12] These models also have column adding-up constraints on the coefficients of each right-hand-side variable. The asset demand equations derived in this chapter have, in addition to these properties, symmetry constraints across equations on their coefficients.[13]

The expected utility hypothesis is based on a set of plausible assumptions[14] concerning the preference ordering of alternative probability

---

[10]William C. Brainard and James Tobin, "Pitfalls in Financial Model-Building," American Economic Review, LVII (May, 1968), 99-122.

[11]Benjamin M. Friedman, "A Structural Model of the Long-Term Corporate Debt Market," Mimeo, Harvard University, 1974; and Benjamin M. Friedman, "Financial Flow Variables and the Short-Run Determination of Long-Term Interest Rates," Mimeo, Harvard University, 1975.

[12]See chapter V for a discussion concerning portfolio adjustment models.

[13]This implies that there are also row adding-up constraints. The symmetry property is discussed in detail, for the general case, in chapter III.

[14]The modern axiomatic development of the expected utility hypothesis was presented by von Neumann and Morgenstern. See J. von Neumann and O. Morgenstern, Theory of Games and Economic Behavior (Princeton: Princeton

distributions of returns.[15] A preference ordering is consistent, with respect to the von Neumann-Morgenstern axioms, if for any two distributions $F_i(X)$ and $F_j(X)$, $F_j(X)$ is preferred to $F_i(X)$ if, and only if, it can be represented by a utility function U(X) such that

$$E[U(X) \mid F_i(X)] < E[U(X) \mid F_j(X)].^{16}$$

The unrestrictive assumptions concerning expected utility maximization can be contrasted directly to the alternative approaches considered below, i.e., safety-first and the maximization of the market value of an investor's equity. In the first case, an arbitrary preassigned disaster level must be specified; and, in the second case, restrictive behavioral and perfect markets assumptions are often utilized to form the criterion that the investor maximizes.

The application of the expected utility framework, to the diverse set of investors in the U.S.Government securities market, may be rationalized by an argument similar to that set forth, in a somewhat different context, by Lintner.[17] The problem that Lintner examined was the effect

---

University Press, 1947); chapter 1 contains the original von Neumann-Morgenstern approach. Many texts concerning statistical decision theory also include an axiomatic development of the expected utility hypothesis. See, for example, Morris H. DeGroot, Optimal Statistical Decisions (New York: McGraw-Hill, 1970).

[15]The probability distributions are usually either taken to represent stochastic returns, rates of return, or terminal values of wealth. For a discussion concerning the alternative arguments of the utility function, see II.B.2b.

[16]Where $E[U(X) \mid F_i(X)] = \int_{-\infty}^{+\infty} U(X)dF_i(X)$.
See DeGroot, op.cit., p. 113; and K. Borch, "A Note on Uncertainty and Indifference Curves," Review of Economic Studies, XXVI (January, 1969), 1-4.

[17]John Lintner, "The Impact of Uncertainty on the 'Traditional' Theory of the Firm," in J. W. Markham and G. F. Papanek (eds.), Industrial

of uncertainty on the traditional theory of the firm. He assumed that a firm is a profit-maximizer subject to risk aversion. This was represented by having the firm maximize the expected value of a utility function depicting a risk averse preference ordering.[18]

The expected utility methodology, in Lintner's analysis, is demonstrated to be applicable to a wide range of decision problems by varying the degree of absolute risk aversion.[19] In particular, Lintner asserts that absolute risk aversion is a declining function of wealth for "large" decisions,[20] a positive but constant function of wealth for "intermediate" decisions, and zero (risk-neutral) for "small" decisions.[21]

The implications of the above are that expected utility maximization can be adapted to become a good approximation to the portfolio selection criterion of an investor group. The extent to which this framework is applied as an approximation is discussed in greater detail in II.B.5.

Organization and Economic Development: In Honor of E.S. Mason (Boston: Houghton Mifflin, 1970), pp. 238-265.

[18]That is, the axioms of the expected utility hypothesis are satisfied and the utility function has $U'(W) > 0$ and $U''(W) < 0$, where W is terminal wealth. Ibid., p. 242. Also see II.B.7.

[19]Absolute risk aversion is defined as $-U''/U'$. See John W. Pratt, "Risk Aversion in the Small and in the Large," Econometrica, XXXII (January/April, 1964), 122-136; Kenneth J. Arrow, Essays in the Theory of Risk Bearing,(Chicago: Markham Publishing Company, 1971), pp. 94-96; or II.B.7b.

[20]This is also the position taken in the portfolio selection problem considered by Arrow. Ibid.

[21]"Large" decisions could include capital investments. "Intermediate" decisions could include the pricing of the firm's products. "Small" decisions could include inventory policy. See Lintner, "The Impact of Uncertainty on the 'Traditional' Theory of the Firm," op. cit., p. 242.

2a. Properties of a Utility Function

The following properties are often considered to be desirable for a utility function in expected utility analysis:[22]

(1) $U'(X) > 0$, i.e., marginal utility is positive;

(2) $U''(X) < 0$, i.e., marginal utility is diminishing; and

(3) $\lim_{X \to 0} U(X)$ and $\lim_{X \to +\infty} U(X)$ exist and are finite, i.e., the utility function is bounded from below and above.

The inclusion of property (2) to the list implies, by definition, that the investor is risk averse. That is, the investor prefers a certain outcome, X, over a stochastic outcome, $\tilde{X}$, that has $E(\tilde{X}) = X$.[23] However, this measure of risk aversion, i.e., $U''(X)$, is not unique for a given preference ordering. This follows from the fact that von Neumann-Morgenstern utility functions are unique only up to positive linear transformations.[24] Thus, $U''(X)$ can not be used to measure the degree of risk aversion.

This dilemma is easily escaped by considering absolute risk aversion and relative risk aversion.[25] Each of these measures are invariant under positive linear transformations.

---

[22]See Kenneth J. Arrow, Aspects of the Theory of Risk-Bearing (Helsinki: The Yrjö Jahnsson Foundation, 1965), p. 31. The argument of the utility function, X, is discussed below in II.B.2b.

[23]See II.B.7.

[24]i.e., U^* describes the same preference ordering as U, where $U^* = aU + b$, $a > 0$. See James M. Henderson and Richard E. Quandt, Microeconomic Theory: A Mathematical Approach 2nd edition (New York: McGraw-Hill Book Company, Inc., 1971), p. 46.

[25]The definitions and interpretations of these measures are reviewed below in II.B.7.

The respective degrees of absolute and relative risk aversions have also been shown to have implications for the comparative statics properties of the asset demand equations when there is a riskless asset.[26] However, as indicated in chapter III, the risk characteristics of the assets,[27] and the argument of the utility function, must be considered in conjunction with these measures of risk aversion in order to derive meaningful comparative statics results for asset demand equations.

Property (3) deals with the boundedness of the utility function. The utility function must be bounded in order to discriminate among all possible probability distributions of outcomes. If it is not bounded, then the St. Petersburg paradox could arise.

This boundedness property may be relaxed, however, by placing restrictions on the probability distributions in the choice set. These restrictions may be quite general, as Ryan[28] and Arrow[29] have shown. In addition, by specifically restricting all of the outcomes to be lognormally distributed with finite moments, the logarithmic utility function[30]

---

[26]See Arrow, Aspects of the Theory of Risk-Bearing, op.cit., pp. 43-44; and Joseph E. Stiglitz, "The Effects of Income, Wealth, and Capital Gains Taxation on Risk-Taking," Quarterly Journal of Economics, LXXXIII (May, 1969), 263-283.

[27]i.e., whether the existence of a riskless asset is postulated.

[28]Terence M. Ryan, "Unbounded Utility Functions in Expected Utility Maximization: Comment," Quarterly Journal of Economics, LXXXVIII (February, 1974), 133-135.

[29]Kenneth J. Arrow, "Unbounded Utility Functions in Expected Utility Maximization: Response," Quarterly Journal of Economics, LXXXVIII (February, 1974), 136-138.

[30]i.e., $U(X) = \log X$. The logarithmic utility function is, of course, unbounded.

may be used in the portfolio selection problem.

2b. The Argument of the Utility Function

In a strict theoretical sense, the most desirable specification for any investor group's portfolio selection problem would directly incorporate transactions costs, multiperiod horizons, and other relevant factors directly into the optimization problem. In addition, end-of-period wealth is often considered as the most suitable argument of the utility function, especially for individuals. However, the inclusion of all of these factors leads, in general, to specifications of asset demand equations that are not empirically tractable. Thus, several approximations are utilized in forming specifications of asset demand equations; one of which involves the argument of the utility function.

The approximation concerning the argument of the utility function directly appeals to the functional form of the asset demand equations. In particular, there is at least one justification in specifying the asset demands to be linear homogeneous in portfolio wealth. This concerns the desirability of this specification in the time series estimation of asset demand equations. That is, if the asset demand equations are linear homogeneous in portfolio wealth, then expected holding-period yields remain as important determinants for the proportional holdings of assets regardless of the level of initial portfolio wealth. This may not be the case for alternative specifications of asset demand equations.

Asset demand equations that are linear homogeneous in wealth may be derived from maximizing either expected utility of end-of-period wealth, where the utility function describes constant relative risk aversion, or expected utility of portfolio rate of return. In addition, end-of-period wealth and portfolio rate of return specifications can represent identical preference orderings under certain restrictive assumptions.[31] Each of these cases are examined, with respect to the corresponding properties of the asset demand equations, in section II.E.

Within the set of expected utility maximization frameworks that lead to linear homogeneous asset demand equations in portfolio wealth, utility of portfolio rate of return is the most general of the possible specifications. In particular, the relevant specifications of utility of end-of-period wealth that render linear homogeneous asset demand equations may be equivalently described in terms of portfolio rate of return independent of initial portfolio wealth. Thus, when portfolio rate of return is used as the argument of the utility function, it is done to approximate actual portfolio selection behavior, and to render reasonable

---

[31]See, for example, Jan Mossin, "Optimal Multiperiod Portfolio Policies," Journal of Business, XLI (April, 1968), 215-229. Mossin derives conditions for the equivalence of the rate of return formulation to that of end-of-period wealth. In a very simple case, consider the conditions in which a negative exponential utility function in rate of return describes the same preference ordering as a negative exponential utility function in terminal wealth. That is, compare the following:

(1) $U(1+r_p) = -\exp[-b(1+r_p)]$, and

(2) $U(W) = -\exp(-c\cdot W)$,

where

W_0: initial wealth,

W : terminal wealth, and

$1+r_p$: $1 + (W-W_0)/W_0$.

If $b = c\cdot W$, then case (1) describes the same preferences as case (2); i.e., b must vary over levels of initial wealth.

asset demand equations in a time series context.

Melton[32] considers the above alternatives, in his portfolio selection problem for a financial firm, and concludes that the rate of return on equity is a reasonable choice. He views this as reasonable, in one instance, since management and stockholders commonly judge the performance of the firm by measures concerning the rate of return on equity.

Melton also claims that using the rate of return on equity relieves the utility function from determining the scale[33] of the financial firm. This is implicit using his definition of scale in the rate of return formulation. However, if the scale of the firm is defined as the total value of either side of the balance sheet, with wealth defined as the value of equity, then the utility function does determine the scale of the firm, in the absence of any imperfect markets assumptions, as long as there are at least one endogenous asset and one endogenous liability.[34] If this was not the case, then the solution to the portfolio selection problem would be indeterminate.

2c. Summary

It has been argued that representing the portfolio selection problem in terms of expected utility maximization is a good approximation to

---

[32]William C. Melton, Simultaneous Restricted Estimation of a New Model of Commercial Bank Portfolio Behavior: Estimates for Swedish Commercial Banks, unpublished Ph.D. dissertation, Harvard University, 1976.

[33]Melton defines scale in terms of the firm's equity.

[34]However, the proportional composition of assets in the portfolio is independent of the level of initial wealth.

actual behavior. Preliminary restrictions on the utility function concerning the first- and second-derivatives, and boundedness, have also been reviewed.

The discussion also indicates that the following elements of the portfolio selection problem should be considered simultaneously:

(1) the investor group,

(2) the utility function,

(3) risk characteristics of the assets,

(4) the argument of the utility function, and

(5) the comparative statics properties of the asset demand equations.

3. Safety-First Analysis

The safety-first criterion has been proposed by several authors as an alternative to expected utility maximization.[35] The primary advantage of this approach is that it specifies the objective of an investor in somewhat more precise terms than those of expected utility maximization. However, the restrictive assumptions that are utilized may not best describe an investor's behavior. The assumptions of safety-first analysis, and its comparison to expected utility maximization, are briefly reviewed in the discussion that follows.

The original proponent of the safety-first approach was Roy.[36] He suggested that an investor specifies a minimum level of acceptable return

---

[35]See, for example, A.D. Roy, "Safety First and the Holding of Assets," Econometrica, XX (July, 1952), 431-449; Shinji Kataoka, "A Stochastic Programming Model," Econometrica, XXXI (January/April, 1963), 181-196; and Lester G. Telser, "Safety-First and Hedging," Review of Economic Studies, XXIII (1955-1956), 1-16.

[36]Roy, op. cit.

such that any amount less than this level would be considered a disaster. The portfolio selection problem involves minimizing the probability of disaster; i.e.,

$$\min \Pr(R_p \leqq d), \tag{2.1}$$

where R_p is portfolio return, and d is the disaster level of return.

Other safety-first models, applicable to portfolio selection, include those presented by Kataoka[37] and Telser.[38] The Kataoka model maximizes d subject to a given probability of disaster; i.e.,

$$\max d \text{ subject to } \Pr(R_p \leqq d) \leqq \alpha. \tag{2.2}$$

The Telser model maximizes expected portfolio return subject to a given probability of a given level of disaster return; i.e.,

$$\max E(R_p) \text{ subject to } \Pr(R_p \leqq d) \leqq \alpha. \tag{2.3}$$

All of the above safety-first models have specific assumptions on the disaster level of return or the acceptable probability of disaster, or both. These assumptions describe an investor's desire to avoid risk with respect to portfolio return. This same type of behavior may be described in the mean-variance expected utility maximization framework by allowing the investor's indifference curve map to reflect his willingness to accept additional variance of portfolio return only with a larger amount of expected portfolio return. In addition, the expected utility maximization framework is flexible enough to describe lesser degrees of risk averse portfolio selection behavior. Thus, it appears

---

[37]Kataoka, op. cit.

[38]Telser, op. cit.

that the specific assumptions utilized in safety-first analysis hinder its general applicability.

It also should be noted that the safety-first critieria in (2.1) and (2.2) yield their most meaningful behavioral implications when all assets are risky. If a riskless asset exists, then the solution is either indeterminate or the entire portfolio is held in the riskless asset.[39] Hence, the portfolio diversification implied by an interior solution of expected utility maximization describes a situation more consistent with observed behavior in the one-riskless asset case.

The safety-first criterion in (2.3) also may have an indeterminate solution. This indeterminancy may occur regardless of the assumption concerning the existence of a riskless asset.[40]

Despite their apparent differences, there are several cases in which safety-first and expected utility maximization analyses describe the same equilibrium solutions. In particular, Pyle and Turnovsky have shown that this may occur, in the all-risky assets case, for the safety-first criteria in (2.1) and (2.2).[41] They have also shown that this could

---

[39]This assumes that the investor can borrow or lend unlimited amounts at the riskless asset's interest rate. See David H. Pyle and Stephen J. Turnovsky, "Safety-First and Expected Utility Maximization in Mean-Standard Deviation Portfolio Analysis," Review of Economics and Statistics, LII (February, 1970), 75-81.

[40]See Pyle and Turnovsky, op. cit.

[41]Levy and Sarnat have also found a situation implying the same equilibrium portfolio. However, this case is based on rather untenable behavior allowing only the expected utility maximizer to borrow and lend unlimited amounts at the riskless asset's interest rate. See, Haim Levy and Marshall Sarnat, "Safety-First--An Expected Utility Principle," Journal of Financial and Quantitative Analysis, IX (December, 1974), 1057-1061; Nicolas Gressis, "Comment: 'Safety First-An Expected Utility

occur when (2.3) is used in the one-riskless asset case. Even though equilibrium solutions may be identical for both frameworks, the comparative statics properties may differ substantially.[42] Thus, in a model of portfolio selection behavior using time series data, one can not claim that both frameworks are applicable.

A safety-first criterion is not used to model the portfolio selection behavior in the U.S. Governmental securities market because of some of the above considerations. In particular, the safety-first model imposes assumptions concerning risk aversion that may, to some extent, be subsumed in the expected utility maximization framework.

4. Maximization of Market Value of Equity

An objective defined as maximizing the market value of equity may not be applied to most of the investor groups in this study. For the investor groups where it is applicable, such as nonfinancial corporate businesses, insurance companies, and commercial banks, it is sometimes thought to be an appealing alternative to expected utility maximization. The researchers that prefer this criterion usually do so because it is somewhat less arbitrary in describing the goals of a firm than expected utility maximization. Some problems inherent in this specification are briefly discussed below.

Principle," Journal of Financial and Quantitative Analysis, IX (December, 1974), 1057-1061; and Haim Levy and Marshall Sarnat, "Reply: 'Safety First--An Expected Utility Principle," Journal of Financial and Quantitative Analysis, IX (December, 1974), 1063-1064.

[42]See David H. Pyle and Stephen J. Turnovsky, "Risk Aversion in Chance Constrained Portfolio Selection," Management Science, XVIII (November, 1971), 218-225.

The expression for the market value of equity may be taken from the equilibrium solution of the Sharpe-Lintner[43] capital asset pricing model (CAPM).[44] It is usually assumed, in this model, that investors in the market for equities are individuals that maximize single-period expected utility of terminal wealth.

There appear to be at least two potential problems in applying the equity market value maximization model to financial firms. First, as Michaelson and Goshay have indicated, the balance sheet of the financial firm may be indeterminate because of possible "homemade diversification" by shareholders.[45] Secondly, there are probably some inconsistencies, in the current usage of this framework, resulting from the neglect of the general equilibrium solution for the prices of all financial assets.

Therefore, the portfolio selection behavior of this class of investor groups, i.e., the categories of financial firms listed above, is also based on expected utility maximization. The expected utility maximization framework may also be capable of approximating the risk averse

---

[43]William F. Sharpe, "Capital Asset Prices: A Theory of Market Equilibrium Under Conditions of Risk," Journal of Finance, XIX (September, 1964), 425-442; and John Lintner, "The Valuation of Risk Assets and the Selection of Risky Investments in Stock Portfolios and Capital Budgets," Review of Economics and Statistics, XLVII (February, 1965), 13-37.

[44]Pringle, for example, has used this framework. See, Pringle, "The Imperfect-Markets Model of Commercial Bank Financial Management," op. cit.; and John J. Pringle, "The Capital Decision in Commercial Banks," Journal of Finance, XXIV (June, 1974), 779-795.

[45]However, under certain conditions on loan and deposit yields, Pyle has formulated a model for commercial banks with a determinate solution. See, Jacob B. Michaelson and Robert C. Goshay, "Portfolio Selection in Financial Intermediaries: A New Approach," Journal of Financial and Quantitative Analysis, II (June, 1967), 166-199; and Pyle, "On the Theory of Financial Intermediation," op. cit.

behavior implicit in the maximization of the market value of equity formulation.

The maximization of the CAPM's market valuation of equity also is not used in the portfolio selection problem of nonfinancial corporate businesses. Their portfolio selection problem, for the purposes of this study, focuses on the selection of liquid assets. An expected utility maximization framework is likely to best represent this portion of a firm's operations.[46]

5. Endogenous Assets in the Portfolio Selection Problems of the Categories of Investors Exclusive of Depository Financial Intermediaries

Before proceeding with the actual expected utility maximization problem that is taken to represent the portfolio selection of the investor groups, several areas should be considered that relate to the assumptions concerning the assets and liabilities in the portfolio. These areas may be summarized as follows: first, assumptions concerning the exogeneity of certain assets and liabilities; secondly, the selection of quantity or price (interest rate) instruments in the optimization problem; thirdly, the relation of the assumptions to the actual portfolio behavior of the investor groups.

Again, the point should be made that the portfolio selection theory developed herein is used as an approximation. Several large scale studies would be necessary to successfully model all of the important aspects

---

[46]See II.B.5.

in each investor group. However, this theory may be thought of as the microeconomic foundation for many of the current specifications of asset demand equations found in the literature.[47]

The discussion immediately below also excludes the depository financial intermediaries from any explicit analysis. This set of investor groups is handled separately because of the special nature of their portfolio selection problem.

In general, the most desirable specification of the portfolio selection problem includes the joint determination of the assets and liabilities in the balance sheet.[48] If the analysis incorporates this feature, then certain questions should be posed regarding the scale[49] and the conditions for the existence of financial intermediation.[50]

For the set of investor groups in this chapter, however, the liability side of the balance sheet is abstracted from, and liabilities and

---

[47]e.g., Brainard and Tobin, op. cit.; Friedman, "Financial Flow Variables and the Short-Run Determination of Long-Term Interest Rates," op. cit.; Barry Bosworth and James S. Duesenberry, "A Flow of Funds Model and its Implications," in Issues in Federal Debt Management (Boston: Federal Reserve Bank of Boston, 1973), pp. 39-149; Franco Modigliani, "The Dynamics of Portfolio Adjustment and the Flow of Savings Through Financial Intermediaries," in Gramlich and Jaffee (eds.) Savings Deposits, Mortgages and Housing (Lexington: D. C. Heath and Company, 1972), pp. 63-102; and others.

[48]A summary of the characteristics that are desirable to include in the portfolio selection problem is provided in David H. Pyle, "Descriptive Theories of Financial Institutions Under Uncertainty," Journal of Financial and Quantitative Analysis, VII (December, 1972), 2009-2029.

[49]The scale may be defined, in this case, as the dollar amount of one side of the balance sheet.

[50]These issues are only introduced here, but are taken up in greater detail in the analysis concerning depository financial intermediaries.

net worth are assumed to be exogenous. This approach conforms to many previous presentations of portfolio theory, such as Markowitz's[51] and Tobin's,[52] where the value of the total amount of financial assets was assumed to be fixed.

This separation of the decisions concerning assets and liabilities is posited to be a reasonable approximation to actual behavior because of the nature of this set of investor groups' portfolios. This same approximation has been made on several previous occasions, and it will be discussed below in the context of each investor group.

The investor groups in this chapter may also be regarded as price takers in their portfolio selection problems. Once again, this consideration is relevant primarily to depository financial intermediaries.

5a. Life Insurance Companies, Other Insurance Companies, Private Pension Funds, and State and Local Government Retirement Funds

The common characteristic of this somewhat diverse set of investor groups is that they specialize essentially in long-term liabilities. In addition, the current period's new investable financial flow is usually known at the beginning of the period with a fairly high degree of accuracy. Thus, the portfolio selection problems for these investor groups are modeled in terms of the asset side of the balance sheet. The yearend 1975 stocks of financial assets for these investor groups are exhibited in Tables 2.1, 2.2, 2.3, and 2.4.

---

[51]Harry Markowitz, "Portfolio Selection," Journal of Finance, VII (March, 1952), 77-96.

[52]Tobin, "Liquidity Preference as Behavior Toward Risk," op. cit.

TABLE 2.1

THE HOLDINGS OF FINANCIAL ASSETS BY LIFE INSURANCE COMPANIES

AS OF YEAREND 1975

Asset	Amount	Percentage
Corporate Bonds	$105.5	37.7 %
Mortgages	89.4	31.9
Corporate Equities	28.1	10.0
Policy Loans	24.5	8.8
Open-Market Paper	4.8	1.7
U.S. Treasury Securities	4.7	1.7
State and Local Obligations	4.5	1.6
Demand Deposits and Currency	1.9	0.7
Miscellaneous Assets	16.5	5.9
Total	279.9	100.0

Notes to Table:

Source: Flow of Funds Accounts 1946-1975

Amounts are in millions of dollars.

Detail may not add to total because of rounding.

TABLE 2.2

THE HOLDINGS OF FINANCIAL ASSETS BY OTHER INSURANCE COMPANIES

AS OF YEAREND 1975

Asset	Amount	Percentage
State and Local Obligations	$ 34.3	44.3 %
Corporate Equities	14.3	18.5
Corporate Bonds	12.2	15.8
Trade Credit	7.7	10.0
U.S. Treasury Securities	4.7	6.1
Demand Deposits and Currency	1.7	2.2
Commercial Mortgages	0.2	0.3
Miscellaneous Assets	2.3	3.0
Total	77.4	100.0

Notes to Table:

Source: Flow of Funds Accounts 1946-1975.

Amounts are in millions of dollars.

Detail may not add to total because of rounding.

TABLE 2.3

THE HOLDINGS OF FINANCIAL ASSETS BY PRIVATE PENSION FUNDS AS OF YEAREND 1975

Asset	Amount	Percentage
Corporate Equities	$ 88.6	59.5 %
Corporate Bonds	37.8	25.4
U.S. Treasury Securities	7.9	5.3
Time Deposits	2.4	1.6
Mortgages	2.4	1.6
Demand Deposits and Currency	1.5	1.0
Miscellaneous Assets	8.4	5.6
Total	149.0	100.0

Notes to Table:

Source: *Flow of Funds Accounts 1946-1975*.

Amounts are in millions of dollars.

Detail may not add to total because of rounding.

TABLE 2.4

THE HOLDINGS OF FINANCIAL ASSETS BY STATE AND LOCAL GOVERNMENT RETIREMENT FUNDS AS OF YEAREND 1975

Asset	Amount	Percentage
Corporate Bonds	$ 60.9	57.5 %
Corporate Equities	25.8	24.3
Mortgages	8.3	7.8
U.S. Government Agency Securities	4.6	4.3
State and Local Obligations	2.5	2.4
U.S. Treasury Securities	2.2	2.1
Demand Deposits and Currency	1.7	1.6
Total	106.0	100.0

Notes to Table:

Source: *Flow of Funds Accounts 1946-1975*.

Amounts are in millions of dollars.

Detail may not add to total because of rounding.

The portfolio selection problem for these investor groups consists of choosing the composition of assets in the portfolio. This is modeled in a "pure" portfolio selection model. That is, there is assumed to be an absence of interperiod "liquidity" adjustments from a forecast error in the level of a liability. Furthermore, the asset demands are derived in a framework that renders them linear homogeneous in wealth.[53] In a time series context, this property insures the continual importance of asset holding-period yields on the desired proportional holdings of assets.

5b. Households

Whereas the previous set of investor groups appears to be well suited to the intended approximation regarding portfolio behavior, there are some obvious problems with respect to households. This is particularly the case when considering their holdings of liquid assets. The financial assets of households as of yearend 1975 are exhibited in Table 2.5.

Duesenberry[54] has indicated that the portfolio selection problem for households may be separated into stages. In particular, given the value of the household's stock of assets, the first stage of the problem is to determine the proportions of liquid and nonliquid assets in the portfolio. Next, the allocation of liquid assets should be determined.

---

[53]See II.E.; in this case, wealth is defined as the total value of the assets in the portfolio.

[54]James S. Duesenberry, "The Portfolio Approach to the Demand for Money and Other Assets," Review of Economics and Statistics, XLV (February, 1963), 9-31.

TABLE 2.5

THE HOLDINGS OF FINANCIAL ASSETS BY HOUSEHOLDS

AS OF YEAREND 1975

Asset	Amount	Percentage
Time and Savings Accounts	$ 776.2	31.1 %
Corporate Equities	630.5	25.3
Pension Fund Reserves	368.6	14.8
Demand Deposits and Currency	165.6	6.6
Life Insurance Reserves	164.6	6.6
State and Local Obligations	74.2	3.0
Mortgages	72.7	2.9
U.S. Government Savings Bonds	67.4	2.7
Corporate and Foreign Bonds	65.9	2.6
U.S. Treasury Securities	49.0	2.0
U.S. Government Agency Securities	9.1	0.4
Open-Market Paper	6.8	0.3
Security Credit	4.0	0.2
Money Market Fund Shares	3.6	0.1
Miscellaneous Assets	38.5	1.5
Total	2496.7	100.0

Notes to Table:
Source: Flow of Funds Accounts 1946-1975.
Amounts are in millions of dollars.
Detail may not add to total because of rounding.

This is also the methodology accepted by Fortune;[55] and he empirically investigates only the allocation among liquid assets.

The motives given by Duesenberry and Fortune, for holding liquid assets, correspond to those usually given for the demand for money. That is, one source of liquid asset demand arises from transactions motives, and another source results from speculative or "pure" portfolio motives. Portfolio selection models such as Tobin's[56] only analyze this latter consideration.

The implication of the framework, advanced by Duesenberry and Fortune, is that the level of liquid assets demanded depends, in one instance, on the level of income and expenditures; and, in another, on the degree of risk aversion in the "pure" portfolio problem. Once the level of liquid assets is determined, households determine the optimal allocation among liquid assets.

Alternatively, one may view the composition of liquid assets as being determined by two distinct sources. In particular, the problem may be separated according to the motives indicated earlier instead of the liquid-nonliquid asset distinction. Hence, a certain amount and composition of liquid assets may be demanded as a result of transactions motives, and this may merely be added to the amount and composition demanded from the "pure" portfolio problem. This methodology incorporates the joint

---

[55]Peter Fortune, A Constrained Econometric Analysis of Household Sector Liquid Asset Allocation (Boston: Federal Reserve Bank of Boston, 1972).

[56]Tobin, "Liquidity Preference as Behavior Toward Risk," op. cit. Portfolio selection problems of this type will be continued to be called "pure" portfolio selection problems.

determination of <u>both</u> the size and composition of liquid asset holdings, as well as the size and composition of nonliquid asset holdings. This may be directly contrasted to the Duesenberry-Fortune methodology, where the size of the respective classifications are determined in the first stage of the portfolio selection problem.

This latter approach is the one that is utilized to model household portfolio selection herein. It is the more useful of the two approximations since a primary focus of this study is the investigation of the substitutability between different maturities of U.S. Government securities.

This approach is illustrated below using a model of portfolio selection based on some preliminary observations on the functional form of asset demand equations. The asset demands are expressed in desired levels, and the adjustment model is not specified until chapter V. Let the model be represented as follows:

$$W^{*T} = \sum_j \beta_j Z_j, \qquad (2.4)$$

$$\frac{a_i^{*T}}{W^{*T}} = \delta_{i0} + \sum_k \delta_{ik}\mu_k, \qquad i = 1,\ldots,I, \qquad (2.5)$$

$$\frac{a_i^{*P}}{W^P} = \alpha_{i0} + \sum_m \alpha_{im}\mu_m, \qquad i = 1,\ldots,I, \qquad (2.6)$$

$$W^P = W - W^{*T}, \qquad (2.7)$$

where

W^{*T} : the desired level of financial assets devoted to transactions demand,

Z_j : the jth independent variable that determines the transactions demand,

a_i^{*T} : the desired dollar amount of transactions holdings of asset i,

a_i^{*P} : the desired dollar amount of "pure" portfolio holdings of asset i,

W^P : "pure" portfolio wealth (defined as a residual),

W : total dollar value of financial assets,

μ_m : expected holding-period yield on asset m.

Equation (2.4) is the linearlized demand for transactions holdings. This is assumed to be the first decision of the household. That is, the respective amounts of portfolio wealth allocated to transactions and speculative demands is determined in the first stage.

The decisions described in (2.5) and (2.6) may be made contemporaneously and independently in this model. That is, the proportion of asset i in transactions holdings is independent of the proportion of asset i in the "pure" portfolio selection problem, and vice versa. This results from the two separate optimization problems, concerning the composition of assets, hypothesized in the household portfolio selection problem.

Solving equations (2.4) through (2.7) for the desired asset levels yields

$$a_i^* = a_i^{*T} + a_i^{*P} = \sum_m \alpha_{im}\mu_m W + \alpha_{i0}W + \sum_{jn}\sum \beta_j \gamma_{in}\mu_n Z_j + (\delta_{i0} - \alpha_{i0}) \sum_j \beta_j Z_j, \quad (2.8)$$

where

$$\sum_n \gamma_{in}\mu_n = \sum_k \delta_{ik}\mu_k - \sum_m \alpha_{im}\mu_m,$$

with range of n extending over [1, max(k,m)]. The coefficients in the first term of (2.8) are from the "pure" portfolio selection problem. The coefficients in the remaining terms result from the determination of the amount and composition of liquidity holdings.

Previous specifications of asset demand equations, that have allowed for effects additional to those in a "pure" portfolio selection model, have occasionally specified these variables in a manner that allows the asset demand equations to be linear homogeneous in wealth, i.e.,

$$a_i^* = \sum_j \alpha_{ij}\mu_j W + \alpha_{i0}W + \sum_k \alpha_{ik}Z_k W. \qquad (2.9)$$

Friedman,[57] for example, has estimated the household demand for corporate bonds using an equation that allows for possible non-yield variables, Z_k, in the manner indicated in (2.9).[58]

Bosworth and Duesenberry[59] have specified asset demand equations as

$$a_i^* = \sum_j \alpha_{ij}\mu_j W + \alpha_{i0}W + \sum_k \delta_{ik}Z_k. \qquad (2.10)$$

---

[57]Friedman, "Financial Flow Variables and the Short-Run Determination of Long-Term Interest Rates," op. cit.

[58]For a discussion of these non-yield variables, see Friedman, "A Structural Model of the Long-Term Corporate Debt Market," op. cit.

[59]Bosworth and Duesenberry, "A Flow of Funds Model and its Implications," op. cit.

Also see Michael J. Hamburger, "The Demand for Money by Households, Money Substitutes, and Monetary Policy," Journal of Political Economy, LXXIV (December, 1966), 600-623; Michael J. Hamburger, "Household Demand for Financial Assets," Econometrica, XXXVI (January, 1968), 97-118; and Mitsuo Saito, "Household Flow-of-Fund Equations: Specification and Estimation," Journal of Money, Credit and Banking, lX (February, 1977), 1-20. All of these studies include both income and wealth variables in the demand for financial assets by households. The specification developed herein differs from these previous studies in that the mechanisms for including income and wealth variables are explicitly developed.

They explicitly include the Z_k variables to represent income and transactions requirements. Equation (2.10) is used in the flow-of-funds model to describe household purchases of short-term financial assets. The difference between (2.8) and (2.10) is the addition of terms, in the former, consisting of products of expected holding-period yields and Z_k variables.

In summation, the household portfolio selection problem is modeled in an explicit framework that allows for the potential substitutability between short- and long-term financial assets. This is accomplished by introducing stages in the decision process. The first stage is to determine the desired level of portfolio wealth for transactions. The second stage involves the contemporaneous, although independent, solutions to the desired allocations of financial assets held for transactions purposes, and the asset selection from the "pure" portfolio problem involving the residual portfolio wealth from the first stage. The underlying portfolio selection theory for the linear homogeneous demand equations in (2.6) is discussed below in II.E.

5c. Nonfinancial Corporate Businesses and State and Local Government General Funds

All assets and liabilities, except holdings of credit market securities, are taken as exogenous in the modeling of nonfinancial corporate businesses and state and local government general funds. In addition, it is assumed that their portfolio selection (or cash management) behavior can be approximated by a risk averse utility function.[60] The relevant

---

[60]The use of a utility function to represent risk averse behavior is discussed in II.B.2.

portions of their balance sheets are exhibited in Tables 2.6 and 2.7.

The above assumptions, that leave only certain categories of assets as endogenous, also determine the scale of the asset allocation problem. Thus, one potential area of interaction between the corporate bond rate and the short-term interest rate on U.S. Government securities is obscured. This concerns the possibility of using liquid assets to facilitate the postponement of new corporate debt issues when the corporate bond rate is high.[61] A similar effect is obscured between the interest rate on state and local government bonds and the amount of security holdings by state and local government general funds.[62] However, the effects of current period net portfolio wealth flows are introduced in the portfolio adjustment mechanism described in chapter V.

The factors that determine the composition of liquid assets are assumed to be based on optimizing behavior similar to that postulated for the other investor groups. The fact that their portfolios contain a sizeable proportion of U.S. Government securities beyond both one year and two years to maturity indicates that they are not merely matching liquid asset maturities to future short-run cash expenditures.

---

[61]See Duesenberry, "The Portfolio Approach to the Demand for Money and Other Assets," op. cit. Maddala and Vogel include the corporate bond rate in their liquid asset allocation problem in G. S. Maddala and Robert C. Vogel, "Estimating Lagged Relationships in Corporate Demand for Liquid Assets," Review of Economics and Statistics, LI (February, 1969), 53-61.

[62]See Paul F. McGouldrick and John E. Petersen, "Monetary Restraint and Borrowing and Capital Spending by State and Local Governments in 1966," in Gibson and Kaufman (eds.), Monetary Economics: Readings on Current Issues (New York: McGraw-Hill, Inc., 1971), pp. 474-482.

TABLE 2.6

THE HOLDINGS OF SHORT-TERM FINANCIAL ASSETS BY NONFINANCIAL CORPORATE BUSINESSES AS OF YEAR END 1975

Asset	Amount	Percentage
Demand Deposits and Currency	$ 47.5	38.2 %
Commercial Paper	27.9	22.4
Time Deposits	22.4	18.0
U.S. Treasury Securities	14.3	11.5
Security R.P.'s	4.7	3.8
State and Local Obligations	4.5	3.6
Miscellaneous Short-Term Assets	3.2	2.6
Total	124.5	100.0

Notes to Table:

Source: Flow of Funds Accounts 1946-1975.

Amounts are in millions of dollars.

Detail may not add to total because of rounding.

TABLE 2.7

THE HOLDINGS OF FINANCIAL ASSETS BY STATE AND LOCAL GOVERNMENT GENERAL FUNDS AS OF YEAREND 1975

Asset	Amount	Percentage
Time Deposits	$ 48.1	34.6 %
U.S. Treasury Securities	30.6	22.0
U.S. Government Agency Securities	22.3	16.0
Demand Deposits and Currency	14.3	10.3
Mortgages	12.8	9.2
Taxes Receivable	6.6	4.7
State and Local Obligations	4.4	3.2
Total	139.1	100.0

Notes to Table:

Source: *Flow of Funds Accounts 1946-1975*.

Amounts are in millions of dollars.

Detail may not add to total because of rounding.

Bosworth and Duesenberry[63] implicitly make similar assumptions concerning these investor groups. However, their level of aggregation is different from that used herein. In particular, the flow-of-funds categories of state and local government general funds, and state and local government retirement funds, are apparently combined. In addition, short-term securities are usually aggregated throughout.

6. Portfolio Selection in an Inflationary Environment

The early research in portfolio selection under uncertainty, e.g., Tobin,[64] systematically included a riskless asset. However, in many cases, this assumption is now obsolete because of persistent and uncertain price inflation. That is, price inflation makes all assets risky when real holding-period yields are considered, and the portfolio selection model should be modified accordingly.

Lintner[65] has investigated the effects of price inflation in a capital asset pricing model. It is also desirable, however, to investigate the intermediate results, i.e., the asset demand equations, apart from the resulting equilibrium market prices for assets.

---

[63]Bosworth and Duesenberry, "A Flow of Funds Model and Its Implications," op. cit.

[64]Tobin, "Liquidity Preference as Behavior Toward Risk," op. cit.

[65]Three pertinent references are: John Lintner, "The Aggregation of Investor's Diverse Judgements and Preferences in Purely Competitive Security Markets," Journal of Financial and Quantitative Analysis, IV (December, 1969), 347-400; John Lintner, "The Effect of Short Selling and Margin Requirements in Perfect Capital Markets," Journal of Financial and Quantitative Analysis, VI (December, 1971), 1173-1195; John Lintner, "The Lognormality of Security Returns, Portfolio Selection and Market Equilibrium," Mimeo, Harvard University, undated. Additional references may be obtained therein.

Along these lines, Bierwag and Grove[66] have analyzed the comparative statics properties of asset demand equations assuming all assets risky. Their results serve as a starting point for a portion of the analysis in chapter III. In anticipation of these results, it may be noted that the inclusion of price inflation in the analysis alters the comparative statics that would otherwise result in its absence. For example, an increase in initial wealth may actually cause maximum expected utility to decline in several common specifications of utility of end-of-period wealth.

The asset demand equations in II.E are derived under the assumption that all assets are risky; i.e., there is an uncertain rate of price inflation and investors select portfolios on the basis of subjective probability distributions of real holding-period yields. Nevertheless, some investors, such as insurance companies, must meet nominal liabilities; and they may view cash and short-term assets as riskless. This behavior, if relevant, is easily incorporated into the asset demand equations.

7. Measures of Risk Aversion

Measures of risk aversion are briefly reviewed immediately below. This is done since their interpretations are important in later analysis concerning the comparative statics properties of asset demand equations.

Pratt and Arrow have somewhat different interpretations of these measures. Pratt's analysis[67] is in terms of a risk or insurance premium;

---

[66] G. O. Bierwag and M. A. Grove, "Indifference Curves in Asset Analysis," Economic Journal, LXXVI (June, 1966), 337-343; and G. O. Bierwag and M. A. Grove, "Slutsky Equations for Assets,: Journal of Political Economy, LXXVI (January/February, 1968), 114-127.

[67] Pratt, op. cit.

and Arrow[68] considers the probability, associated with a symmetric bet, necessary for an individual to be indifferent between a nonstochastic level of wealth and the bet. Arrow's methodology is used in the discussion that follows.

7a. The Second Derivative of the Utility Function With Respect to End-of-Period Wealth

A risk averse individual, by definition, prefers a nonstochastic level of end-of-period wealth, W, to a random level of wealth described by winning or losing an amount h; i.e., W + h or W - h, each with probability equal to one-half. That is,

$$U(W) > \tfrac{1}{2}U(W-h) + \tfrac{1}{2}U(W+h),$$

or

$$U(W) - U(W-h) > U(W+h) - U(W).$$

This further implies that $U'(W)$ is a decreasing function of W, i.e.,

$$U''(W) < 0.$$

However, this measure is not unique for a given preference ordering since von Neumann-Morgenstern utility functions are unique only up to positive linear transformations. This observation led to the introduction of absolute risk aversion and relative risk aversion, both of which are invariant up to positive linear transformations.

7b. Absolute Risk Aversion

The measure of absolute risk aversion is defined as

---

[68] Arrow, Aspects of the Theory of Risk-Bearing, op. cit., 33-34.

$$R_A(W) = \frac{-U''(W)}{U'(W)} . \quad (2.11)$$

Arrow shows that given a nonstochastic amount of wealth, W, and the possible outcomes of a bet, W+h or W-h, with probabilities p and 1-p respectively, then there is a probability, p(W,h), such that the individual is indifferent between W and the bet.[69] For small values of h, this implies that

$$p(W,h) = \frac{1}{2} + \frac{R_A(W)}{4} h + \text{terms of higher order in } h. \quad (2.12)$$

Thus, $R_A(W)$ measures the individual's desire for a bet that is actuarily unfair in his favor.

In addition, there are comparative statics results, involving changes in initial wealth, that are usually associated with increasing, decreasing, or constant absolute risk aversion. However, if a riskless asset does not exist, then these comparative statics results could have ambiguous signs. This area of investigation is discussed in chapter III.

Finally, this measure also defines the functional form of a utility function given the functional form of $R_A(W)$. If absolute risk aversion is constant, then the utility functions corresponding to zero, positive, and negative values are the following:[70]

$$U(W) = W, \text{ if } R_A(W) = 0, \quad (2.13)$$

$$U(W) = -\exp(-cW), \text{ if } R_A(W) = c > 0, \quad (2.14)$$

$$U(W) = \exp(-cW), \text{ if } R_A(W) = c < 0. \quad (2.15)$$

---

[69] Ibid.

[70] See Pratt, op. cit.

The utility function given in (2.14) is the only one in this group with $U'(W) > 0$ and $U''(W) < 0$.

7c. Relative or Proportional Risk Aversion

Relative risk aversion is defined as

$$R_R(W) = \frac{-WU''(W)}{U'(W)}. \qquad (2.16)$$

This measure may be interpreted, following Arrow,[71] in the same framework as that used for absolute risk aversion. In the case of relative risk aversion, the bet now involves a fraction of wealth, n, instead of an absolute amount, h. Therefore, setting $h = nW$, and substituting into (2.12) yields

$$p(W,nW) = \frac{1}{2} + \frac{R_R(W)}{4} n + \text{terms of higher order in } n. \qquad (2.17)$$

Thus, for bets involving proportions of W, $R_R(W)$ measures the insistence of an individual for more than actuarily fair bets.

If relative risk aversion is constant, then the following utility functions result:[72]

$$U(W) = W^{1-c}, \text{ if } R_R(W) = c < 1, \qquad (2.18)$$

$$U(W) = \log W, \text{ if } R_R(W) = 1, \qquad (2.19)$$

$$U(W) = -W^{-(c-1)}, \text{ if } R_R(W) = c > 0. \qquad (2.20)$$

All of the above utility functions have $U'(W) > 0$ and $U''(W) < 0$.

Again, there are comparative statics results, with respect to changes

---

[71]Arrow, Aspects of the Theory of Risk-Bearing, op. cit., p. 34.

[72]See Pratt, op. cit.

in initial wealth, that correspond to characteristics of relative risk aversion. These are also postponed until chapter III.

C. Expected Utility in Terms of Mean-Variance Analysis

In order to apply the expected utility maximization methodology to an empirical investigation of asset demands, it is desirable to reduce the number of parameters necessary to describe a given specification of expected utility. This may be facilitated by specifying expected utility in a manner that reduces to a preference ordering with respect to the mean and variance of the argument of the utility function. The empirical tractability of this approach is readily apparent upon inspection of previous research; e.g., Parkin[73] and Melton.[74]

Portfolio selection in terms of mean-variance analysis may be viewed as an approximation, or as the result of explicit assumptions concerning the utility function and probability distribution of the outcome, or both. Samuelson[75] regards mean-variance analysis as a useful approximation, especially when the variance is near zero, i.e., for a small amount of risk. The Borch, Feldstein, and Tobin exchange[76] also indicates that quadratic utility or joint normally distributed asset rates of return are sufficient conditions for expected utility to reduce

---

[73]Michael Parkin, "Discount House Portfolio and Debt Selection," Review of Economic Studies, XXXVII (October, 1970), 469-497.

[74]Melton, op. cit.

[75]Paul A. Samuelson, "The Fundamental Approximation Theorem of Portfolio Analysis in Terms of Means, Variances and Higher Moments," Review of Economic Studies, XXVII (October, 1970), 537-542.

[76]Borch, "A Note on Uncertainty and Indifference Curves," op. cit.; Martin S. Feldstein, "Mean-Variance Analysis in the Theory of Liquidity Preference and Portfolio Selection," Review of Economic Studies, XXXVI (January, 1969), 5-12; and James Tobin, "Comment on Borch and Feldstein," Review of Economic Studies, XXXVI (January, 1969), 13-14.

to a function of mean and variance.

Furthermore, if the portfolio rate of return is distributed lognormally, and the utility function is logarithmic, then mean-variance analysis is applicable. However, if the asset rates of return are lognormally distributed, then it is well known that a linear combination of these rates of return is not lognormally distributed. This case is investigated below using an approximation developed by Lintner.[77]

The remainder of this section further discusses the conditions for, and implications of, mean-variance analysis.

1. Joint Normally Distributed Asset Rates of Return and Quadratic Utility

It is easily demonstrated that joint normally distributed asset rates of return[78] or quadratic utility are sufficient conditions for expected utility analysis to be reduced to a preference ordering in terms of the mean and variance of the argument of the utility function. This is done immediately below.

If U(X) is the utility associated with a value of X, where X is either portfolio rate of return, return, or end-of-period wealth, then U(X) may be represented by an exact Taylor series expansion around E(X) as follows:

---

[77]Lintner, "The Lognormality of Security Returns, Portfolio Selection and Market Equilibrium," op. cit.

[78]If the asset rates of return are normally distributed, then, of course, the argument of the utility function is normally distributed regardless of its definition; i.e., whether it is defined as rate of return, return, or end-of-period wealth.

$$U(X) = \sum_{n=0}^{\infty} \frac{U^{(n)}[E(X)]}{n!} \cdot (X - E(X))^n. \tag{2.21}$$

Taking the expectation of (2.21) yields

$$E[U(X)] = U[E(X)] + \sum_{n=0}^{\infty} \frac{U^{(n)}[E(X)]}{n!} \cdot E[X - E(X)]^n. \tag{2.22}$$

If the utility function is quadratic, i.e., $U(X) = X - bX^2$, then

$$E[U(X)] = U[E(X)] + \frac{U''[E(X)]}{2} \cdot V(X),$$

or

$$E[U(X)] = E(X) - b[V(X) + E(X)^2]. \tag{2.23}$$

Equation (2.23) is independent of the probability distribution of X.

If X is a normally distributed random variable, then[79]

$$E[U(X)] = U[E(X)] + \sum_{n=1}^{\infty} \frac{U^{(2n)}[E(X)]}{2^n n!} \cdot V(X)^n. \tag{2.24}$$

This is conditional on the existence of both $U^{(2n)}[E(X)]$ (n=1,2,...), and U(X) for all values of X. This excludes the applications of normal probability distributions to the logarithmic utility function, since X can not have negative values in this case.

---

[79]See, for example, M. E. Rubenstein, "The Fundamental Theorem of Parameter-Preference Security Valuation," Journal of Financial and Quantitative Analysis, VIII (January, 1973), 61-69.

If X is normally distributed, then

$$E[X-E(X)]^m = \begin{cases} \dfrac{m!}{2^{m/2}(m/2)!} \cdot V(X)^{\frac{m}{2}}, & \text{if m is even,} \\ 0, & \text{if m is odd.} \end{cases}$$

The expectation of the negative exponential utility function, i.e., $U(X) = \exp(-bX)$, may be evaluated using (2.24) assuming normality. The derivatives of the negative exponential utility function may be represented as

$$U^{(2n)}[E(X)] = -b^n \exp[-bE(X)], \quad n=1,2,\ldots; \tag{2.25}$$

and substituting this expression into (2.24) yields

$$E[U(X)] = U[E(X)] + \sum_{n=1}^{\infty} \frac{-b^n \exp[-bE(X)]}{2^n n!} \cdot V(X)^n, \tag{2.26}$$

or

$$E[U(X)] = -\exp[-bE(X)][1 + \sum_{n=1}^{\infty} \frac{[(b/2)\cdot V(X)]^n}{n!}], \tag{2.27}$$

which further reduces to

$$E[U(X)] = -\exp(-b[E(X) - (b/2)\cdot V(X)]). \tag{2.28}$$

The signs of $U'(X)$ and $U''(x)$ also translate into unambiguous signs on the derivatives of $E[U(X)]$, with respect to $E(X)$ and $V(X)$, when X is normally distributed. This may be demonstrated by the use of Taylor series expansions of $U'(X)$ and $U''(X)$ around $E(X)$, and taking the expectations to yield[80]

$$E[U'(X)] = \sum_{n=0}^{\infty} \frac{U^{(2n+1)}[E(X)]}{2^n n!} \cdot V(X)^n, \tag{2.29}$$

and

$$E[U''(X)] = \sum_{n=1}^{\infty} 2n \cdot \frac{U^{(2n)}[E(X)]}{2^n n!} \cdot V(X)^{n-1}. \tag{2.30}$$

---

[80]See M. E. Rubinstein, "A Comparative Statics Analysis of Risk Premiums," Journal of Business, XLVI (October, 1973), 605-615.

Differentiating (2.24) with respect to E(X), and comparing this result to (2.29), implies that

$$\frac{\partial E[U(X)]}{\partial E(X)} = E[U'(X)]. \tag{2.31}$$

Similarly, differentiating (2.24) with respect to V(X), and comparing this result to (2.30), implies that

$$\frac{\partial E[U(X)]}{\partial V(X)} = (1/2) \cdot E[U''(X)]. \tag{2.32}$$

Therefore, if $U'(X) > 0$ for all X, then $\partial E[U(X)]/\partial E(X) > 0$, from (2.31); and if $U''(X) < 0$ for all X, then $\partial E[U(X)]/\partial V(X) < 0$, from (2.32)

There is another unambiguous correspondence between U(X) and E[U(X)] that should be noted. This deals with the Pratt-Arrow measure of absolute risk aversion, $R_A(X)$, and the slope of an indifference curve in mean-variance space. In particular, it has been shown that if $R_A(X)$ is constant, then $dE(X)/dV(X)$ is constant.[81] This result is directly applicable to the negative exponential utility function.

2. Lognormally Distributed Portfolio Rate of Return and Logarithmic Utility

A logarithmic utility function with end-of-period wealth as the argument, is analyzed in conjunction with a theoretical framework proposed by Lintner.[82] This framework is based on an extensive study of

---

[81]See Stephen M. Miller, "Measures of Risk Aversion: Some Clarifying Comments," Journal of Financial and Quantitative Analysis, X (June, 1975), 299-309.

[82]Lintner, "The Lognormality of Security Returns, Portfolio Selection and Market Equilibrium," op. cit.

actual equity returns from 569 companies on the Chicago tapes with continuous records over 20 postwar years. In addition, extensive portfolio simulations were performed under the assumption that individual security returns were distributed lognormally. The results of this excellent study may be summarized, in a rather cursory manner, as follows:

(1) with respect to the aforementioned 569 companies, the assumption of lognormal returns is superior to the assumption of normal returns over all time intervals greater than one month;

(2) on the basis of simulation experiments involving a group of empirically relevant portfolios, the hypothesis of lognormally distributed portfolios is preferable to the hypothesis that they are normally distributed when individual security returns are lognormally distributed; and

(3) a good second-order estimate of the logarithmic expected portfolio return may be formulated, from a Taylor series expansion, that performs significantly better than the usual first-order approximation.

Lintner actually introduces two approximations with respect to the case involving a joint lognormal distribution on individual security returns and a lognormally distributed portfolio return. His "second-best" second-order approximation is used in what follows. In particular, end-of-period wealth may be represented as

$$W = W_0(1+r_p) = W_0\exp(g_p), \tag{2.33}$$

where

W : end-of-period wealth,

W_0 : initial wealth,

$1+r_p$: rate of return on the portfolio, and

g_p : the logarithm of the rate of return on the portfolio with $g_p \sim N(m_p, v_p)$.

Lintner's "second-best" second-order estimate of the logarithm of expected portfolio rate of return, derived from a truncated Taylor series expansion, is

$$m_p = \underline{h}'\underline{m} + (1/2)\cdot\underline{h}'\underline{v} - (1/2)\cdot(\underline{h}'S\underline{h}), \qquad (2.34)$$

where

$\underline{h}$: vector of the asset proportions to initial wealth such that $\sum_i h_i = 1$,

$\underline{m}$: vector of logarithmic means with typical element $E[\log(1+r_i)] = E[g_i] = m_i$,

$\underline{v}$: vector of logarithmic variances with typical element $V[\log(1+r_i)] = V(g_i) = v_i$,

S : variance-covariance matrix of logarithmic rates of return, i.e., $E[(\underline{g}-\underline{m})(\underline{g}-\underline{m})']$,

$1+r_i$: rate of return on asset i in natural units, and

$\underline{g}$: vector of logarithmic rates of return with typical element $\log(1+r_i) = g_i$.

If the utility function is logarithmic, then

$$E[U(W)] = E[\log W] = \log W_0 + m_p. \qquad (2.35)$$

Substituting (2.34) into (2.35) yields

$$E[U(W)] = \log W_0 + \underline{h}'\underline{m} + (1/2)\cdot\underline{h}'\underline{v} - (1/2)\cdot(\underline{h}'S\underline{h}), \qquad (2.36)$$

and this expression is used below in the derivation of asset demand equations. This problem, as formulated, has once again reduced to an analysis of means, variances, and covariances. In addition, the investor is not risk neutral with respect to logarithmic portfolio mean, which has not usually been the case in the utilization of this framework of analysis.

D. Multiperiod Versus One-Period Optimization

Previous empirical studies of portfolio behavior, based on expected utility maximization, have used one-period optimization models.[83] Empirical tractability especially plays a role in this choice between multiperiod and one-period portfolio selection models. Even though Fama[84] concludes that observed multiperiod behavior is analogous to one-period horizon behavior, the parameters to be considered are still overly complex. In Mossin's[85] general version of his multiperiod portfolio selection model, the investor must form subjective means and variances for holding-period yields over the entire horizon of the problem, despite the fact that portfolio selection in the initial planning period only involves choosing the optimal levels of assets for that period. The modeling of the parameters of subjective probability distributions beyond one period is, at best, a formidable task. The complexity is increased when factors such as serially correlated holding-periods yields, transactions costs, and the elimination of one of the perfect markets assumptions are considered.

There are conditions, however, that lead to optimal portfolio selection behavior that is myopic.[86] This case is usually analyzed in a framework that includes utility of terminal wealth, no transactions costs,

---

[83] See, for example, Melton, op. cit.; and Parkin, op. cit.

[84] Fama, op. cit.

[85] Mossin, op. cit.

[86] Myopic behavior is defined as using only the information concerning the current period, such as subjective probability distributions of holding-period yields for the current period.

no taxes, and the same distributions of holding-period yields in all future periods. Under these assumptions, Mossin has shown that if an investor has constant relative risk aversion, then the optimal multiperiod portfolio strategy is myopic.[87] This result is independent of the existence of a riskless asset.

A myopic multiperiod portfolio selection strategy implies that an investor's preference ordering is reducible to a function of portfolio rate of return. This follows from the properties of utility functions with constant relative risk aversion. However, specifying portfolio rate of return as the argument of the utility function does not necessarily lead to myopic behavior. The same theorems for myopic behavior are valid, in this case, by setting initial wealth equal to unity, causing the asset demands to equal proportional amounts of initial wealth. Again, only power utility functions[88] satisfy the conditions for myopic multiperiod portfolio selection behavior.

An alternative criterion of multiperiod portfolio selection has been advanced, most recently, by Hakansson.[89] This approach consists of the maximization of expected average compound rate of return. Hakansson's

---

[87]Mossin, op. cit. See II.B.7 and III.E for discussions concerning relative risk aversion.

[88]For a description of this class of utility functions, see II.B.7.

[89]Nils H. Hakansson, "Multiperiod Mean-Variance Analysis: Toward a General Theory of Portfolio Choice," Journal of Finance, XXVI (September, 1971), 857-774. For a criticism of this criterion, see Paul A. Samuelson, "Lifetime Portfolio Selection by Dynamic Stochastic Programming," Review of Economics and Statistics, LI (August, 1969), 239-246; and Robert C. Merton and Paul A. Samuelson, "Fallacy of the Log-Normal Approximations to Optimal Portfolio Decision Making Over Many Periods," Journal of Financial Economics, I (May, 1974), 67-94.

results imply that for every portfolio policy consisting of the maximization of expected average compound rate of return, there exists a power utility function that represents the same criterion. If the number of periods is great, then the model reduces to the maximization of the expectation of the logarithm of portfolio rate of return. Thus, in either case, the optimal portfolio selection strategy is myopic.

Maximizing the expectation of the logarithm of portfolio rate of return has also been shown to be "growth-optimal" in the sense that it is efficient and results in greater wealth than any other policy with probability approaching one as the number of periods become large.[90] However, this criterion implies that an investor is risk neutral with respect to the variance around the expected growth path of compound rate of return.[91]

The multiperiod framework, as reviewed above, would preclude a "liquidity motive"[92] and less than instantaneous portfolio adjustment in the portfolio selection problem. These would be a particularly serious omissions when considering the U.S. Government securities market. Thus, a one-period framework is used in the empirical analysis of asset demands; this framework allows for less than instantaneous portfolio adjustment, due to transactions costs, by combining it with a portfolio adjustment model.

---

[90]See Hakansson, op. cit.

[91]See the references in footnote 89. Also see Lintner, "The Lognormality of Security Returns, Portfolio Selection and Market Equilibrium," op. cit.

[92]For a discussion of this point, see Melton, op. cit.

E. Asset Demand Equations

This section develops alternative specifications of asset demand equations derived from the mean-variance expected utility models reviewed in II.C. Five specific models of portfolio selection, based on three different utility functions, are presented. The three utility functions include quadratic utility, negative exponential utility, and logarithmic utility. The quadratic and negative exponential cases are analyzed with both portfolio rate of return and end-of-period wealth as the arguments. A logarithmic utility function on end-of-period wealth is analyzed using Lintner's approximation.[93] When portfolio rate of return is utilized as the argument of the utility function, it is done in the sense of the approximation described in II.B.2b.

The properties that are examined, in the context of the models considered in this section, are symmetry constraints, adding-up constraints, and wealth homogeneity. In chapter III, these are considered for general cases, along with an analysis of bliss (or saturation) points in expected utility analysis.

The asset demand equations are derived under the assumption that investors form subjective estimates of means, variances, and covariances on real holding-period yields associated with the individual assets. Implicit in this assumption is that investors are calculating the effects of persistent and uncertain price inflation. This, of course, also implies that all assets are risky in the absence of a default-free inflation-indexed security. However, the specifications of asset demand equations

---

[93] See II.C.2.

have the same general properties, in terms of the properties of the coefficient matrix on the vector of expected holding-period yields, if an investor's assessments are in nominal, instead of real, terms. This is demonstrated, for the general case, in chapter III.

The measure of end-of-period wealth may be interpreted, for the purposes of the asset demand derivations, either as the total dollar value of assets (i.e., one side of the balance sheet), or net worth. For the seven investor groups in this chapter, the former interpretation is utilized. In addition, it is assumed that non-negativity constraints on asset levels are not binding.[94]

The "coefficients" corresponding to the expected asset holding-period yields are functions of variances and covariances. That is, they are not predetermined constants dependent only on the specifications of the utility function. This implies that estimation over different partitions of the sample period may be especially important in determining the stability of the coefficients in the absence of an explicit treatment of variances and covariances. This area was empirically examined along with the possibility of structural shifts from institutional changes. In addition, variances of asset holding-period yields are included in the

---

[94]Analyses incorporating non-negativity constraints may be found in Lintner, "The Valuation of Risk Assets and the Selection of Risky Investment in Stock Portfolios and Capital Budgets," op. cit.; and W. M. Jones-Lee, "Some Portfolio Adjustment Theorems for the Case of Non-Negativity Constraints on Security Holdings," Journal of Finance, XXVI (June, 1971), 763-775.

It is shown in these articles that the explicit recognition of non-negativity constraints complicates the specifications of asset demand equations, and the corresponding comparative statics results. Hence, these are neglected in order to form tractable asset demand specifications. Hopefully, this is done at a small cost.

the asset demand specifications used in the empirical investigation.

The notation used throughout the remainder of this chapter is the following:

W_0 : initial wealth,

W : end-of-period wealth,

$1+r_p$: rate of return on the portfolio, where $r_p = (W/W_0) - 1$,

$1+r_i$: rate of return on asset i, where r_i is defined as interest received or paid, plus capital gain or loss received, on a dollar investment in asset i,

$\underline{r}$: vector consisting of all r_i,

a_i : dollar amount invested in asset i,

$\underline{a}$: vector consisting of all a_i,

$\underline{\mu}$: vector consisting of all μ_i, where $E(r_i) = \mu_i$,

Σ : variance-covariance matrix of asset rates of return; $E(\underline{r}-\underline{\mu})(\underline{r}-\underline{\mu})' = \Sigma$,

$\underline{\sigma}$: vector of the diagonal elements of Σ,

$\underline{\ddot{r}}$: vector consisting of all $1+r_i$,

$\underline{\ddot{\mu}}$: vector consisting of all $1+\mu_i$,

λ : Lagrangean multiplier,

$\underline{1}$: vector of 1's.

The definitions of g_p, m_p, $\underline{h}$, $\underline{m}$, $\underline{v}$, S, and $\underline{g}$ correspond to those given in II.C.2.

The following relationships immediately result from the above definitions:

$$W_0 = \underline{a}'\underline{1}, \tag{2.37}$$

$$E(W) = \underline{a}'\underline{\ddot{\mu}} = W_0 + \underline{a}'\underline{\mu}, \tag{2.38}$$

$$V(W) = \underline{a}'\Sigma\underline{a}, \tag{2.39}$$

$$E(1+r_p) = (1/W_0)\cdot \underline{a}'\underline{\mu} = 1 + \underline{h}'\underline{\mu}, \tag{2.40}$$

$$V(1+r_p) = (1/W_0)^2\cdot \underline{a}'\Sigma\underline{a} = \underline{h}'\Sigma\underline{h}, \tag{2.41}$$

The expected utility maximization problem may be formulated as

$$\max_{\underline{a},\lambda} L = E[U(W)] + \lambda(W_0 - \underline{a}'\underline{1}), \tag{2.42}$$

or

$$\max_{\underline{h},\lambda} L = E[U(1+r_p)] + \lambda(1 - \underline{h}'\underline{1}), \tag{2.43}$$

depending on the argument of the utility function.

1. Expected Utility Maximization with a Quadratic Utility Function

The expected utility maximization problem, involving quadratic utility of end-of-period wealth, is developed by substituting (2.38) and (2.39) into (2.23), and then substituting this expression into (2.42) to yield

$$\max_{\underline{a},\lambda} L = W_0 + \underline{a}'\underline{\mu} - b\underline{a}'\Sigma\underline{a} - bW_0^2 - 2bW_0\underline{a}'\underline{\mu} - b\underline{a}'\underline{\mu\mu}'\underline{a} + \lambda(W_0 - \underline{a}'\underline{1}). \tag{2.44}$$

The first-order conditions for the maximization of L are

$$\frac{\partial L}{\partial \underline{a}} = (1 - 2bW_0)\underline{\mu} - 2b(\Sigma+\underline{\mu\mu}')\underline{a} - \lambda\underline{1} = 0, \tag{2.45}$$

$$\frac{\partial L}{\partial \lambda} = W_0 - \underline{a}'\underline{1} = 0.$$

The second-order conditions for the constrained maximum are satisfied if the principal minors of the bordered Hessian,

$$\begin{bmatrix} -2b(\Sigma+\underline{\mu\mu}'), & -\underline{1} \\ -\underline{1}', & 0 \end{bmatrix}, \tag{2.46}$$

alternate in sign starting with positive for the principal minor described by the determinant of a 3x3 matrix, and then continuing for all principal minors described by the determinants of progressively higher order matrices.

The first-order conditions imply that

$$\begin{bmatrix} \underline{a} \\ \lambda \end{bmatrix} = \begin{bmatrix} 2b(\Sigma+\underline{\mu}\underline{\mu}'), & \underline{1} \\ \underline{1}', & 0 \end{bmatrix}^{-1} \begin{bmatrix} \underline{\mu}-2bW_0\underline{\mu} \\ W_0 \end{bmatrix} \quad (2.47)$$

By applying block inversion to (2.47), the asset demand equations may be expressed as

$$\underline{a} = \begin{cases} (1-2bW_0)Q_{11}\underline{\mu} + \underline{q}_{12}W_0, & \text{for } W_0 < W_0^*, \\ (1-2bW_0^*)Q_{11}\underline{\mu} + \underline{q}_{12}W_0^*, & \text{for } W_0 \geq W_0^*, \end{cases} \quad (2.48)$$

where

$$Q_{11} = (1/2b)\cdot(\Sigma+\underline{\mu}\underline{\mu}')^{-1} - (1/2b)(\underline{1}'(\Sigma+\underline{\mu}\underline{\mu}')^{-1}\underline{1})^{-1} (\Sigma+\underline{\mu}\underline{\mu}')^{-1}\underline{1}\underline{1}'(\Sigma+\underline{\mu}\underline{\mu}')^{-1}, \quad (2.49)$$

$$\underline{q}_{12} = (\underline{1}'(\Sigma+\underline{\mu}\underline{\mu}')^{-1}\underline{1})^{-1}(\Sigma+\underline{\mu}\underline{\mu}')^{-1}\underline{1}, \quad (2.50)$$

$$W_0^* = \frac{E^* - (\underline{\mu}'Q_{11}\underline{\mu})}{(1 + \underline{\mu}'\underline{q}_{12} - 2b\underline{\mu}'Q_{11}\underline{\mu})}, \text{ and} \quad (2.51)$$

$$E^* = \frac{(\ddot{\underline{\mu}}'\Sigma^{-1}\ddot{\underline{\mu}})}{2b[(\ddot{\underline{\mu}}'\Sigma^{-1}\ddot{\underline{\mu}}) + 1]}. \quad (2.52)$$

The conditions presented in (2.48) represent the <u>global</u> maximization of (2.44). The derivations of E^* and W_0^* are presented for the general case in chapter III.

If a riskless asset exists, then it is well known that the highest expected utility for (2.23), in the entire positive quadrant of mean-variance space, occurs at (E,V) = [(1/2b),0]. That is, there exists a level of initial wealth such that a further increase would result in a lower level of expected utility. However, if a riskless asset does not exist, then maximum attainable expected utility occurs at (E^*,V^*), where E^* is defined in (2.52), and

$$V^* = \frac{(\ddot{\underline{\mu}}'\Sigma^{-1}\ddot{\underline{\mu}})}{4b^2[(\ddot{\underline{\mu}}'\Sigma^{-1}\ddot{\underline{\mu}}) + 1]^2} . \tag{2.53}$$

The point (E^*, V^*) is derived conditional on the envelope of all efficiency loci corresponding to all values of initial wealth. Hence, the bliss point usually associated with quadratic utility can not be obtained since $E^* < (1/2b)$ and $V^* > 0$; but a different bliss point arises at a lower level of expected utility. In addition, the bliss point (E^*,V^*) depends on conditions that are not unique to quadratic utility.

Therefore, in applying expected quadratic utility of end-of-period wealth in the all risky assets case, expected utility will never reach 1/4b, which is the maximum over all values in the entire mean-variance space. Thus, one undesirable property of quadratic utility is eliminated. However, a different bliss point arises, and it is also evident in a wide class of utility functions.

Quadratic utility of end-of-period wealth does have some additional undesirable properties upon reflection of certain a priori economic considerations.[95] In addition, a major problem involving the empirical tractability of the model is that Q_{11} and $\underline{q}_{12}$ both depend, in a non-trivial way, on $\underline{\mu}$. In the analysis that follows, it is assumed that

---

[95]e.g., the asset demand equations are not linear homogeneous in wealth.

Q_{11} and $\underline{q}_{12}$ may be approximated as being constant. This implies that the asset demand equations have the following properties:

(1) the coefficient matrix of $\underline{\mu}$, i.e., $(1-2bW_0)Q_{11}$, is symmetric, and the sum of the elements of each individual column and row equals zero;

(2) if $W_0^* \leqq E^*$, then $(1-2bW_0) > 0$;[96]

(3) if the condition in property (2) is satisfied, then $(1-2bW_0)Q_{11}$ is the matrix of a positive semi-definite quadratic form;[97] and this further implies that the own-rate coefficients are non-negative;

(4) the sum of the elements of $\underline{q}_{12}$ equals one; and

(5) the asset demand equations are not linear homogeneous in wealth.

Formulating the expected utility maximization problem in terms of the portfolio rate of return approximation involves the use of (2.40), (2.41), (2.23), and (2.43). The derivation of the asset demand equations then proceeds analogously to the end-of-period wealth case. In particular, the first-order conditions for the relevant constrained maximization problem imply that

$$\begin{bmatrix} 2b(\Sigma+\underline{\mu}\underline{\mu}'), & \underline{1} \\ \underline{1}', & 0 \end{bmatrix} \begin{bmatrix} \underline{h} \\ \lambda \end{bmatrix} = \begin{bmatrix} (1-2b)\underline{\mu} \\ 1 \end{bmatrix}; \tag{2.54}$$

---

[96]If $W_0^* \leqq E^*$, then $W_0 \leqq W_0^* < \frac{1}{2b}$. This implies that $1-2bW_0 > 0$.

[97]See Paul A. Samuelson, Foundations of Economic Analysis (New York: Atheneum, 1972), pp. 376-379.

and the second-order conditions are identical to those corresponding to (2.46).

The block inversion of the matrix in (2.54) allows the asset demand equations to be represented as

$$\underline{h} = (1-2b)Q_{11}\underline{\mu} + \underline{q}_{12} , \qquad (2.55)$$

which is equivalent to

$$\underline{a} = (1-2b)Q_{11}\underline{\mu}\cdot W_0 + \underline{q}_{12}\cdot W_0 . \qquad (2.56)$$

The asset demand equations in (2.56), employing the assumption that Q_{11} and $\underline{q}_{12}$ are constants, have the following properties:

(1') the coefficient matrix of $\underline{\mu}\cdot W_0$ is symmetric, and the sum of the elements of each individual column and row equals zero;

(2') if $U'(1+r_p) > 0$ at $r_p = 0$, then $(1-2b) > 0$;

(3') if the condition in property (2') is satisfied, then $(1-2b)Q_{11}$ is the matrix of a positive semi-definite quadratic form; and this further implies that the own-rate coefficients are non-negative;

(4') the sum of the elements of $\underline{q}_{12}$ equals one; and

(5') the asset demand equations are linear homogeneous in wealth.

In addition, by specifying the argument of the utility function as portfolio rate of return, there is no longer a bliss point in $E(W)-V(W)$ space;[98] and the point of maximum utility in $E(1+r_p)-V(1+r_p)$ space is invariant with respect to changes in wealth.[99]

---

[98]Expected utility maximization problems may be transformed from $E(W)-V(W)$ space to $E(1+r_p)-V(1+r_p)$ space, and vice versa. See Mossin, "Optimal Multiperiod Portfolio Policies," op. cit.

[99]See chapter III for the general case.

Therefore, the rate of return specification leads to a much more desirable set of asset demand equations in comparison to the end-of-period wealth specification. However, the desirability of the former specification, in comparison to those that follow, is critically dependent on the assumption that the $\underline{\mu}\underline{\mu}'$ matrix may be approximated as being constant.[100] The remaining models that are considered in this section do not rely on this assumption.

2. Expected Utility Maximization with a Negative Exponential Utility Function

It is assumed that asset holding-period yields are normally distributed, and this implies that the negative exponential utility function on end-of-period wealth may be represented by (2.28). This expression is maximized if

$$\theta = E(W) - (b/2)\cdot V(W) \qquad (2.57)$$

is maximized.

Substituting (2.38) and (2.39) into (2.57), and substituting this result for expected utility in (2.42) yields

$$\max_{\underline{a},\lambda} L = W_0 + \underline{a}'\underline{\mu} - (b/2)\cdot\underline{a}'\Sigma\underline{a} + \lambda(W_0 - \underline{a}'\underline{1}) \qquad (2.58)$$

The first-order conditions for the constrained maximization problem described in (2.58) are

---

[100]Variances and covariances of asset rates of return are also assumed to be constant, but this assumption is by no means unique to these particular demand equations.

$$\frac{\partial L}{\partial \underline{a}} = \underline{\mu} - b\Sigma\underline{a} - \lambda\underline{1} = 0,$$

$$\frac{\partial L}{\partial \lambda} = W_0 - \underline{a}'\underline{1} = 0. \tag{2.59}$$

The second-order conditions for the constrained maximum are satisfied if the principal minors of the bordered Hessian,

$$\begin{bmatrix} -b\Sigma, & -\underline{1} \\ -\underline{1}', & 0 \end{bmatrix}, \tag{2.60}$$

alternate in sign starting positive for the principal minor described by the determinant of a 3x3 matrix, and then continuing for all principal minors described by the determinants of progressively higher order matrices.

The first-order conditions imply that

$$\begin{bmatrix} \underline{a} \\ \lambda \end{bmatrix} = \begin{bmatrix} b\Sigma, & \underline{1} \\ \underline{1}', & 0 \end{bmatrix}^{-1} \begin{bmatrix} \underline{\mu} \\ W_0 \end{bmatrix}, \tag{2.61}$$

By applying block inversion to (2.61), the asset demand equations may be expressed as

$$\underline{a} = \begin{cases} P_{11}\underline{\mu} + \underline{p}_{12}W_0 , & \text{for } W_0 < W_0^* , \\ P_{11}\underline{\mu} + \underline{p}_{12}W_0^* , & \text{for } W_0 \geq W_0^* , \end{cases} \tag{2.62}$$

where

$$P_{11} = (1/b)\cdot\Sigma^{-1} - (1/b)\cdot(\underline{1}'\Sigma^{-1}\underline{1})^{-1}\Sigma^{-1}\underline{\underline{11}}'\Sigma^{-1}, \tag{2.63}$$

$$\underline{p}_{12} = (\underline{1}'\Sigma^{-1}\underline{1})^{-1}\Sigma^{-1}\underline{1}, \tag{2.64}$$

$$W_0^* = \frac{E^* - \underline{\mu}'P_{11}\underline{\mu}}{1 + \underline{\mu}'\underline{p}_{12}}, \text{ and} \tag{2.65}$$

$$E^* = (1/b)\cdot(\underline{\ddot{\mu}}'\Sigma^{-1}\underline{\ddot{\mu}}). \tag{2.66}$$

The conditions presented in (2.62) represent the global maximization of (2.58). Previous research, based on the maximization of (2.58), has not incorporated the conditions described in (2.62).[101] Thus, these previous analyses are only valid for levels of initial wealth less than W_0^*.

The initial wealth necessary to obtain the maximum possible utility is given by (2.65). In mean-variance space, this level of utility corresponds to the point (E^*,V^*), where E^* is given in (2.66), and

$$V^* = (1/b)^2(\underline{\ddot{\mu}}'\Sigma^{-1}\underline{\ddot{\mu}}). \tag{2.67}$$

This bliss point is derived and interpreted for the general case in chapter III.

The "coefficients" in the asset demand equations, P_{11} and $\underline{p}_{12}$, depend only on variances, covariances, and the degree of absolute risk aversion, b. Hence, these have a distinct advantage to those in the quadratic utility case because of the exclusion of terms involving $\underline{\mu}$. Interpreting P_{11} and $\underline{p}_{12}$ as coefficient matrices implies that the asset demand equations have the following properties:

(1) the coefficient matrix of $\underline{\mu}$, i.e., P_{11}, is symmetric, and the

---

[101] For example, Parkin, op. cit.; and Lintner, "The Effect of Short Selling and Margin Requirements in Perfect Capital Markets," op. cit.

sum of the elements in each individual column and row equals zero;

(2) P_{11} is the matrix of a positive semi-definite quadratic form;[102] and this further implies that the own-rate coefficients are non-negative;

(3) the sum of the elements of $\underline{p}_{12}$ equals one; and

(4) the asset demand equations are not linear homogeneous in wealth.

The expected utility maximization problem in terms of portfolio rate of return approximation may be formulated by replacing (2.57) with

$$\theta = E(1+r_p) - (b/2)\cdot V(1+r_p). \tag{2.68}$$

The derivation of the asset demand equations proceeds analogously to that of the end-of-period wealth case by substituting (2.40) and (2.41) into (2.68), and forming the Lagrangean corresponding to (2.43).

The first-order conditions for this constrained maximization problem imply that

$$\begin{bmatrix} \underline{h} \\ \lambda \end{bmatrix} = \begin{bmatrix} b\Sigma, & \underline{1} \\ \underline{1}', & 0 \end{bmatrix}^{-1} \begin{bmatrix} \underline{\mu} \\ 1 \end{bmatrix}; \tag{2.69}$$

and the second-order conditions are identical to those corresponding to (2.60).

The block inversion of the matrix in (2.69) allows the asset demand equations to be represented as

$$\underline{h} = P_{11}\underline{\mu} + \underline{p}_{12}, \tag{2.70}$$

---

[102] See footnote 97.

which is equivalent to

$$\underline{a} = P_{11}\underline{\mu} \cdot W_0 + \underline{p}_{12} \cdot W_0 \ . \qquad (2.71)$$

Properties (1) through (3) listed for the asset demand equations presented in (2.62) are directly applicable to the asset demand equations in (2.71). However, property (4) is replaced by

(4') the asset demand equations described by (2.71) are linear homogeneous in wealth.

Therefore, the model conforms to *a priori* economic considerations that are often thought to be desirable, i.e., wealth homogeneity and non-negative coefficients on own-rates of return. In addition, the model introduces symmetry constraints into the usual specification of asset demand equations,[103] and suggests that changes in subjective estimates of variances and covariances of asset holding-period yields could cause the asset demand relationship to shift.

Melton[104] also compares the specifications in (2.62) and (2.70). He chooses the latter as his basic model primarily because of its wealth homogeneity property. A further and perhaps even greater motive for this choice originates from the conditions in (2.62), i.e., the existence of a saturation or bliss point.

Nevertheless, this model is based on the assumption of normality. Actual asset holding-period yields have often been posited to have an alternative joint probability distribution.[105] The final model considered

---

[103]See the references in footnote 47.

[104]Melton, *op. cit.*

[105]See, for example, Feldstein, *op. cit.*; and Lintner, "The Lognormality of Security Returns, Portfolio Selection and Market Equilibrium," *op.cit.*

in this section is formulated under the assumption of lognormality, which is at least as tenable as the assumption involving the normal distribution.[106]

3. Expected Utility Maximization with a Logarithmic Utility Function

The assumptions that are utilized in conjunction with a logarithmic utility function are described in II.C.2. In particular, the asset demand equations are derived from the maximization of expected logarithmic utility of end-of-period wealth, where end-of-period wealth is lognormally distributed. In addition, the asset holding-period yields are assumed to be joint lognormally distributed, and Lintner's "second-best" second-order approximation is utilized for the mean of logarithmic portfolio rate of return.[107]

The constrained maximization of expected utility may be formulated, using (2.36), as

$$\max_{\underline{a},\lambda} L = \log W_0 + \underline{h}'\underline{m} + \frac{1}{2}\underline{h}'\underline{v} - \frac{1}{2}(\underline{h}'S\underline{h}) + \lambda(1 - \underline{h}'\underline{1}). \quad (2.72)$$

The first-order conditions are

$$\frac{\partial L}{\partial \underline{h}} = \underline{m} + \frac{1}{2}\underline{v} - S\underline{h} - \lambda\underline{1} = 0,$$

$$\frac{\partial L}{\partial \lambda} = 1 - \underline{h}'\underline{1} = 0. \quad (2.73)$$

---

[106] Ibid.

[107] See II.C.2 and Lintner, "The Lognormality of Security Returns, Portfolio Selection and Market Equilibrium," op. cit.

The second-order conditions for the constrained maximum are satisfied if the principal minors of the bordered Hessian,

$$\begin{bmatrix} -S, & \underline{1} \\ -\underline{1}', & 0 \end{bmatrix}, \tag{2.74}$$

alternate in sign starting with positive for the principal minor described by the determinant of a 3x3 matrix, and then continuing for all principal minors described by the determinants of progressively higher order matrices.

The first-order conditions imply that

$$\begin{bmatrix} \underline{h} \\ \lambda \end{bmatrix} = \begin{bmatrix} S, & \underline{1} \\ \underline{1}', & 0 \end{bmatrix}^{-1} \begin{bmatrix} \underline{m} + \frac{1}{2}\underline{v} \\ 1 \end{bmatrix}. \tag{2.75}$$

The application of block inversion to (2.75) allows the asset demand equations to be represented as

$$\underline{h} = B_{11}\underline{m} + \frac{1}{2} B_{11}\underline{v} + \underline{b}_{12}, \tag{2.76}$$

where

$$B_{11} = S^{-1} - (\underline{1}'S^{-1}\underline{1})^{-1}S^{-1}\underline{1}\underline{1}'S^{-1}, \tag{2.77}$$

$$\underline{b}_{12} = (\underline{1}'S^{-1}\underline{1})^{-1}S^{-1}\underline{1}. \tag{2.78}$$

The asset demands in (2.76) may also be expressed as

$$\underline{a} = B_{11}\underline{m}\cdot W_0 + (\frac{1}{2} B_{11}\underline{v} + \underline{b}_{12})\cdot W_0. \tag{2.79}$$

Even though this expected utility maximization problem is expressed in terms of end-of-period wealth, a bliss point does not emerge.[108] Additional properties of (2.79) are the following:

(1) the coefficient matrix of $\underline{m}$, i.e., B_{11}, is symmetric, and the sum of the elements in each individual column and row equals zero;

(2) B_{11} is the matrix of a positive semi-definite quadratic form;[109] this further implies that the own rate coefficients are non-negative;

(3) the sum of the elements of $(\frac{1}{2} B_{11}\underline{v} + \underline{b}_{12})$ equals one;

(4) the asset demand equations are linear homogeneous in wealth.

These properties are analogous to those presented for negative exponential utility of portfolio rate of return. The primary difference involves the use of logarithmic means, variances, and covariances in (2.79).

Equation (2.79) may be used directly in empirical estimation with the logarithmic holding-period yields, or an approximation may be utilized in order to transform the logarithmic holding-period yields into natural units. In particular, an approximation may be based on the marginal log-normal distribution of $1+r_i$. This implies that the logarithmic mean, m_i, may be expressed as[110]

$$m_i = \log\,(1+\mu_i) - \frac{1}{2}\log\,[\frac{\sigma_{ii}^2}{(1+\mu_i)^2} + 1]\ , \qquad (2.80)$$

---

[108] This is because the maximization of expected logarithmic utility of end-of-period wealth is equivalent to the analogous maximization with the argument of the utility function defined as portfolio rate of return. See chapter III.

[109] See footnote 97.

[110] See, for example, Felstein, op. cit.

and using log (1+x) $\simeq$ x, for small x, reduces this expression to

$$m_i \simeq \mu_i - \frac{1}{2}\left[\frac{\sigma_{ii}^2}{(1+\mu_i)^2}\right] \tag{2.81}$$

A somewhat less satisfactory approximation may be applied to (2.81) to yield[111]

$$m_i = \mu_i - \frac{1}{2}\sigma_{ii}^2. \tag{2.82}$$

Substituting (2.82) into (2.79) yields

$$\underline{a} = B_{11}\underline{\mu}\cdot W_0 - \frac{1}{2}B_{11}\underline{\sigma}\cdot W_0 + (\frac{1}{2}B_{11}\underline{v} + \underline{b}_{12})\cdot W_0. \tag{2.83}$$

Some very heroic assumptions (and approximations) must be exploited in order to allow $\underline{\sigma}$ to vary while keeping B_{11} and $(\frac{1}{2}B_{11}\underline{v} + \underline{b}_{12})$ constant. Nevertheless, in the estimation of the asset demand equations, the effects of the variances of asset holding-period yields are incorporated in the manner indicated in (2.83). However, similar specifications also follow from the linearization of expressions for desired holdings of assets from other models of expected utility maximization.

---

[111]If μ_i = .03, then the percentage error in using the denominator of (2.82) instead of the denominator of (2.81) is 6%. If μ_i = .05, then the percentage error is 10%. These approximations are presented primarily for reasons of empirical tractability in the specification of asset demand equations.

F. Summary and Conclusions

The portfolio selection problem in this chapter is developed in a general framework to facilitate its applicability to seven out of the ten investor groups in this study. Although each of the investor groups included has special characteristics associated with their individual operations, the models that are specified may be utilized as approximations to their portfolio selection behavior.

The asset demand equations derived in this chapter are not in their final form. The implications of this portfolio selection framework, from which the demand equations are derived, are that there is either a costless instantaneous portfolio adjustment, or that the asset demand equations merely indicate the desired, instead of the actual, holdings of assets. The final form of the asset demand equations are not specified until chapter V, when models of portfolio adjustment are considered.

It should be noted that even though a complete set of asset demand equations is derived as the solution to a portfolio selection problem, only a subset of these asset demands is estimated for each investor group. In particular, demand equations for U.S. Government securities that are disaggregated across certain maturity boundaries are the primary products of the portfolio selection problem analyzed herein.

This chapter also includes a comparison of alternative portfolio selection theories. These include expected utility maximization, safety-first analysis, and the maximization of the market value of equity given by the Sharpe-Lintner capital asset pricing model. The choice of the portfolio theory that is utilized to form asset demand specifications is based, in part, on these comparisons. In particular, the expected utility maximization framework is selected due to its explicit treatment of risk aversion along with its general applicability.

CHAPTER III

PROPERTIES OF ASSET DEMAND EQUATIONS DERIVED FROM MEAN-VARIANCE ANALYSIS: SOME GENERAL RESULTS

A. Introduction

This chapter considers some important properties of asset demand equations that result from the maximization of expected utility. In most cases, it is assumed that expected utility is described by a function of the mean and variance of the argument of the utility function.[1] In addition, a one-period optimization framework is utilized for this analysis.

The results in this chapter are used for the general specification of the desired levels of asset demands for the seven investor groups considered in chapter II.[2] The specific properties of the asset demand equations previously introduced in II.E may then be empirically tested for the constraints inherent in their specifications.[3]

The general specifications of mean-variance expected utility maximization problems are presented in section III.B. Both the one-riskless

---

[1]Sufficient conditions for expected utility to become a function of only the mean and variance of the argument of the utility function are discussed in II.C.

[2]The unifying characteristic for these seven investor groups is that only the asset side of the balance sheet is considered. The portfolio selection problem is to determine the allocation of total portfolio wealth among the individual assets.

[3]e.g., symmetry and adding-up constraints on the coefficients.

and all-risky assets cases are examined.

The derivations in section III.B are utilized in the analysis of section III.C where symmetry and adding-up constraints on the coefficient matrix of expected holding-period yields are considered. In section III.C, a condition is presented that is, in general, necessary and sufficient for the existence of a symmetric coefficient matrix. A general specification of expected utility, in terms of the mean and variance of the argument of the utility function, is also presented that satisfies this condition.

A comparative statics analysis of wealth effects is presented in section III.D. The important, although largely neglected, existence of a bliss point for certain specifications of expected utility is discussed. In addition, alternative specifications for the argument of utility function are examined in conjunction with their indifference curve maps in mean and variance of end-of-period wealth space. The implications of a bliss point are most clearly seen in this framework.

Implications of the various measures of risk aversion found in the literature are investigated in section III.E. These measures are examined in the context of their usefulness in comparative statics analysis. In the all-risky assets case, the implications of the Pratt-Arrow measures of risk aversion on the comparative statics properties of asset demands are, by definition, ambiguous in most instances.[4] However, an unambiguous case results from specifying the utility function to have constant relative risk aversion.

---

[4]The usual comparative statics properties involve either the absolute or proportional changes in the riskless asset as a result of a change in initial wealth.

B. General Mean-Variance Expected Utility Maximization Problems

Four general specifications of the expected utility maximization problem are considered in this section. They are described by combinations of asset risk characteristic assumptions, and assumptions concerning the argument of the utility function. In particular, the portfolio selection problem is examined for cases with or without the existence of a riskless asset, and with either end-of-period wealth or portfolio rate of return as the argument of the utility function. As discussed previously in II.B.2b, the portfolio rate of return case is used as an approximation to form specifications of asset demand equations for use in time series estimation. The desirability of this specification results from the wealth homogeneity property of the asset demand equations; i.e., in this case, the asset demand equations are homogeneous of the first degree in portfolio wealth.

The analysis in this section focuses primarily on the derivations and general similarities of the four alternative specifications. That is, the first-order conditions for maximum expected utility are derived, and then contrasted among the possibilities considered. Of particular interest is the comparison between the cases with and without a riskless asset. It is shown that the first-order conditions, and, therefore, the implicit asset demand equations, are very similar in these two cases.

The primary use of the derivations is, however, for the analyses of later sections in this chapter. In particular, the analysis concerning possible symmetry and adding-up properties, inherent in the coefficient matrix on the vector of expected holding-period yields, directly utilizes the first-order conditions derived below.

The asset demand equations previously presented in section II.E are a subset of those attainable from the general analysis presented in this section.

1. Utility of End-of-Period Wealth

If the argument of the utility function is assumed to be end-of-period wealth, then the mean-variance expected utility maximization problem may be represented as[5]

$$\max_{\underline{a},\lambda} L = U[E(W),V(W)] + \lambda(\underline{a}'\underline{1} - W_0), \tag{3.1}$$

where

$$E(W) = \begin{cases} W_0 + \underline{a}'\underline{\mu} & \text{, if all assets are risky,} \\ W_0 + a_0 r_0 + \hat{\underline{a}}'\hat{\underline{\mu}} & \text{, if } a_0 \text{ is riskless} \end{cases} \tag{3.2}$$

$$V(W) = \begin{cases} \underline{a}'\Sigma\underline{a} & \text{, if all assets are risky,} \\ \hat{\underline{a}}'\hat{\Sigma}\hat{\underline{a}} & \text{, if } a_0 \text{ is riskless,} \end{cases} \tag{3.3}$$

$$\underline{a} = \begin{bmatrix} a_0 \\ \hat{\underline{a}} \end{bmatrix}, \tag{3.4}$$

$$\underline{\mu} = \begin{bmatrix} \mu_0 \\ \hat{\underline{\mu}} \end{bmatrix}, \text{ and} \tag{3.5}$$

[5]The notation used in this chapter is introduced in chapter II.

$$\Sigma = \begin{bmatrix} \sigma_{00} & \sigma_{01} \cdots \sigma_{0,n-1} \\ \sigma_{10} & \\ \cdot & \hat{\Sigma} \\ \cdot & \\ \cdot & \\ \sigma_{n-1,0} & \end{bmatrix}, \tag{3.6}$$

If a_0 is riskless, then $\mu_0 = r_0$ and $\sigma_{i0} = \sigma_{0i} = 0$, $i=0,\ldots,n-1$.

The asset demands are derived from the first-order conditions for the constrained maximization problem in (3.1). If a riskless asset is postulated, then the first-order conditions may be rewritten as

$$\begin{bmatrix} a_0 \\ \underline{a} \end{bmatrix} = -(1/2)(U_E/U_V)P_1 \begin{bmatrix} r_0 \\ \underline{\mu} \end{bmatrix} + \underline{p}_1 W_0, \tag{3.7}$$

where

$$P_1 = \begin{bmatrix} \underline{1}'\hat{\Sigma}^{-1}\underline{1}, & -\underline{1}'\hat{\Sigma}^{-1} \\ -\hat{\Sigma}^{-1}\underline{1}, & \hat{\Sigma}^{-1} \end{bmatrix}, \text{ and} \tag{3.8}$$

$$\underline{p}_1 = \begin{bmatrix} 1 \\ \underline{0} \end{bmatrix} . \tag{3.9}$$

It is easily verified that the matrix P_1 is symmetric with non-negative main diagonal elements. In addition, the sum of the elements in each individual row and column of P_1 equals zero. This matrix does not, however, fully describe the properties of the matrix of partial derivatives $\partial \underline{a}/\partial \underline{\mu}$ since U_E/U_V is not independent of $\underline{\mu}$.[6] The conditions for a symmetric matrix of partial derivatives $\partial \underline{a}/\partial \underline{\mu}$ are discussed in section III.C.

If a riskless asset does not exist because of the presence of persistent and uncertain price inflation and the absence of an adequately indexed instrument, then the relevant first-order conditions may be rewritten as

$$\underline{a} = -(1/2)(U_E/U_V)\ P_2\underline{\mu} + \underline{p}_2 W_0, \qquad (3.10)$$

where

$$P_2 = \Sigma^{-1} - (\underline{1}'\Sigma^{-1}\underline{1})^{-1}\ \Sigma^{-1}\underline{1}\underline{1}'\Sigma^{-1}, \text{ and} \qquad (3.11)$$

$$\underline{p}_2 = (\underline{1}'\Sigma^{-1}\underline{1})^{-1}\ \Sigma^{-1}\underline{1}. \qquad (3.12)$$

For many specifications of expected utility of end-of-period wealth that reduce to a function of the mean and variance of end-of-period wealth, the asset demands implicit in (3.10) do <u>not</u> represent the solution to the global maximization of (3.1). For example, in II.E, it was claimed that quadratic and negative exponential utilities of end-of-period wealth have bliss points in mean-variance space conditional on the set of attainable portfolios over all levels of initial wealth in the all-risky assets case. The existence of a bliss point implies that (3.10) represents a global maximum only for particular levels of

---

[6]The expression $-(U_E/U_V)$ is the reciprocal of the slope of an indifference curve in mean-variance space; i.e., $(dE/dV) = -(U_V/U_E)$.

initial wealth. Sufficient conditions for the existence of a bliss point, and the implications of its existence, are examined in section III.D.

If the second-order conditions for the constrained maximum in (3.1) are satisfied for the case described in (3.10), then it can be shown that the matrix P_2 is symmetric with non-negative main diagonal elements. In addition, the sum of the elements in each individual row and column of P_2 equals zero.

The same qualifications concerning the symmetry of $\partial \underline{a}/\partial \underline{\mu}$ are relevant for (3.10), as they were for (3.7), because of the presence of U_E/U_V. The expression U_E/U_V has additional importance in (3.10) because of the previously mentioned possibility of a bliss point. These properties are considered in detail in later sections of this chapter.

The final property of (3.10) concerns the vector $\underline{p}_2$. It is easily shown that the sum of the elements of this vector equals one.

Despite assuming the existence of a riskless asset for the derivation of (3.7), and assuming its absence for (3.10), these systems of equations have similar properties. In particular, the P_1 and P_2 matrices are both symmetric with positive main diagonal elements; and the $\underline{p}_1$ and $\underline{p}_2$ vectors have identical sums for their elements.

Thus, to the extent that some investor groups may be basing their portfolio selection on nominal instead of real holding-period yields, the specification of asset demand equations for empirical implementation would be similar to those of investor groups basing their optimization on real holding-period yields. The primary difference would be the exclusion in the former, of variables representing the mean and variance of expected price inflation except for nominal interest rate forecasts based on "Fisher effect" considerations.

2. Utility of Portfolio Rate of Return

If the argument of the utility function is assumed to be portfolio rate of return, then the mean-variance expected utility maximization problem may be represented as

$$\max_{\underline{a},\lambda} L = U[E(1+r_p),V(1+r_p)] + \lambda(\underline{a}'\underline{1} - W_0), \tag{3.13}$$

where

$$E(1+r_p) = \begin{cases} 1 + (1/W_0)\underline{a}'\underline{\mu} & \text{, if all assets are risky,} \\ 1 + (1/W_0)a_0r_0 + (1/W_0)\hat{\underline{a}}'\hat{\underline{\mu}} & \text{, if } a_0 \text{ is riskless,} \end{cases} \tag{3.14}$$

$$V(1+r_p) = \begin{cases} (1/W_0)^2\underline{a}'\Sigma\underline{a} & \text{, if all assets are risky,} \\ (1/W_0)^2\hat{\underline{a}}'\hat{\Sigma}\hat{\underline{a}} & \text{, if } a_0 \text{ is riskless.} \end{cases} \tag{3.15}$$

The asset demands are derived from the first-order conditions for the constrained maximization problem in (3.13). If a riskless asset is assumed to exist, then the first-order conditions may be rewritten as

$$\begin{bmatrix} a_0 \\ \hat{\underline{a}} \end{bmatrix} = -(1/2)(U_{ER}/U_{VR})P_1 \begin{bmatrix} r_0 \\ \underline{\mu} \end{bmatrix} W_0 + \underline{p}_1 W_0, \tag{3.16}$$

where P_1 and $\underline{p}_1$ are defined in (3.8) and (3.9), respectively.[7]

---

[7]Also note that $\partial U(1+r_p)/\partial E(1+r_p) = U_{ER}$ and $\partial U(1+r_p)/\partial V(1+r_p) = U_{VR}$.

The fundamental difference between (3.16) and the similar specification for the end-of-period wealth case in (3.7) is that, in the former, both terms in the expression are scaled by initial wealth W_0. Thus, if U_{ER}/U_{VR} is independent of initial wealth, then the asset demands implicit in (3.16) are first-degree homogeneous in initial wealth. For utility functions satisfying this condition, the portfolio selection problem is independent of the level of initial wealth with respect to the proportional allocation among the assets. That is, the wealth of the investor does not effect desired asset proportions. This characteristic was claimed to be desirable for the portfolio selection problems of the seven investor groups considered in this and the previous chapters.[8]

Additional properties pertaining to the expression in (3.16) are similar to those already discussed in conjunction with (3.7). In both cases, the matrix P_1 and the vector $\underline{p}_1$ appear; and similar considerations concerning the matrix of partial derivatives $\partial \underline{a}/\partial \underline{\mu}$ are relevant.

A property of particular importance in this case, however, is that $-(U_{ER}/U_{VR})$ represents the reciprocal of the slope of an indifference curve in the mean and variance of portfolio rate of return space. Thus, when transforming this preference ordering into E(W)-V(W) space, the indifference curves shift for changes in initial wealth.[9] This is particularly important for the all-risky assets case, which is considered immediately below, since this property alleviates the possibility of a

---

[8]See II.B.5 for a discussion concerning the approximations utilized in specifying the portfolio selection problems of these investor groups. Also see II.B.2b for a discussion concerning the desirability of asset demand equations that are linear homogeneous in wealth.

[9]See section III.D.

bliss point in E(W)-V(W) space if the investor is initially fully invested.

If a riskless asset does not exist, then the first-order conditions from the relevant constrained maximum problem may be rewritten as

$$\underline{a} = -(1/2)(U_{ER}/U_{VR})P_2\underline{\mu}\cdot W_0 + \underline{p}_2W_0, \qquad (3.17)$$

where P_2 and $\underline{p}_2$ are defined in (3.11) and (3.12), respectively.

Again, an important difference between (3.17) and the similar specification for the end-of-period wealth case in (3.10) is that, in the former, both terms in the expression are scaled by initial wealth W_0. Thus, an investor's level of wealth does not affect the proportional allocation of his assets if U_{ER}/U_{VR} is independent of initial wealth.

An important advantage of (3.17), in comparison to (3.10), is that the possibility of a bliss point in E(W)-V(W) space is eliminated under very general conditions on the utility of portfolio rate of return.[10] Thus, in the all-risky assets case, the specification described by (3.17) conforms much more closely to observed portfolio selection behavior.

Additional properties of the expression in (3.17) are similar to those already discussed for (3.10). In both cases, the implicit asset demands are dependent on the matrix P_2 and the vector $\underline{p}_2$.

C. Symmetry and Sum Constraints on the Coefficient Matrix

The analysis concerning the possible existence of a symmetric coefficient matrix on the vector of expected holding-period yields is investigated using the general framework presented in the previous section. Sum (or adding-up) constraints on rows and columns of the coefficient

---

[10]The implications of this difference are further discussed in section III.D.

matrix are also examined in this framework. The results are presented for the case where an investor's assessments are in real terms; however, similar results are valid for the nominal case.

The imposition of symmetry and adding-up constraints are important for the specification and estimation of asset demand relationships. For an investor's entire set of demand equations, it is necessary that the column sums of this coefficient matrix equal zero. This property allows the budget (or wealth) constraint to be satisfied at all times.

Symmetry and row adding-up constraints on the coefficient matrix of the vector of expected real holding-period yields need not be imposed in order to form a consistent set of demand equations.[11] These additional constraints may arise, however, from the specific choice-theoretic framework underlying an investor's portfolio selection.

Given that a coefficient matrix has zero column sums, the symmetry property implies zero row sums. Thus, if an investor forms expected real holding-period yields by the subtraction of the expected rate of price inflation from expected nominal holding-period yields, then the expected rate of price inflation would have a coefficient identically equal to zero in each asset demand equation.

Even if the asset demands are determined entirely by expected nominal holding-period yields, the rate of price inflation may be important via the formation of the expectations.[12] However, if <u>all</u> expected nom-

---

[11] i.e., consistent in the sense that the budget constraint is satisfied at all times.

[12] See, for example, Martin Feldstein and Gary Chamberlain, "Multimarket Expectations and the Rate of Interest," <u>Journal of Money, Credit and Banking</u>, V (November, 1973), 873-902; Martin Feldstein and Otto

inal holding-period yields incorporated the "Fisher effect", then, given zero row sums, the level of expected price inflation again would not have any affect on an investor's portfolio allocation in the absence of cash as a potential asset. The importance of price inflation on the demand for U.S. Government securities is an area that is empirically examined.

In order to investigate the above conditions on the coefficient matrix, only the asset demands implicitly specified in (3.10) and (3.17) may be considered without any loss of generality. That is, these two sets of asset demands are used to represent all four cases. This may be done since the matrices P_1 and P_2, and the vectors $\underline{p}_1$ and $\underline{p}_2$, have similar properties; i.e., both matrices are symmetric, and all relevant sums of elements of these matrices and vectors are identical.

As a preliminary observation, it may be noted that if U_E/U_V is equal to a constant (or assumed to be constant as an approximation)[13] then all of the previously discussed conditions result for the asset demands in (3.10); i.e., the coefficient matrix on the vector of expected real holding-period yields is symmetric with row and column sums equal to zero. This same result is true for the asset demands in (3.17) when U_{ER}/U_{VR} is constant.

Eckstein "The Fundamental Determinants of the Interest Rate," Review of Economics and Statistics, LII (November, 1970), 363-375; and Franco Modigliani and Robert J. Shiller, "Inflation, Rational Expectations, and the Term Structure of Interest Rates," Economica, XL (February, 1973), 12-43. Price inflation plays a role in the determination of nominal long-term interest rates in these analyses.

[13]This is the approximation used for the quadratic utility case in II.E. For negative exponential utility, this ratio is a constant.

The investigation of symmetry, for the coefficient matrix on the vector of expected real holding-period yields in (3.10), focuses on the following Jacobian matrix:

$$\frac{\partial \underline{a}}{\partial \underline{\mu}} = [I + (1/2)\left[\frac{U_{EE}U_V - U_{VE}U_E}{(U_V)^2}\right] P_2\underline{\mu\mu}' + \left[\frac{U_{EV}U_V - U_{VV}U_E}{(U_V)^2}\right] P_2\underline{\mu a}'\Sigma]^{-1}$$

$$\cdot\ (-1/2)[(U_E/U_V)P_2 + \left[\frac{U_{EE}U_V - U_{VE}U_E}{(U_V)^2}\right] P_2\underline{\mu a}'], \tag{3.18}$$

The similar expression for the asset demands in (3.17) is

$$\frac{\partial \underline{a}}{\partial \underline{\mu}} = [I + (1/2)\left[\frac{U_{ER,ER}U_{VR} - U_{VR,ER}U_{ER}}{(U_{VR})^2}\right] P_2\underline{\mu\mu}'$$

$$+ (1/W_0)\left[\frac{U_{ER,VR}U_{VR} - U_{VR,VR}U_{ER}}{(U_{VR})^2}\right] P_2\underline{\mu a}'\Sigma]^{-1}$$

$$\cdot\ (-1/2)[W_0(U_{ER}/U_{VR})P_2 + \left[\frac{U_{ER,ER}U_{VR} - U_{VR,ER}U_{ER}}{(U_{VR})^2}\right] P_2\underline{\mu a}'], \tag{3.19}$$

The expressions in (3.18) and (3.19) are directly applicable to specifications utilized in empirical work since, in many cases, it is desirable to employ a linearized version of an economic relationship. Thus, symmetry is discussed with respect to (3.18) and (3.19).

The Jacobian matrices in (3.18) and (3.19) each consist of several terms. These terms are pairwise identical except for the scaling of (3.19) by functions of initial wealth.

The overall symmetry of the Jacobians is dependent on the properties of each term. For the expressions (3.18) and (3.19) to be symmetric, each of the terms must be symmetric. However, the terms $P_2\underline{\mu a'}\Sigma$ and $P_2\underline{\mu a'}$ are not, in general, symmetric. This is the case since $\underline{\mu a'}$ is not symmetric except for certain restrictive values of P_2, $\underline{\mu}$, or $\underline{p}_2$.[14]

In general, necessary and sufficient conditions for the existence of a symmetric Jacobian matrix in (3.18) are

$$U_V U_{EE} - U_E U_{VE} = 0, \text{ and}$$
$$U_V U_{EV} - U_E U_{VV} = 0; \tag{3.20}$$

and the corresponding expressions for (3.19) are

$$U_{VR} U_{ER,ER} - U_{ER} U_{VR,ER} = 0, \text{ and}$$
$$U_{VR} U_{ER,VR} - U_{ER} U_{VR,VR} = 0. \tag{3.21}$$

If (3.20) and (3.21) are satisfied, then the expressions in (3.18) and (3.19) reduce to

$$\frac{\partial \underline{a}}{\partial \underline{\mu}} = -(1/2)(U_E/U_V)P_2, \text{ and} \tag{3.18'}$$

$$\frac{\partial \underline{a}}{\partial \underline{\mu}} = -(1/2)\cdot W_0(U_{ER}/U_{VR})P_2. \tag{3.19'}$$

For $-(U_E/U_V),-(U_{ER}/U_{VR}) > 0$,[15] the own-rate coefficients are unambiguously non-negative in each asset demand equation. In addition, these matrices have zero row and column sums. The existence of a symmetric coefficient matrix also has a distinct interpretation in terms of risk aversion. This is demonstrated in section III.E.

---

[14] e.g., $\underline{\mu}_2 = \underline{p}_2$, which sets the vector of expected real holding-period yields equal to a function of the variance-covariance matrix Σ. However, certain properties of the utility function may cause the expressions with $\underline{\mu a}'$ to equal the zero matrix. This is discussed immediately below in the text.

[15] Following Tobin, these are the conditions for an investor to be risk averse. See Tobin, "Liquidity Preference as Behavior Toward Risk," op. cit.

A general functional form of utility that satisfies the necessary and sufficient conditions for symmetry is

$$U(E,V) = g[E-bV]. \qquad (3.22)$$

This may be shown by substituting (3.22) into each of the equations in (3.20). Similar derivations are valid for the case involving the mean and variance of portfolio rate of return.

The mean-variance preference ordering involving the negative exponential utility function, as described in II.C., satisfies the conditions in (3.20) and (3.21). Thus, as previously noted in II.E., the coefficient matrix on the vector of expected real holding-period yields is symmetric. However, quadratic utility does not satisfy the necessary and sufficient condition for symmetry.[16]

The approach taken for the empirical investigation, concerning the demand for U.S. Government securities, appeals directly to the above analysis. Since it is not the case that all mean-variance utility functions are consistent with symmetric coefficient matrices on the vector of expected real holding-period yields, the asset demands are initially estimated unconstrained. In addition, the unconstrained case does not impose row adding-up constraints. A second set of regressions is also performed in order to test the hypothesis that this matrix is symmetric.[17]

---

[16]The other specification in II.E involving logarithmic utility of end-of-period wealth is not applicable to this framework. This is because of the approximation used for the logarithm of the mean of portfolio rate of return is not strictly in terms of the mean and variance of the argument of the utility function.

[17]A complete set of an investor's asset demands is not estimated;

D. A Comparative Statics Analysis of Wealth Effects on Expected Utility

This section investigates the effects of changes of initial wealth on an investor's expected utility. This is examined for both of the previous specifications of the argument of the utility function; i.e., end-of-period wealth and portfolio rate of return. When comparing these alternative specifications for changes in initial wealth, it is demonstrated that the relationship between their respective indifference curve maps in E(W)-V(W) space is of particular importance.

1. The General Case for the Existence of a Bliss Point

The possible existence of a bliss point in E(W)-V(W) space, conditional on the set of all attainable portfolios obtained by varying the level of initial wealth, has been introduced by Bierwag and Grove.[18] They, however, dismiss this property as an extreme case occuring only for "large" values of initial wealth. They also attempt to rationalize this phenomenon in terms of "risk saturation."

Nevertheless, this bliss point has implications similar to those of the much maligned quadratic utility function. In particular, the applications of quadratic utility, and the additional general cases considered below, should be restricted to levels of initial wealth satisfying the property that marginal expected utility is positive.

---

but within any subset of asset demands, involving two or more equations, the symmetry constraint is testable on certain pairs of coefficients.

[18]Bierwag and Grove, "Indifference Curves in Asset Analysis," op. cit.; and, Bierwag and Grove, "Slutsky Equations for Assets," op. cit. The bliss point represents the highest attainable level of expected utility for all values of initial wealth.

The existence of a bliss point is predominant only in the case where all assets are risky, with a non-singular variance-covariance matrix for the vector of holding-period yields, and where end-of-period wealth is the argument of the utility function. This is consistent with the specification in (3.10); and sufficient conditions for the existence of a bliss point are given in terms of this specification.

The implications of the existence of a bliss point are highly untenable. In particular, for some values of initial wealth, an investor would maximize expected utility by simply disposing of a certain portion of his wealth. That is, a higher level of expected utility is reached with a lower level of initial wealth. It appears that this implication is more of a reflection on the models that have a bliss point than on the economics of portfolio selection.

For any given level of initial wealth, an investor characterized as a risk averse diversifier will restrict his portfolio selection to a set of efficient portfolios. An efficient portfolio may be described as one in which the variance of end-of-period wealth is at a minimum for a given level of expected end-of-period wealth. The set of efficient portfolios may be described by an efficiency locus (or frontier) as depicted in Figure 3.1 for W_0^* and W_0^+, where $W_0^* < W_0^+$.[19] There is an efficiency locus corresponding to every level of initial wealth.

The set of all attainable portfolios, subsuming all levels of initial wealth, has a boundary that corresponds to the envelope of all efficiency loci. This is represented by V' in Figure 3.1.

---

[19]See, for example, Markowitz, op. cit.; or Roy, op. cit.

FIGURE 3.1

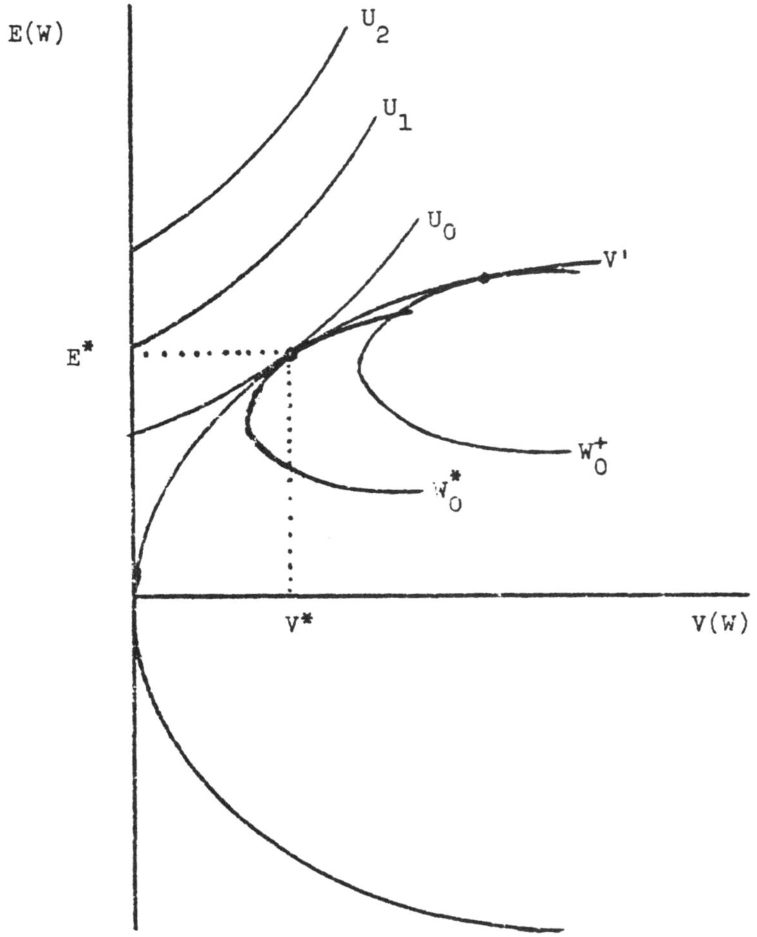

UTILITY OF END-OF-PERIOD WEALTH

The algebraic expression for V' may be obtained from the first-order conditions of the following constrained minimization problem:

$$\min_{\underline{a},\lambda} L = \underline{a}'\Sigma\underline{a} + \lambda(\underline{a}'\underline{1} + \underline{a}'\underline{\mu} - E_0), \qquad (3.23)$$

where E_0 is a constant level of expected end-of-period wealth. It follows that

$$V' = \frac{E_0^2}{(\underline{\ddot{\mu}}'\Sigma^{-1}\underline{\ddot{\mu}})}. \qquad (3.24)$$

A set of indifference curves consistent with that of a risk averse diversifier[20] is represented in Figure 3.1 as U_0, U_1, and U_2, where $U_0 < U_1 < U_2$. It is apparent upon the inspection of Figure 3.1 that the highest point of attainable utility, conditional on V', is reached at (E^*,V^*). In general, a sufficient condition for the existence of a bliss point is satisfied if, along every indifference curve,

$$\frac{dE}{dV} > 0, \text{ and} \qquad (3.25)$$

$$\frac{d^2E}{dV^2} \geqq 0. \qquad (3.26)$$

The values of E^*, V^*, and W_0^* may be obtained from

$$\max_{E,V,\lambda} L = U(E,V) + \lambda\left(V - \frac{E^2}{(\underline{\ddot{\mu}}'\Sigma^{-1}\underline{\ddot{\mu}})}\right). \qquad (3.27)$$

The first-order conditions for the constrained maximization problem in (3.27) imply that

---

[20]See Tobin, "Liquidity Preference as Behavior Toward Risk," op. cit.

$$E^* = -(1/2)(U_E/U_V)(\underline{\ddot{\mu}}'\Sigma^{-1}\underline{\ddot{\mu}}), \tag{3.28}$$

$$V^* = -(1/4)(U_E/U_V)^2(\underline{\ddot{\mu}}'\Sigma^{-1}\underline{\ddot{\mu}}), \text{ and} \tag{3.29}$$

$$W_0^* = \frac{E^* + (1/2)(U_E/U_V)\underline{\mu}'P_2\underline{\mu}}{(1 + \underline{\mu}'\underline{p}_2)} . \tag{3.30}$$

Thus, when using a specification of (3.10) that satisfies (3.25) and (3.26), the vector of asset demands implicit in (3.10) is a solution to the expected utility maximization problem for levels of initial wealth W_0 such that $W_0 \leqq W_0^*$. For $W_0 > W_0^*$, the vector of asset demands represents a local maximum that does not correspond to the global maximum. In particular, if $W_0 = W_0^+ > W_0^*$, as in Figure 3.1, then the global maximum is obtained by disposing of an amount of initial wealth equal to $W_0^+ - W_0^*$.

If a riskless asset exists, then the bliss point described by (E^*,V^*) does not exist. That is, the specification of asset demands implicit in (3.7) implies a global maximization of expected utility under the usual convexity assumptions on the indifference curves. This is the case since the boundary of all attainable portfolios is no longer described by V' in (3.24); instead, the set of attainable portfolios consists of the entire E(W)-V(W) space conditional on $V(W) \geqq 0$. In other words, if an investor's level of initial wealth is W_0, then a portfolio may always be selected such that $E(W) \geqq W_0$ and $V(W) = 0$ assuming that the riskless asset has a non-negative rate of return.

Returning to the all-risky assets case, it is useful to consider utility functions that are consistent with the asset demands implicit in (3.10) and also have a bliss point. Two specifications that were previously claimed to have bliss points are the negative exponential and quadratic cases.[21] The indifference curves associated with negative exponential utility unambiguously satisfy the sufficient conditions for the existence of a bliss point in (3.25) and (3.26). In addition, the sufficient conditions are also satisfied at the point of tangency of V' with the indifference curve map of quadratic utility.[22] These cases are illustrated in Figures 3.2 and 3.3.

If portfolio rate of return is the argument of the utility function, then the expected utility maximization problem excludes the possibility of wealth disposal as long as the investor is initially fully invested. This is also true if expected utility of end-of-period wealth reduces to a function of portfolio rate of return independent of initial wealth. This latter condition is satisfied for utility represented by the logarithm of end-of-period wealth when portfolio rate of return is lognoramlly distributed. The indifference curve map for this case is illustrated in Figure 3.4.[23]

---

[21]See II.E for a discussion concerning the specific properties of these specifications.

[22]A major source of the misunderstanding and neglect, with respect to the bliss point described by (E^*,V^*), is a result of it being confused with the point U^* in Figure 3.3. However, Bierwag and Grove were not concerned with E(W)-V(W) space, but with asset space. They have shown that, under certain conditions, the indifference curve map in asset space is described by a set of concentric circles, the center being the point of highest utility conditional on V'. See Borch, "A Note on Uncertainty and Indifference Curves," op. cit.; and Bierwag and Grove, "Indifference Curves in Asset Analysis," op. cit.

[23]See Feldstein, "Mean-Variance Analysis in the Theory of Liquidity Preference and Portfolio Selection," op. cit. In this case, the indifference curves are initially convex for small values of E and V, and then they become concave. Every indifference curve intersects V'.

FIGURE 3.2

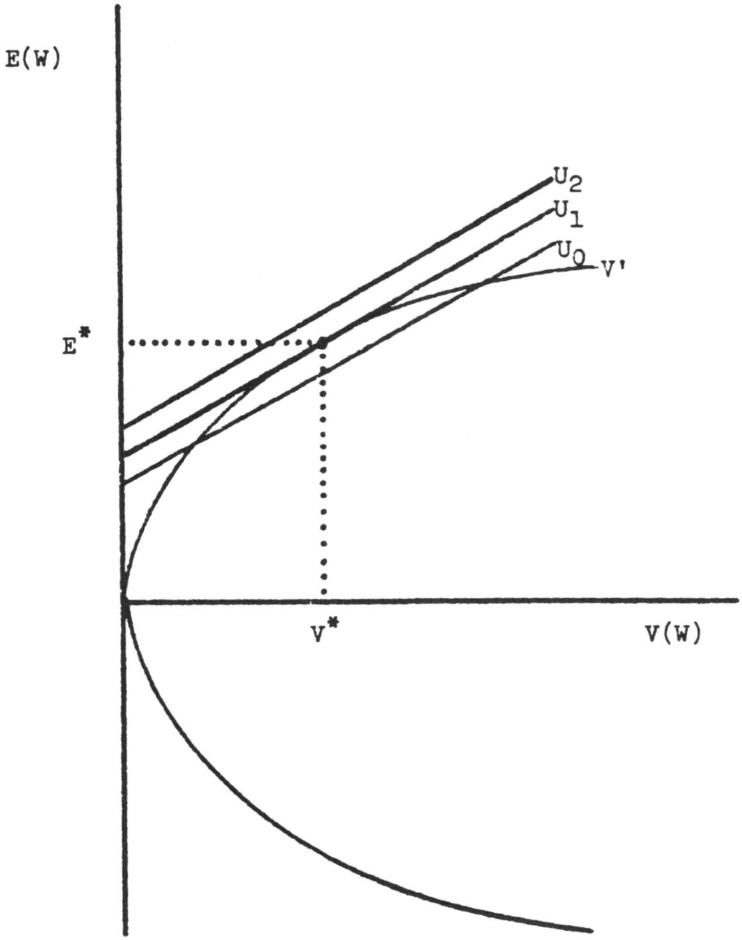

NEGATIVE EXPONENTIAL UTILITY OF END-OF-PERIOD WEALTH

WITH NORMALLY DISTRIBUTED ASSET RATES OF RETURN

FIGURE 3.3

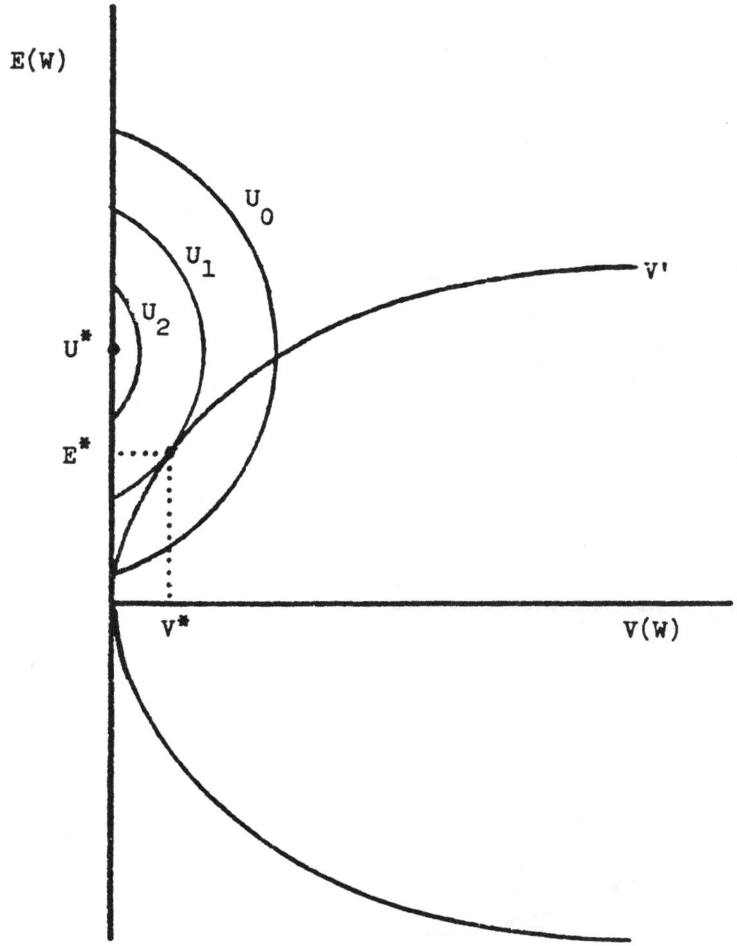

QUADRATIC UTILITY OF END-OF-PERIOD WEALTH

FIGURE 3.4

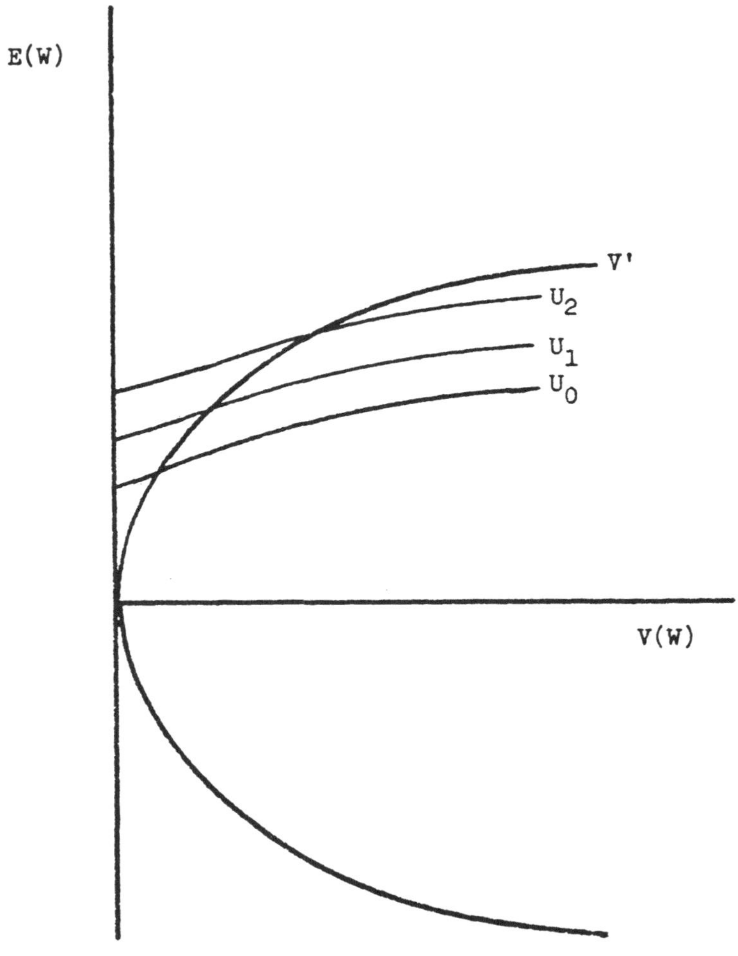

LOGARITHMIC UTILITY WITH LOGNORMALLY DISTRIBUTED PORTFOLIO RATE OF RETURN

The specification involving expected utility of portfolio rate of return is discussed immediately below in III.D.2.

2. Comparative Statics Properties When Portfolio Rate of Return is the Argument of the Utility Function

Portfolio selection problems for expected utility of portfolio rate of return are considered for the all-risky assets case. The asset demands resulting from the general specification of this case are given in (3.17).

An investor characterized as a risk averse diversifier will again only consider a set of efficient portfolios. In the rate of return case, however, there is a single efficiency locus in $E(1+r_p)-V(1+r_p)$ space for all levels of initial wealth given that the investor is fully invested; i.e., $\underline{a}'\underline{1}=W_0$. However, a family of efficiency loci again exist, and they correspond to different proportions of the portfolio that are invested; i.e., $\underline{a}'\underline{1}\cdot(1/W_0)\leqq 1$. (I am indebted to David Jones for this point.)

The envelope of these efficient loci may be described as the minimum variance of portfolio rate of return for a given level of expected portfolio rate of return. It may be derived from the first-order conditions of the following constrained minimization problem:

$$\min_{\underline{h},\lambda} L = \underline{h}'\Sigma\underline{h} + \lambda[\underline{h}'\underline{\mu} - E_0(1+r_p)], \tag{3.31}$$

where $E_0(1+r_p)$ is a given level of expected portfolio rate of return. In particular, the envelope of the efficiency loci may be expressed as

$$V'(1+r_p) = E_0^2(1+r_p)/(\underline{\ddot{\mu}}'\Sigma^{-1}\underline{\ddot{\mu}}). \tag{3.32}$$

This expression is illustrated in Figure 3.5.

FIGURE 3.5

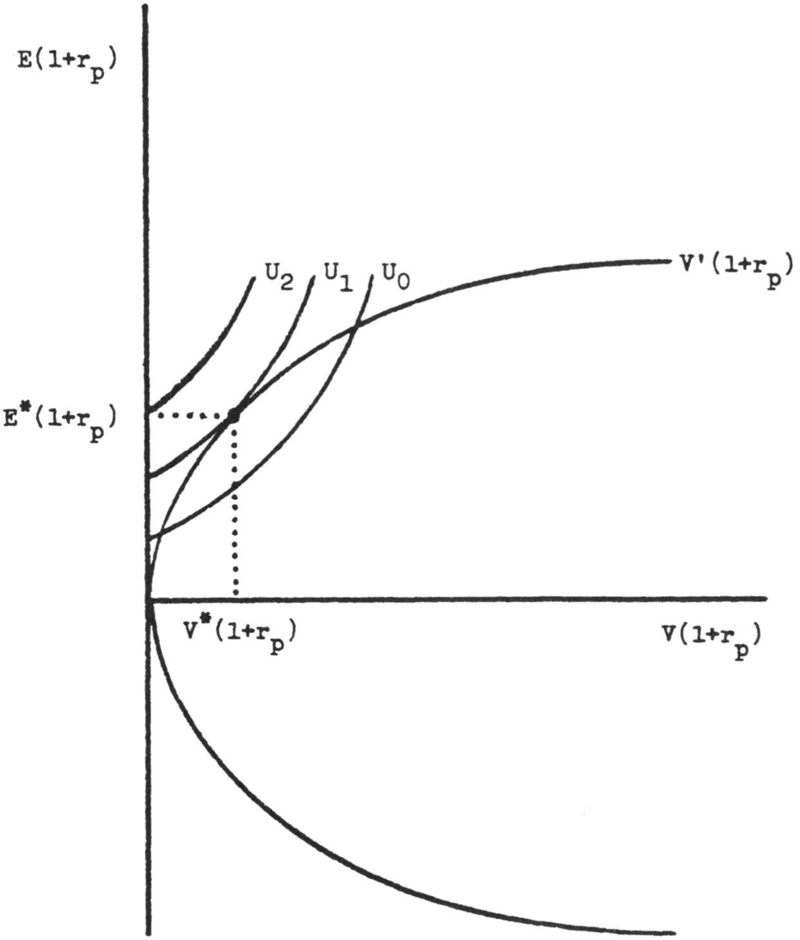

UTILITY OF PORTFOLIO RATE OF RETURN

Figure 3.5 also contains a set of indifference curves consistent with an investor that is a risk averse diversifier. These are labeled as U_0, U_1, and U_2, where $U_0 < U_1 < U_2$. The investor maximizes expected utility at the point $[E^*(1+r_p),V^*(1+r_p)]$.

Given that the investor's utility of portfolio rate of return is independent of initial wealth, the ratio of the mean to the variance of portfolio rate of return is constant for all levels of initial wealth at maximum expected utility; i.e.,

$$\frac{E^*(1+r_p)}{V^*(1+r_p)} = c_0, \quad \text{for all levels of } W_0, \tag{3.33}$$

where c_0 is a constant. These observations directly facilitate the transformation of this framework into E(W)-V(W) space.[24]

Expected utility of portfolio rate of return may be expressed as a function of the mean and variance of end-of-period wealth as follows:

$$U[E(1+r_p),V(1+r_p)] = U[(1/W_0) \cdot E(W),(1/W_0)^2 \cdot V(W)]. \tag{3.34}$$

Hence, along an indifference curve, the marginal rate of substitution between mean and variance of end-of-period wealth becomes

$$\frac{dE(W)}{dV(W)} = -\frac{U_{VR}}{U_{ER}} \cdot \frac{1}{W_0}. \tag{3.35}$$

In addition, the ratio of the mean to the variance of portfolio rate of return in (3.33) implies that

---

[24]Utility of portfolio rate of return may also be considered as utility of end-of-period wealth scaled by initial wealth. This is a useful way of considering the analysis that follows. See Melton, op. cit.; and Mossin, "Optimal Multiperiod Portfolio Policies," op. cit.

$$\frac{E(W)}{V(W)} = \frac{c_0}{W_0} .$$

These relationships, with (3.36) denoted as EV*, along with the efficiency locus for a given level of initial wealth W_0^* are illustrated in Figure 3.6. The point of maximum expected utility occurs at (E*,V*).

It should also be noted that the envelope of all efficiency loci in E(W) - V(W) space, as illustrated in Figure 3.1, is no longer relevant when portfolio rate of return is the argument of the utility function. In particular, the same efficiency locus in $E(1+r_p) - V(1+r_p)$ space consistent with the optimal portfolio is applicable for all levels of initial wealth, even though different efficiency loci in E(W) - V(W) space correspond to different levels of initial wealth. The envelope of all efficiency loci in E(W) - V(W) space does not lead to wealth disposal provided $\underline{a}'\underline{1} = W_0$ because the indifference curves and the line EV* shift for changes in initial wealth. This is illustrated in Figure 3.7 for an increase in initial wealth from W_0 to W_1.[25] In this case, maximum expected utility remains at U_1 as is apparent in Figure 3.5.

Therefore, in the all-risky assets case, utility of portfolio rate of return, or specifications of expected utility of end-of-period wealth

---

[25]The effects of this change in wealth may be seen from (3.35) and (3.36). The efficiency locus also changes from that described by W_0^* to one conditional W_1. The tangency of the new efficiency locus to the indifference curves is the intersection of EV_1^* with U_1. As a specific example concerning the shift in indifference curves, consider the negative exponential case which, for $U_0 = E(1+r_p) - (b/2)V(1+r_p)$, may be expressed as

$$E(W) = W_0 \cdot U_0 + (b/2)(1/W_0)V(W).$$

FIGURE 3.6

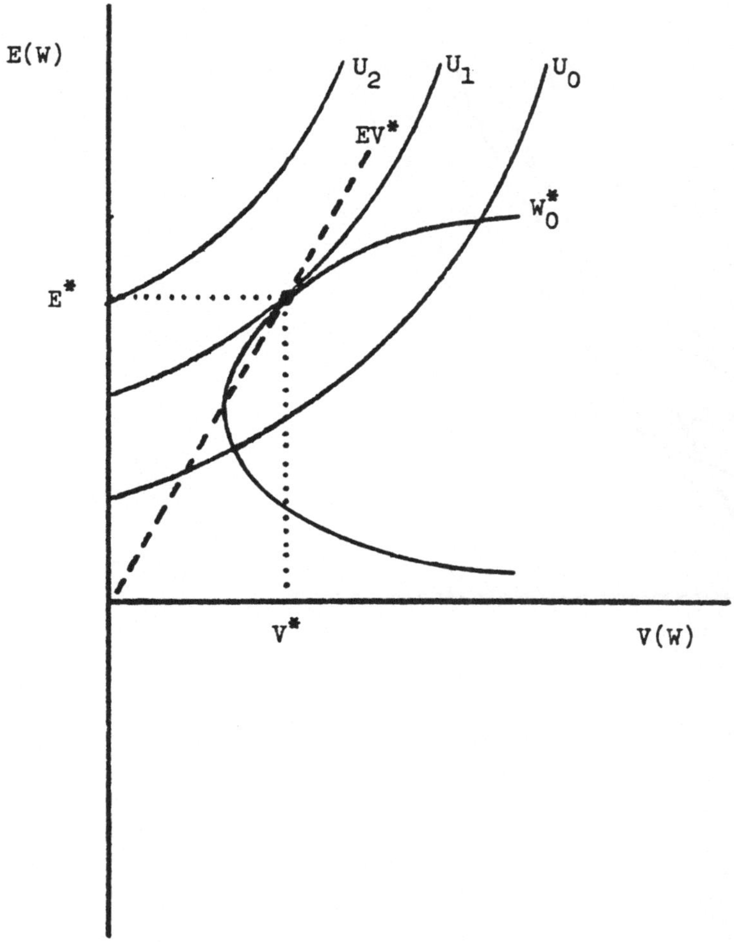

UTILITY OF PORTFOLIO RATE OF RETURN

IN E(W)-V(W) SPACE

FIGURE 3.7

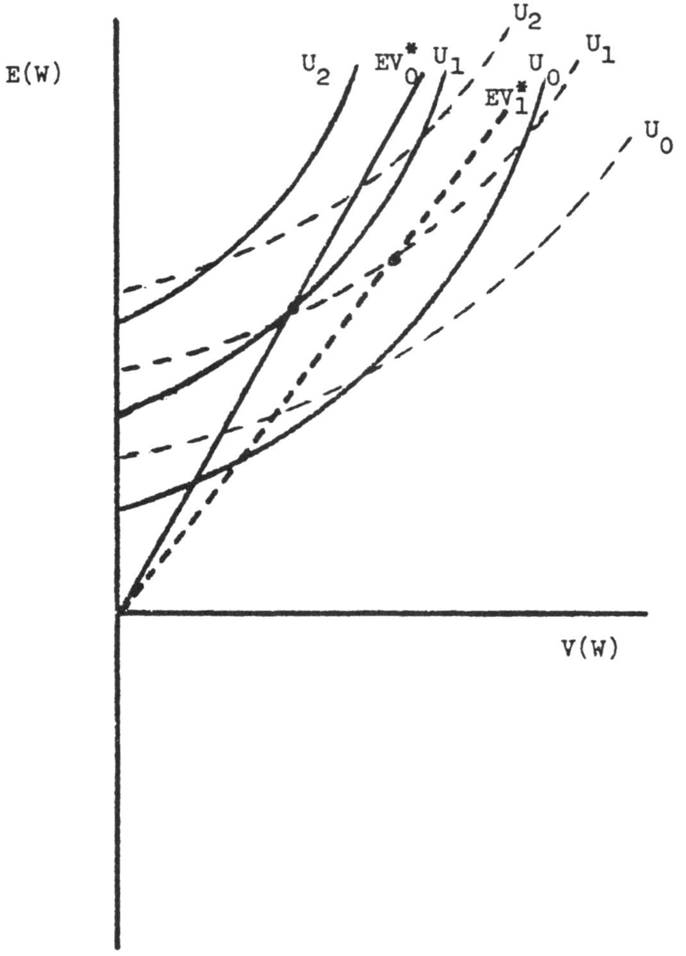

THE EFFECTS OF AN INCREASE IN INITIAL WEALTH ON THE INDIFFERENCE CURVES REPRESENTING UTILITY OF PORTFOLIO RATE OF RETURN IN E(W)-V(W) SPACE

that reduce to expected utility of portfolio rate of return independent of initial wealth, have a distinct advantage to the general end-of-period wealth specification. This results from the implications of the bliss point that may arise in the end-of-period wealth case. Additional comparisons concerning these alternatives are given in II.B.2.

The portfolio rate of return case implies that the proportional allocation of initial wealth among assets is independent of the investor's scale. For the investor groups considered in this study, this appears to be a reasonable assumption.

E. Implications of Measures of Risk Aversion

Measures of risk aversion have two major uses. First, they describe effects, from changes of initial wealth, on an investor's portfolio of risky and riskless assets. These effects may alternatively be described in terms of holding-period yields on the risky assets and the corresponding certainty equivalents. Secondly, they define functional forms of utility based on their assumed mathematical properties. The relevance of this latter consideration is dependent on the former's importance.

The major focus of this section is on the implications of the Pratt-Arrow measures of risk aversion.[26] Some additional results are obtained for a related measure of risk aversion that explicitly concerns mean-variance analysis.[27] In particular, the analysis concerning symmetry in section III.C is related to this measure of risk aversion. The measure of partial risk aversion is not discussed.[28]

It is assumed throughout that the argument of the utility function is end-of-period wealth. Specifying the argument of the utility function

---

[26]The Pratt-Arrow measures of risk aversion are also discussed in II.B.7.

[27]This measure is described by Adler and generalized by Miller. See Michael Adler, "On the Risk-Return Trade-Off in the Valuation of Assets," Journal of Financial and Quantitative Analysis, IV (December, 1969), 493-512; and Stephen M. Miller, op. cit.

[28]For a description of this measure, see Peter A. Diamond and Joseph E. Stiglitz, "Increase in Risk and in Risk Aversion," Journal of Economic Theory, VIII (July, 1974), 481-487; and Richard Zeckhauser and Emmett Keeler, "Another Type of Risk Aversion," Econometrica, XXXVIII (September, 1970), 661-665. For the purposes of this section, the comparative statics properties of asset demand equations are adequately described by the included measures of risk aversion.

as portfolio rate of return yields comparative statics properties, for changes in initial wealth, similar to those represented by constant relative risk aversion in the end-of-period wealth specification.

The analysis also assumes a two asset world. Initially, it is assumed that one of the assets, denoted as a_1, is riskless. The all-risky assets case is considered in III.E.1.

If a riskless asset exists, then the comparative statics results may be summarized as [29]

$$R_A'(W) \gtreqless 0 \text{ implies } \frac{\partial a_2}{\partial W_0} \lesseqgtr 0, \text{ and}$$

$$R_R'(W) \gtreqless 0 \text{ implies } \frac{\partial a_1}{\partial W_0} \cdot \frac{W_0}{a_1} \gtreqless 1.$$

Thus, if absolute risk aversion is decreasing, for example, then increases in initial wealth increase the amount of the risky asset in the portfolio; and, if relative risk aversion is increasing, then increases in initial wealth proportionally increase the amount of the riskless asset. These are empirically testable hypotheses in the specification including a riskless asset.

The measures of risk aversion for E(W)-V(W) specifications are considered by Miller.[30] Given an infinitesimal change in variance, these measures result from the risk premium that must be paid in order to leave an investor at the same level of expected utility. These cases may be

---

[29]See Arrow, Aspects of the Theory of Risk-Bearing, op. cit., p. 43. The notation follows that given in section II.B.7.

[30]Stephen M. Miller, op. cit. Miller considers mean-standard deviation space. However, the results hold for mean-variance space.

labeled, following the Pratt-Arrow terminology, as the measures of absolute and relative mean-variance risk aversion.

The measure of absolute mean-variance risk aversion is

$$r_A(E,V) = -(U_V/U_E). \tag{3.37}$$

The measure of relative mean-variance risk aversion is

$$r_R(E,V) = -(U_V/U_E)(1/E). \tag{3.38}$$

Absolute mean-variance risk aversion is the only measure considered in the discussion that follows. Parallel results are obtainable for the case involving relative mean-variance risk aversion.

Miller has shown that

$$\frac{\partial r_A}{\partial E} < 0, \text{ and}$$

$$\frac{\partial r_A}{\partial V} > 0,$$

imply that an investor is a risk averse diversifier that treats the risky asset as a normal good. That is, this represents behavior compatible with an investor that has decreasing Pratt-Arrow absolute risk aversion.

Miller also shows that the measure of absolute mean-variance risk aversion increases, decreases, or is constant with respect to changes in E and V, respectively, corresponding to the signs of

$$-U_E U_{VE} + U_V U_{EE}, \text{ and}$$
$$-U_E U_{VV} + U_{EV} U_V.$$[31]

The equality of these expressions to zero is also given as necessary and

---

[31] *Ibid.*

sufficient conditions for symmetry in (3.20). Thus, an investor has constant absolute mean-variance risk aversion with respect to E and V if, and only if, his vector of asset demands has a symmetric coefficient matrix on the vector of expected holding-period yields.

A similar correspondence between the symmetry property and a mean-variance measure of risk aversion also exists for the mean-variance specification in terms of portfolio rate of return. In this case, however, the measure of risk aversion must be defined in terms of portfolio rate of return, instead of end-of-period wealth.

In the all-risky assets case, the comparative statics results based on measures of risk aversion involving the changes in actual asset categories are usually ambiguous. This is investigated immediately below.

1. Measures of Risk Aversion in the All-Risky Assets Case

An important utilization of measures of risk aversion is negated, by definition, when all assets are risky. That is, one may no longer discuss an investor's behavior concerning the choice between the two risky assets in terms of the comparative statics properties given in the one-risky asset and one-riskless asset case. In addition, a set of useful comparative statics results may *not*, in general, be obtained in the all-risky assets case. This is demonstrated below.[32]

The measures of risk aversion continue as a useful way of classifying certain functional forms of utility. For example, even though constant absolute risk aversion in the all-risky assets case is without

---

[32]In the discussion that follows, only Pratt-Arrow measures of risk aversion are considered. The implications of measures of mean-variance risk aversion are also dependent on the one-riskless asset assumption.

implications for the comparative statics analysis of asset demands, it still defines a functional form of utility.

The definitions of the measures of risk aversion indicate the problems inherent in their applications to the all-risky assets case.[33] In particular, they may be explicitly derived conditional on the assumption that an investor may either keep his wealth in a riskless asset, or gamble on a symmetric bet involving stochastic levels of end-of-period wealth.[34]

For an intuitive explanation of this inapplicability of risk aversion measures, one must consider the difficulty in defining risk aversion in terms of the choice between assets in the all-risky assets case. It is somewhat appealing to consider the comparative statics properties of the asset that possesses either the smallest or the largest variance on its holding-period yield as indicative of an investor's risk aversion. However, the covariances associated with the holding-period yields may dominate the signs of the comparative statics results. Hence, this interpretation is not generally valid.

To illustrate the problems inherent in measures of risk aversion in the all-risky assets case, consider the comparative statics properties for asset demands obtained from negative exponential utility.[35]

---

[33]The definitions of absolute and relative risk aversions are given in II.B.7.

[34]This is Arrow's interpretation. See II.B.7. Pratt's interpretation also involves the trade-off between holding a riskless or risky asset. See Pratt, op. cit.

[35]Again, the analysis assumes the existence of only two assets, both of which are risky. In addition, it is assumed that initial wealth is not sufficiently large for a bliss point to occur.

The asset demands are obtained from (2.55) to yield

$$a_1 = \frac{(\mu_1 - \mu_2)}{b(\sigma_{11} + \sigma_{22} - 2\sigma_{12})} + \frac{(\sigma_{22} - \sigma_{12})}{(\sigma_{11} + \sigma_{22} - 2\sigma_{12})} \cdot W_0, \text{ and} \quad (3.39)$$

$$a_2 = \frac{(\mu_2 - \mu_1)}{b(\sigma_{11} + \sigma_{22} - 2\sigma_{12})} + \frac{(\sigma_{11} - \sigma_{12})}{(\sigma_{11} + \sigma_{22} - 2\sigma_{12})} \cdot W_0. \quad (3.40)$$

Thus, the effects on the assets from changes in initial wealth are

$$\frac{\partial a_1}{\partial W_0} = \frac{(\sigma_{22} - \sigma_{12})}{(\sigma_{11} + \sigma_{22} - 2\sigma_{12})}, \text{ and} \quad (3.41)$$

$$\frac{\partial a_2}{\partial W_0} = \frac{(\sigma_{11} - \sigma_{12})}{(\sigma_{11} + \sigma_{22} - 2\sigma_{12})}. \quad (3.42)$$

The denominators of (3.41) and (3.42) are unambiguously positive.[36] Thus, the signs of the expressions in (3.41) and (3.42) depend on the signs of their numerators.

If a_1 is riskless, then

$$\frac{\partial a_2}{\partial W_0} = 0;$$

and this result follows from the consequences of constant absolute risk aversion. However, in the all-risky assets case, the sign of (3.42) depends on σ_{11} and σ_{12}. In particular, assuming that $\sigma_{11} < \sigma_{22}$ is not sufficient to determine the sign of (3.42). Thus, the riskier of the

---

[36]The denominator equals the determinant of the matrix of a positive definite quadratic form.

two assets, in terms of variance, may increase, decrease, or remain constant for increases in initial wealth.[37]

The negative exponential case may also be used to illustrate similar problems for relative risk aversion. Negative exponential utility has increasing relative risk aversion; and if a_1 is riskless, then this implies that the wealth elasticity of demand for a_1 is greater than one, i.e.,

$$\frac{\partial a_1}{\partial W_0} \cdot \frac{W_0}{a_1} > 1.$$

If all assets are risky, and a_1 again has the smallest variance, then the corresponding wealth elasticity of demand is

$$\frac{\partial a_1}{\partial W_0} \cdot \frac{W_0}{a_1} = \frac{(\sigma_{22} - \sigma_{12}) \cdot bW_0}{(\mu_1 - \mu_2) + b(\sigma_{22} - \sigma_{12})W_0} \tag{3.43}$$

From this expression, it follows that[38]

$$\frac{\partial a_1}{\partial W_0} \cdot \frac{W_0}{a_1} \gtreqless 1 \text{ if, and only if, } (\mu_1 - \mu_2) \lesseqgtr 0.$$

Thus, the assumptions concerning relative risk aversion may lead to

---

[37]In the two assets case, the asset with the smallest variance always increases with an increase in initial wealth. If more than two assets are considered, however, this is not always true. This may be verified by considering specific examples of

$(\partial \underline{a}/\partial W_0) = (1'\Sigma^{-1}\underline{1})^{-1}\Sigma^{-1}\underline{1}$, which follows from (2.62).

[38] $\sigma_{22} - \sigma_{12} > 0$ since $\sigma_{11} < \sigma_{22}$ and $\sigma_{11} + \sigma_{22} - 2\sigma_{12} > 0$. See footnote 37.

ambiguous comparative statics results.

A special case arises, however, when relative risk aversion is constant. In particular, if relative risk aversion is constant, then all wealth elasticities equal one regardless of the assumption concerning the existence of a riskless asset.

To demonstrate this, consider the following general expected utility maximization problem:

$$\max_{a_2} E\,[U(W)], \tag{3.44}$$

such that

$$W = W_0(1 + r_1) + a_2(r_2 - r_1).$$

The first- and second-order conditions for a maximum are

$$E[U'(W)(r_2 - r_1)] = 0, \text{ and} \tag{3.45}$$

$$E[U''(W)(r_2 - r_1)^2] < 0. \tag{3.46}$$

The wealth elasticity of demand for a_1 is[39]

$$\frac{\partial a_1}{\partial W_0} \cdot \frac{W_0}{a_1} = 1 + \frac{E[U''(W)(r_2 - r_1) \cdot W]}{a_1 \cdot E[U''(W)(r_2 - r_1)^2]} \,. \tag{3.47}$$

The denominator of the second term is negative from the second-order conditions for expected utility maximization in (3.46). Thus the magnitude of the elasticity in (3.47) depends on the numerator; i.e.,

$$\frac{a_1}{W_0} \cdot \frac{W_0}{a_1} \gtreqless 1 \text{ if, and only if, } E[U''(W)(r_2 - r_1) \cdot W] \gtreqless 0.$$

---

[39]See Arrow, Aspects of the Theory of Risk-Bearing, op. cit., p. 43.

From the definition of constant relative risk aversion, it follows that

$$R_R(W) = \frac{U''(W)\cdot W}{U'(W)} = R_R(W_0), \text{ or} \tag{3.48}$$

$$U''(W)\cdot W = -R_R(W_0) \cdot U'(W). \tag{3.49}$$

Multiplying both sides of (3.49) by $(r_2 - r_1)$, and taking the expectation yields

$$E[U''(W)(r_2 - r_1)\cdot W] = -R_R(W_0) \cdot E[U'(W)(r_2 - r_1)] = 0.$$

Therefore, if relative risk aversion is constant, then

$$\frac{\partial a_1}{\partial W_0} \cdot \frac{W_0}{a_1} = \frac{\partial a_2}{\partial W_0} \cdot \frac{W_0}{a_2} = 1.$$

This result holds for any number of assets in the portfolio selection problem.

For expected utility maximization problems specified in terms of portfolio rate of return, the asset demands are homogeneous of the first degree in wealth. Thus, for a one-period framework, the wealth elasticities are analogous to the case where the utility of end-of-period wealth has constant relative risk aversion. These are the specifications that are used on this study in order to approximate the behavior of the investor groups excluding depository financial intermediaries. The fact that these specifications are relatively insensitive to assumptions concerning the existence of a riskless asset facilitates their general applicability.

F. Summary and Conclusions

This chapter has examined some general results applicable to asset demand equations derived from mean-variance analysis. These results are used to formulate a general specification for the asset demand equations of the investor groups in this study. More restrictive specifications are then tested to determine whether their constraints are empirically evident.

The properties of the coefficient matrix on the vector of expected holding-period yields were discussed in section III.B. It was demonstrated that the coefficient matrix is similar for alternative assumptions concerning the argument of the utility function and the existence of a riskless asset. In particular, all coefficient matrices have zero column sums as a result of the wealth constraint.

A necessary and sufficient condition for a symmetric coefficient matrix was also discussed in section III.B. This condition is valid for both specifications of the argument of the utility function, i.e., end-of-period wealth and portfolio rate of return.

The existence of a symmetric coefficient matrix implies that the coefficients on holding-period yields in each asset demand equation sum to zero. Thus, if expectations for real holding-period yields are formed by subtracting expected price inflation from expected nominal holding-period yields, then the resulting coefficient on the price inflation term would equal zero. However, this neglects the possibility that expected price inflation may be used in the formulation of expected nominal holding-period yields. The possible effects of price inflation on the demand for U.S. Government securities is empirically examined in chapter V.

The discussion in section III.D, concerning the effects of changes of an investor's initial wealth on his expected utility, indicates that there are some important differences between utility of end-of-period wealth and utility of portfolio rate of return. In addition, assumptions concerning the existence of a riskless asset are very important in the end-of-period wealth case.

If all assets are risky, then there are many specifications regarding utility of end-of-period wealth that lead to a bliss point in E(W)-V(W) space. This bliss point occurs at the highest attainable expected utility conditional on the set of all possible portfolios obtained by varying the level of initial wealth. It was shown that if an investor is a risk averse diversifier, then this bliss point exists. Its existence implies that there is a level of initial wealth such that an investor will dispose of a portion of his wealth in order to maximize expected utility. This is a very untenable situation.

A similar bliss point does not emerge when using utility of portfolio rate of return. Thus, in this context, there is a distinct advantage in using this specification. This is especially true in the time series estimation of asset demands.

The final section concerns the implications of measures of risk aversion. In particular, this section primarily focuses on the general inapplicability of these measures to the comparative statics properties of asset demands when all assets are risky. Constant relative risk aversion is the only measure that implies comparative statics results that are independent of assumptions concerning the existence of a riskless asset. In this case, the wealth elasticity of demand for each asset equals one. This result is also true when portfolio rate of return is the argument of the utility function. Thus, either of these assumptions are attractive because of their general applicability.

The analysis in section III.E also relates the symmetry property investigated in section III.C to a measure of risk aversion. It is shown that the property involving a symmetric coefficient matrix on the vector of expected holding-period yields has a distinct behavioral implication.

The results of this chapter coincide with the conclusions of chapter II concerning the functional form of asset demand equations. In chapter II, it was argued that, for the investor groups in this study, linear homogeneous asset demands may be used to approximate actual portfolio selection behavior. The analysis of this chapter indicated that this specification may be preferred for the additional reasons cited above.

CHAPTER IV

THE PORTFOLIO SELECTION PROBLEM OF DEPOSITORY FINANCIAL INTERMEDIARIES, AND THE DEMAND FOR U.S. GOVERNMENT SECURITIES

A. Introduction

This chapter considers the principle determinants of the demand for U.S. Government securities by the depository financial intermediaries in this study. These investor groups consist of commercial banks, mutual savings banks, and savings and loan associations. The balance sheets for these investor groups, in terms of the flow-of-funds accounts[1] for year-end 1975, are shown in Tables 4.1, 4.2, and 4.3.

Commercial banks, mutual savings banks, and savings and loan associations are considered apart from the other seven investor groups for several reasons. First, the structure and characteristics of the liability side of the balance sheet may have both direct and indirect effects on the selection of assets. Secondly, the perfect markets assumption relating to the asset side of the balance sheet is violated in several cases. Thirdly, in conjunction with the above, the most desirable framework for considering the portfolio selection problem of these investor groups is in a multiperiod setting.

While all of the aforementioned depository financial intermediaries participate in the U.S. Government securities market, this chapter focuses

---

[1]Board of Governors of the Federal Reserve System, op. cit.

TABLE 4.1

THE ASSETS AND LIABILITIES OF COMMERCIAL BANKS

AS OF YEAREND 1975

Assets	Amount	Percentage
Bank Loans	$257.3	31.3 %
Mortgages	134.8	16.4
State and Local Obligations	102.0	12.4
Consumer Credit	90.3	11.0
U.S. Treasury Securities	84.6	10.3
Interbank Claims	43.7	5.3
U.S. Government Agency Securities	34.4	4.2
Security Credit	14.3	1.7
Open-Market Paper	10.2	1.2
Corporate Bonds	8.1	1.0
Miscellaneous Assets	42.6	5.2
Total	822.3	100.0
Liabilities		
Other Time Deposits	370.2	47.8
Other Demand Deposits	233.7	30.2
Large Negotiable CD's	82.9	10.7
Interbank Liabilities	15.0	1.9
Security R.P.'s	10.2	1.3
Corporate Bonds	4.5	0.6
U.S. Government Deposits	3.1	0.4
Profit Taxes Payable	0.6	0.1
Miscellaneous Liabilities	54.9	7.1
Total	775.1	100.0

Notes to Table:

Source: Flow of Funds Accounts 1946-1975.
Amounts are in millions of dollars.
Detail may not add to total because of rounding.

TABLE 4.2

THE ASSETS AND LIABILITIES OF MUTUAL SAVINGS BANKS

AS OF YEAREND 1975

Assets	Amount	Percentage
Mortgages	$ 77.2	63.9 %
Corporate Bonds	17.5	14.5
U.S. Government Agency Securities	6.1	5.1
U.S. Treasury Securities	4.7	3.9
Corporate Equities	4.4	3.6
Consumer Credit	1.8	1.5
State and Local Obligations	1.5	1.2
Demand Deposits and Currency	1.2	1.0
Security R.P.'s	1.1	0.9
Commercial Paper	1.1	0.9
Time Deposits	1.1	0.9
Miscellaneous Assets	3.2	2.7
Total	121.1	100.0

Liabilities		
Savings Deposits	109.9	97.6
Miscellaneous Liabilities	2.8	2.5
Total	112.6	100.0

Notes to Table:

Source: Flow of Funds Accounts 1946-1975.
Amounts are in millions of dollars.
Detail may not add to total because of rounding.

TABLE 4.3

THE ASSETS AND LIABILITIES OF SAVINGS AND LOAN ASSOCIATIONS

AS OF YEAREND 1975

Assets	Amount	Percentage
Mortgages	$278.7	82.4 %
U.S. Government Agency Securities	17.2	5.1
Time Deposits	7.4	2.2
U.S. Treasury Securities	5.4	1.6
Consumer Credit	2.8	0.8
Open-Market Paper	2.7	0.8
Federal Funds and R.P.'s	2.6	0.8
State and Local Government Securities	1.1	0.3
Demand Deposits and Currency	0.7	0.2
Miscellaneous Assets	19.8	5.9
Total	338.4	100.0

Liabilities		
Savings Shares	286.0	89.8
FHLB Advances	17.8	5.6
Mortgage Loans in Process	5.2	1.6
Bank Loans	3.2	1.0
Profit Taxes Payable	0.4	0.1
Miscellaneous Liabilities	6.0	1.9
Total	318.6	100.0

Notes to Table

Source: Flow of Funds Accounts 1946-1975.
Amounts are in millions of dollars.
Detail may not add to total because of rounding.

primarily on commercial banks. In several cases, the discussion is directly applicable to the portfolio selection problems of the other two investor groups.

A general discussion of the determinants of the demand for U.S. Government securities for these investor groups is presented in section IV.B. The sources of these determining factors include the "pure" portfolio problem, liquidity considerations, other interactions with assets and liabilities, and institutional requirements. Thus, the approximations utilized in modeling the other seven investor groups do not appear to be applicable to this case. However, this is a hypothesis that may be empirically tested.

Section IV.C surveys several normative models that have been devised for the portfolio selection of depository financial intermediaries. Considering these models is useful for at least two reasons. First, these models facilitate the identification, and hypothesize the effects, of factors that influence the demand for U.S. Government securities. Secondly, these models demonstrate the desirability of a multiperiod framework when considering optimal portfolio selection. A comparison is also made between these normative models and prevailing portfolio selection practices.

Section IV.D considers portfolio selection models that focus primarily on either the "pure" portfolio problem or the liquidity problem. All of these models are formulated in a one-period framework. The model that is used in the empirical investigation of the demand for U.S. Government securities is based, to a large degree, on these types of models.

Multiperiod models of depository financial intermediaries are discussed in section IV.E. While a multiperiod model appears to be the most desirable framework to model these investor groups, the simplifying assumptions that are necessary to devise a tractable model abstract from several important aspects of the portfolio selection problem. For example, a common simplifying assumption has been to assume complete certainty about future yields. However, even the simple models surveyed in section IV.E demonstrate the desirability of ultimately considering portfolio selection in a multiperiod framework.

The specification of the demand for U.S. Government securities, that is used in the empirical investigation, is presented in section IV.F. In order to develop an empirically tractable model, several approximations are utilized. In particular, desired holdings of government securities are determined from a one-period framework that includes only a part of the actual portfolio. Many of the interesting factors that influence the actual holdings of government securities are delegated to the adjustment model.

The motive to formulate an empirically tractable model that includes many of the determinants of the demand for government securities led to the final specification. All of the other models considered that are based _entirely_ on an optimization problem were inappropriate in several respects as is indicated in the sections that follow.

B. Determinants of the Demand for U.S. Government Securities by Depository Financial Intermediaries

In order to facilitate the comparison of the models considered in subsequent sections, this section examines the factors that jointly determine the composition and size of the holdings of U.S. Government securities by depository financial intermediaries. The inclusion of this discussion is necessitated by the dearth of tractable theoretical models that are flexible enough to include all of these important determinants.

Thus, the basic determinants of the actual holdings of government securities are itemized in the subsections that follow. These include demand from "pure" portfolio selection, liquidity considerations arising from the composition and stochastic nature of deposits, other interactions with assets and liabilities in the balance sheet, and institutional requirements.

1. "Pure" Portfolio Selection Motives as Determinants of the Demand for U.S. Government Securities

Two fundamental, and interdependent, factors in portfolio selection behavior may be described in terms of "pure" portfolio selection motives. These are the return and risk characteristics of the alternative portfolios obtainable by an investor. The effects from these "pure" portfolio selection factors on the demand for U.S. Government securities by depository financial intermediaries are presented in the discussion that follows.

The risk and return trade-off from "pure" portfolio selection motives is apparent in the expected utility maximization framework presented in previous chapters. It is also evident in the framework where an investor (firm) maximizes the market value of its equity. With respect to these optimization models, the "pure" portfolio selection framework is taken to represent portfolio selection behavior without the presence of liquidity effects. In particular, in the mean-variance version of expected utility maximization that has most often been utilized,[2] the demand for any asset depends on expectations, variances, and covariances of asset holding-period yields. In addition, the scale of the portfolio may either be determined within the optimization problem or be taken as exogenous.

Since the determinants of the demand for assets from "pure" portfolio selection considerations may be viewed as fundamental to any portfolio selection problem, they are incorporated into the specification that is used in the empirical analysis. In particular, the final specification utilizes a variant of the "pure" portfolio selection model to specify desired holdings of government securities.

Many of these models based on "pure" portfolio selection motives have assumed perfectly competitive markets for assets and liabilities. However, a feature of actual depository financial intermediary behavior, particularly commercial banks, is the inapplicability of the perfect markets assumption. Melton has successfully incorporated imperfect competition in the loan market into a one-period expected utility maxi-

---

[2]See, for example, Hart and Jaffee, op. cit.; Melton, op. cit.; Parkin, op. cit.; and Pyle, "On the Theory of Financial Intermediation," op. cit. The general properties of these portfolio selection models are discussed in section IV.D.

mization model.[3] In addition, he has considered optimal portfolio selection in terms of quantity-or rate-setting in this framework. In the rate-setting case, the demand for assets in perfectly competitive markets contains additional terms including coefficients from the demand or supply equations of the assets or liabilities in imperfectly competitive markets. Thus, to the extent that important items in a commercial bank's balance sheet are traded in imperfectly competitive markets, the imperfections in these markets may influence the demand for U.S. Government securities.

Pierce[4] and Russell[5] are among the researchers who have empirically investigated commercial bank behavior in terms of "pure" portfolio selection motives. Both utilize an expected utility maximization framework under the assumption of quantity setting behavior in the loan market; however, Pierce allows for some market imperfections.[6] In each case,

---

[3]Klein and Pyle have also considered this problem in a similar framework. See Michael A. Klein, "Imperfect Asset Elasticity and Portfolio Theory," American Economic Review, LX (June, 1970), 491-494; and Pyle, "On the Theory of Financial Intermediation," op. cit.

Pringle has considered the effects of an imperfectly competitive loan market on a commercial bank's portfolio, where the bank maximizes the market value of equity as given by the Sharpe-Lintner capital asset pricing model. Pringle's approach is corrected and further developed by Van Deventer. See, Pringle, "The Imperfect-Markets Model of Commercial Bank Financial Management," op. cit.; and Donald R. Van Deventer, "Optimal Commercial Bank Liquidity and Portfolio Policy," Mimeo, Harvard University, 1977.

[4]See James L. Pierce, "The Monetary Mechanism: Some Partial Relationships," American Economic Review, LIV (May, 1964), 523-531.

[5]William R. Russell, "Commercial Bank Portfolio Adjustments," American Economic Review, LIV (May, 1964), 544-553.

[6]Pierce also tests for affects from cyclical variation in loan demand on a commercial bank's portfolio selection. Pierce, op. cit.

the reported empirical results find government securities and loans as substitutes in the equation for the supply of loan credit by commercial banks. However, these studies neglect several potentially important factors that affect the commercial bank's portfolio selection problem. Some of these omissions, and their likely consequences, are discussed in the subsections below.

2. Liquidity Demand from the Composition and Stochastic Nature of Deposits

The short-run stochastic properties of deposits, and the potential costs of bankruptcy or violations of regulatory constraints, induce a liquidity motive for holding U.S. Government securities. This is an important omission in discussions entirely in terms of "pure" portfolio selection motives. This source of liquidity demand is especially important as an explanatory element in the demand for short-term government securities.[7] These securities are ideally suited for the liquidity problem because of their characteristics; e.g., low transactions costs, interest-bearing, and virtually riskless in nominal terms.

It is often the case that depository financial intermediaries hold a portion of their government securities portfolio in short-term securities to meet these foreseeable liquidity needs arising from deposit

---

[7]Several researchers have discussed the impact of stochastic deposits on commercial bank portfolio selection. See, for example, Leonall C. Anderson and Albert E. Burger, "Asset Management and Commercial Bank Portfolio Behavior," Journal of Finance, XXIV (May, 1969), 207-222; Richard C. Porter, "A Model of Bank Portfolio Selection," in Hester and Tobin (eds.), Financial Markets and Economic Activity (New Haven: Yale University Press, 1967), pp. 12-54; Ira O. Scott, The Government Securities Market (New York: McGraw-Hill Book Company, 1965), pp. 49-58; and Van Deventer, op. cit.

variability. In addition, this secondary reserve component in the balance sheet is often managed separately from the remainder of the portfolio.[8] Thus, an empirical specification of the demand for government securities should definitely allow for the effects from deposit flows. In addition, the specification should incorporate the possible disproportionate effects on securities with different maturities.

The composition of deposits has also been hypothesized to effect the composition of assets in a commercial bank's portfolio.[9] The usual rationale is that time deposits are somewhat more stable than demand deposits; thus, commercial banks are more likely to hold long-term or illiquid investments the higher the proportion of time deposits to total deposits.

In an empirical study using individual commercial bank data, Carson and Scott[10] found that the higher the proportion of time deposits to total deposits, the lower the ratio of cash plus U.S. Government securities to total assets. That is, the size of the government securities portfolio and cash holdings is influenced by deposit mix. They were unsuccessful in finding any effects on the maturity composition of assets within the government securities portfolio. However, their analy-

---

[8]See Charles R. Wolf, "A Model for Selecting Commercial Bank Government Security Portfolios," Review of Economics and Statistics, LI (February, 1969), 40-52.

[9]See, for example, William R. Bryan and Willard T. Carleton, "Short-Run Adjustments of an Individual Bank," Econometrica, XXXV (April, 1967), 321-347; Deane Carson and Ira O. Scott, "Commercial Bank Attributes and Aversion to Risk," in Carson (ed.), Banking and Monetary Studies, (Homewood: Irwin, 1963), pp. 420-433; and Donald D. Hester and James L. Pierce, Bank Management and Portfolio Behavior, (New Haven: Yale University Press, 1975), pp. 118-122.

[10]Carson and Scott, op. cit.

sis completely neglected interest rates and deposit flows.

Goldfeld has estimated disaggregated demand equations for U.S. Government securities by commercial banks.[11] The disaggregation is across two classes of commercial banks and two maturity classes of government securities. In his empirical results, the coefficient on the quarterly flow of time deposits is positive in the demand equation describing the holdings of short-term government securities. In addition, the value of the coefficient was greater than those for alternative measures of quarterly flows of demand deposits. For holdings of long-term government securities, this relationship between the effects from quarterly flows of demand and time deposits was reversed. However, while interest rates were included as explanatory variables, Goldfeld neglected the possibility that these deposit flows may have effects that are dependent on interest rates. The possibility of asymmetrical effects from positive and negative deposit flows also is excluded.

Finally, Hester and Pierce have investigated the effects of the deposit mix on the composition of a commercial bank's portfolio.[12] Using time series and cross-sectional commercial bank data, their results indicate similar effects from demand and time deposits. Their analysis is, however, entirely devoid of any effects of interest rates on any asset or liability in the portfolio.

An additional classification of deposits in a commercial bank's

---

[11]Stephen M. Goldfeld, Commercial Bank Behavior and Economic Activity, (Amsterdam: North-Holland Publishing Company, 1966), pp. 53-59.

[12]Hester and Pierce, *op. cit.*, pp. 118-122.

portfolio, i.e., U.S. Government deposits, is also an important determinant of the demand for government securities. Since tax and loan accounts are a large part of this classification, they are discussed in the context of their institutional characteristics in IV.B.4.

The specification of the demand for government securities, utilized in the empirical estimation in this study, includes the flexibility to allow the disaggregated components of deposit flows to effect the size and composition of the government securities portfolio. This is introduced via a portfolio adjustment model due to the inadequate, or empirically intractable, treatments of these effects from models derived solely from optimization problems. This is discussed further in section IV.C, IV.D, and IV.E, where specific models of depository financial intermediaries are presented.

The previous empirical work on the subject, that was cited above, has demonstrated the importance of deposits and deposit flows on the government securities portfolio. Nevertheless, taken as a whole, there are potentially important omissions in these studies. In particular, the interest rate sensitivity of the effects from deposit flows and the possibility of the asymmetrical influences from positive and negative flows have not been included in previous empirical investigations.

3. Interactions of the Government Securities Portfolio with Other Assets in the Balance Sheet

The government securities portfolio is influenced, in terms of both composition and size, by the characteristics of other assets in the balance sheet. The discussion concerning "pure" portfolio selection motives has identified one important set of factors that influences the joint determination of assets. Effects from the properties of deposits have also been discussed. Nevertheless, these previous discussions have not explicitly examined the specific characteristics of two important categories of assets; i.e., loans and mortgages.

The properties of loans and mortgages, in comparison to deposits, may be equally important in describing the properties of depository financial intermediaries. Other investment decisions are often viewed as subsidiary to the strategies involving these balance sheet items.[13]

Several areas of potential interaction, focusing primarily on commercial bank loan and government securities portfolios, are explicitly examined herein. These include the constrained nature of asset selection resulting from the existence of illiquid loans (or mortgages) in the portfolio; loan-demand-induced liquidity requirements; credit rationing and the lock-in effect; and effects from customer relationships. These areas are discussed immediately below.

In any given period, the demand for assets by a bank is conditional on the existence of illiquid assets in the portfolio. This means, of course, that a bank is unable to completely rearrange its existing portfolio at a single decision point.

The effects of asset illiquidities are apparent for either a one-period or multiperiod investment horizon. In the one-period case, the expected returns and risk characteristics of the illiquid assets affect the selection of the remaining assets. For example, a large proportion

---

[13]See, for example, the discussion presented in Porter, op. cit.

of high-return and high-risk loans, in the total portfolio of a risk averse diversifying commercial bank, may induce the bank to hold relatively riskless securities in its investment portfolio. This same example, disregarding liquidity requirements, may also be applied to the multiperiod problem.

The multiperiod problem, however, would also take into account the effects of current decisions and outcomes on its multiperiod optimization criterian. Avoiding the liquidity problem for the moment, these effects of asset illiquidities are even apparent in multiperiod frameworks assuming the complete certainty of future outcomes. For examnle, Goldfeld and Jaffee[14] consider this problem for savings and loan associations. They view savings and loan associations as setting the deposit rate and holding mortgages in direct proportion to deposits. They find that the stickiness of the deposit rate for these financial institutions is a result of the illiquidities of their mortgages holdings. Expanding this model to include other assets would presumably demonstrate the effects of mortgage illiquidities on the entire portfolio.

In empirical models of depository financial intermediaries, measures of total assets should therefore, be reconciled with possible asset illiquidities. Asset illiquidities would affect the adjustment of existing stocks of assets as well as the allocation of new investable financial flows. This latter consideration results from the return and risk characteristics of the illiquid assets.

---

[14] Stephen M. Goldfeld and Dwight M. Jaffee, "The Determinants of Deposit-Rate Setting by Savings and Loan Associations," Journal of Finance, XXV (June, 1970), 615-632.

A related area of interest, with respect to the characteristics of depository financial intermediaries' portfolios, involves the concept of "loan-demand-induced liquidity requirements".[15] A similar concept is also applicable to mortgage holdings. The particular interaction envisioned, between loans (or mortgages) and the government securities portfolio, involves the effects from expectations of future loan (or mortgage) demand. This may be an important source of liquidity demand in addition to that induced from fluctuations in deposits.

This induced liquidity demand arises from a multiperiod portfolio selection problem. In a multiperiod framework, asset illiquidities and maturity lengths are again important determinants of this particular component of liquidity demand. For example, if a commercial bank desires to realize maximum profit from its loan portfolio during peak loan demand,[16] and not face the possibility of realizing capital losses on securities, it will purchase short-term securities and not make illiquid or long-term investments. This operates as a constraint on the investment portfolio.

It should be noted that this aspect of the portfolio decision is prior to actual increases or decreases in the demand for loan credit.[17]

---

[15]This is the phraseology that Pyle uses in describing this problem. See Pyle, "Descriptive Theories of Financial Institutions under Uncertainty," op. cit., p. 2024.

[16]For a discussion concerning the cyclical nature of loan demand, see John H. Wood, Commercial Bank Loan and Investment Behavior, (New York: John Wiley and Sons, 1975), pp. 1-4; and Pierce, op. cit.

[17]Several normative models for selecting a commercial bank's government securities portfolio may be applied to this problem upon the inclusion of future fluctuations in deposits. See, for example, Stephen P. Bradley and Dwight B. Crane, "A Dynamic Model for Bond Portfolio Manage-

This is in contrast to propositions regarding lock-in effects and credit rationing, which may occur after increases in loan demand or uncertainty. These latter two phenomena are the next topics that are considered.

Credit rationing, and the possibility of a lock-in effect, are examined in the context of their relation to the government securities portfolio. Following the definition of credit rationing given by Friedman,[18] credit rationing is related to the non-interest price of loans in the discussion herein. However, the effect from excess loan demand on the government securities portfolio is the primary emphasis of the investigation. Thus, whether the interest price of loans is at a sufficient level to allow market equilibrium, or certain non-price aspects are employed to ration credit, makes little difference with respect to the size of the government securities portfolio. The latter is, however, probably a better indicator of excess loan demand.

The initial credit rationing argument, advanced by Roosa,[19] placed direct emphasis on the government securities portfolio. In particular, the result of higher yields on long-term securities, in conjunction with increased loan demand and increased uncertainty with respect to all market yields, leads to the lock-in effect. That is, commercial banks are assumed to be unwilling to realize capital losses on securities in

---

ment," Management Science, XIX (October, 1972), 139-151; and Wolf, "A Model for Selecting Commercial Bank Government Security Portfolios," op. cit.

[18]Benjamin M. Friedman, "Credit Rationing: A Review," Mimeo, Board of Governors of the Federal Reserve System, 1972.

[19]Robert V. Roosa, "Interest Rates and the Central Bank," in Money, Trade, and Economic Growth. Essays in Honor of John H. Williams. (New York: The Macmillan Company, 1951), pp. 270-295.

order to accomodate loan demand.[20]

Of particular interest, with respect to the management of a commercial bank's total portfolio, is the related argument advanced by Scott.[21] Scott's formulation explicitly examined the riskiness of a bank's total portfolio. In periods where the loan rate has risen relative to security yields, and the yields on long-term securities are subject to increased uncertainty, a bank may choose to maintain or increase its holdings of government securities in order to satisfy its minimum risk standards on its total portfolio. This could occur since the riskiness of loans is significantly greater than the riskiness of government securities, and the total portfolio risk constraint may be binding.

Some additional arguments concerning the lock-in effect are discussed by Kane[22] and Wolf.[23] They focus on the institutional aspects of a commercial bank's reported earnings and capital. In addition, the tax laws, prior to the Tax Reform Act of 1969, that motivated banks to plan "gain" or "loss" years are related to the government securities portfolio by

---

[20]This assertion led to an extended literature on the subject. For a concise summary and comparison of the credit rationing arguments, see Friedman, "Credit Rationing: A Review," op. cit.

[21]Ira O. Scott, "The Availability Doctrine : Theoretical Underpinnings," Review of Economic Studies, XXV (October, 1957), 41-48.

[22]Edward J. Kane, "Is There a Predilected Lock-in Effect?", National Tax Journal, XXI (December, 1968), 365-385.

[23]Charles R. Wolf, "Bank Preferences and Government Security Yields," Quarterly Journal of Economics, LXXXV (May, 1971), 283-303; and Charles R. Wolf, "Regulation F and the Yield Structure of the U.S. Government Securities Market," Journal of Money, Credit and Banking, II (February, 1970), 112-122.

Also see Sam B. Chase, Jr., "Bank Reactions to Securities Losses," in Cawthorne, et al. (eds.), Essays on Commercial Banking, (Kansas City: Federal Reserve Bank of Kansas City, 1962), pp. 87-98.

these authors. This "gain" or "loss" year consideration is, however, contrary to the purported lock-in effect in the absence of unanticipated yield changes. In particular, certain tax advantages may have arisen from the realization of only losses or long-term gains during a particular year.[24]

The motive for not realizing capital losses on securities relates to the effects on bank capital, and, fairly recently, on bank earnings.[25] In particular, capital losses on securities are reflected in the accounting value of bank capital, and commercial banks are generally inclined to prefer stability in this measure.[26]

With respect to reported bank earnings, commercial bank practices have changed, in most cases, following 1964. In particular, the advent of Regulation F, and other related regulations,[27] have helped to reconcile actual bank earnings with the measures of earnings reported prior to this date. The current practice, resulting from the imposition of these regulations, involves either allowing for capital losses and gains on securities directly in the reported earnings measure, or listing a separate item that reflects capital losses and gains. Wolf has presented

---

[24]See Kane, op. cit.; and Wolf, "Regulation F and the Yield Structure of the U.S. Government Securities Market," op. cit.

[25]Ibid.

[26]In support of this contention, Kane's list of factors includes the fear of misinterpretation and criticism by shareholders, depositors, and examiners; and possible interference by regulatory agencies and other institutional considerations. See Kane, op. cit.

[27]In addition to the Federal Reserve's Regulation F, similar regulations were employed around 1965 by the Federal Deposit Insurance Corporation and the Comptroller of Currency. See Wolf, "Regulation F and the Yield Structure of the U.S. Government Securities Market," op. cit.

evidence that these changes may have led to a structural shift in bank preferences.[28] This hypothesis is tested in the empirical investigation in chapter V.

The previous empirical studies on the lock-in effect have been generally supportive. Gramley[29] and Chase[30] both offer supporting views based on the apparent non-maximizing behavior of commercial banks with respect to capital losses on securities. Kane finds, in a somewhat more rigorous analysis, that "other things equal, the net amount of gains or losses a bank chooses to realize is inversely related to the capital and income position of the bank."[31]

The implications of these analyses are that net purchases of long-term government securities depend predominately on yields and actual capital gains or losses; and they may also be affected by excess demand in the loan market depending on the history of their yields. In addition, there may be asymmetric effects regarding inflows and outflows of investable funds in the government securities portfolio depending on loan demand. However, as indicated above, the introduction of Regulation F could imply that the magnitudes of the effects have been altered. Thus, the possibility of a structural shift in commercial bank behavior is empirically investigated for the demand for government securities.

The final item that is considered in this subsection is the customer

---

[28]Ibid.

[29]Lyle E. Gramley, "Interest Rates and Credit Availability at Commercial Banks," in Cawthorne, et al. (eds.), Essays on Commercial Banking (Kansas City : Federal Reserve Bank of Kansas City, 1962), pp. 77-86.

[30]Chase, op. cit.

[31]Kane, op. cit., p. 380.

deposit relationship of commercial banks. Hodgman introduces the customer deposit relationship as an answer to several observed characteristics of the portfolios of commercial banks over the business cycle.[32]

Regarding the government securities portfolio, Hodgman asks the following question: "If commercial bankers are sensitive to yield changes on securities why have they moved so freely out of these securities whenever the demand for bank loans was strong?"[33] Despite the validity of the empirical observation in this question, it neglects the disaggregation of the government securities portfolio. However, the notion that banks initially sell short-term securities after a rise in yields is assumed explicitly during the course of his explanation concerning the effect of the customer relationship.

The analysis of the customer deposit relationship introduces another element into consideration that affects all aspects of commercial bank portfolio selection. The key proposition afforded by this theory is that commercial banks prefer to lend to those loan applicants that are most likely to maintain long-term deposits with the bank. This is the case since deposits are the principle source of investable funds; so, banks desire to have increasing amounts of deposits with a minimum of fluctuations over time.

The implication of the customer deposit relationship, with respect

---

[32]Donald R. Hodgman, "The Deposit Relationship and Commercial Bank Investment Behavior," Review of Economics and Statistics, XLII (August, 1961), 257-268.

Also see Edward J. Kane and Burton G. Malkiel, "Bank Portfolio Allocation, Deposit Variability, and the Availability Doctrine," Quarterly Journal of Economics, LXXIX (May, 1965), 113-134. These latter researchers explicitly introduce risk into the model.

[33]Hodgman, op. cit., p. 257.

to the government securities portfolio, is that there may be additional factors determining its size and composition apart from the risk and return characteristics discussed previously. This arises from the effects of the intertemporal relation between current loans and future deposits.[34] In addition, this effect potentially dilutes the magnitude of the lock-in effect.

All of the portfolio interactions discussed above are additional to the basic portfolio selection determinants that arise from the "pure" portfolio selection problem. In many respects, these interactions are unique characteristics of depository financial intermediaries. Again, this observation motivates the separate modeling of these investor groups.

4. Institutional Requirements Pertaining to the Government Securities Portfolio

The regulations and requirements applied to depository financial intermediaries vary considerably depending on the specific type of institution, and even within homogeneous categories of financial institutions. Thus, in the discussion that follows, only a subset of these requirements pertaining to the government securities portfolio are briefly itemized.

An important institutional requirement relates to the pledging of U.S. Government securities in conjunction with U.S. Government deposits at commercial banks.[35] Because of the volatility of these deposits,

---

[34]Wood considers this relationship explicitly in a multiperiod framework under the assumption of complete certainty. See Wood, *op. cit.*, pp. 29-39.

[35]See Irving Auerbach, "United States Treasury Cash Balances and the

commercial banks may hold even more than the required amount of securities for this purpose.[36] In the empirical investigation of the demand for U.S. Government securities by commercial banks, deposits are disaggregated in order to disentangle the effects of U.S. Government deposits.

U.S. Government securities are also used by commercial banks to collateralize trust account deposits, some state and local government deposits, and borrowing from the Federal Reserve. These features are not explicitly allowed for in the empirical estimation. This is due primarily to the lack of sufficient detail in the aggregate commercial bank data that are used in estimation.

U.S. Government securities are also important for certain solvency standards imposed on depository financial intermediaries.[37] For example, the amount and composition of U.S. Government securities in a commercial bank's portfolio enter directly into the Federal Reserve's measure of analyzing bank capital adequacy.

Tax laws for commercial banks are additional influences on certain aspects of the government securities portfolio. In particular, the tax laws prior to the Tax Reform Act of 1969 motivated "gain" or "loss" years

---

Control of Member Bank Reserves," in Commission on Money and Credit, Fiscal and Debt Management Policies, (Englewood Cliffs : Prentice-Hall, Inc., 1963), pp. 311-398; Kenneth R. Biederman and John A. Tuccillo, Taxation and Regulation of the Savings and Loan Industry, (Lexington: D. C. Heath and Company, 1976), pp. 56-57; and Scott, The Government Securities Market, op. cit., pp. 49-58.

[36]See Biederman and Tuccillo, op. cit., pp. 56-57; and the references cited therein.

[37]See Scott, The Government Securities Market, op. cit., pp. 49-58; and Dudley G. Luckett, "Compensatory Cyclical Bank Asset Adjustments, Journal of Finance, XVII (March, 1962), 53-62.

as previously reviewed in IV.B.3.

Finally, holdings of short-term government securities may be used as required reserves in some instances. For example, this is the case for savings and loan associations.[38]

Because of the disjoint collection of institutional requirements within any investor group in this study, and the properties of the available data, many of these institutional characteristics are disregarded. In defense of this position, the other motives for holding U.S. Government securities should, in most cases, substantially outweigh these particular institutional factors.[39] The exception to this methodology involves U.S. Government deposits at commercial banks.

---

[38]See Biederman and Tucillio, op. cit., p. 52.

[39]For a supportive view of this assertion, see the discussion concerning commercial banks, mutual savings banks, and savings and loan associations in Scott, The Government Securities Market, op. cit., pp. 49-58 and pp. 62-65.

C. Normative Models for Selecting Government Securities Portfolios

Normative models for selecting government securities portfolios serve to illustrate several aspects of the formulation and implications of portfolio selection for depository financial intermediaries. First, the models facilitate the identification, and may hypothesize the effects, of factors that influence the demand for U.S. Government securities. Secondly, these models demonstrate the desirability of a multiperiod framework when considering optimal portfolio selection. Finally, the complexity of formulating and interpreting a multiperiod model becomes apparent from the properties of the solutions of the multiperiod optimization problem; e.g., the comparative statics properties of asset demands are usually ambiguous rendering the ultimate interpretation dependent on the substitution of numerical values into the formulae.

The normative models that are considered below may be classified as programming models.[40] The primary emphasis is on the fairly recent application of stochastic programming to the portfolio selection problem.

The forebears of the stochastic programming models are the linear programming models of researchers such as Chambers and Charnes,[41] and Cohen and Hammer.[42] These models depend on various arbitrary liquidity constraints, and limits on assets and liabilities, to describe portfolio

---

[40]For a survey of the application of programming models to the microeconomics of banking, see Van Deventer, op. cit.

[41]D. Chambers and A. Charnes, "Intertemporal Analysis and Optimization of Bank Portfolios," Management Science, VII (July, 1961), 393-410.

[42]Kalman J. Cohen and Frederick S. Hammer, "Linear Programming and Optimal Bank Asset Management Decisions," Journal of Finance, XXII (May, 1967), 147-165.

diversification.

The structure of stochastic programming models are exemplified by those presented by Wolf,[43] Crane,[44] and Bradley and Crane.[45] The model developed by Bradley and Crane, which is based on Crane's previous model, is very complex despite the presence of restrictive simplifying assumptions. In particular, their analysis focuses solely on the investment portfolio; and they include stochastic future cash flows and interest rates that affect this segment of the portfolio. In addition, their objective function is the expected value of the investment portfolio. Risk aversion is introduced through the loss constraints that apply to the limits on maximum capital losses that a bank is willing to tolerate.

The multiperiod model presented by Bradley and Crane is solved by an algorithm suitable for computer programming. They focus on this latter aspect of the problem without further considering the qualitative effects on portfolio management.

The model developed by Wolf deals directly with some of the more interesting problems confronting a commercial bank in managing its government securities portfolio. Future interest rates and cash flows are again assumed to be stochastic in this model. In addition, an explicit treatment of the tax laws concerning capital gains and losses, along

---

[43] Wolf, "A Model for Selecting Commercial Bank Government Security Portfolios," <u>op. cit.</u>

[44] Dwight B. Crane, "A Stochastic Programming Model for Commercial Bank Bond Portfolio Management," Journal of Financial and Quantitative Analysis, VI (June, 1971), 955-976.

[45] Bradley and Crane, op. cit.

with the bank's preference for return in the form of current income, is included.

The objective function in Wolf's model is a managerial utility function. The utility function includes both current income and capital gains to reflect the actual preferences of commercial banks. In a multi-period setting, the utility function is assumed to be additive. Nevertheless, this specification of the multiperiod programming problem allows explicit recognition of the trade-off that commercial banks face between current return and uncertain future capital changes.

Using data collected from a sample of commercial banks, and including five maturities of government securities, Wolf finds that the optimal portfolio consists of either one or two maturities during the sample period. The superiority of this configuration results from three factors: "(1) the structure of the portfolio manager's forecast of interest rates, (2) the fact that bankers are risk averters and (3) the differential tax treatment of capital gains and losses."[46] This solution is again obtained through the use of computer programming techniques.

Wolf also makes a useful comparison of his normative model with prevailing commercial bank portfolio management. He asserts that the practice of managing a secondary reserve component of the government securities portfolio consisting of short-term securities is sub-optimal in terms of his model. In addition, actual practices of portfolio managers involve, in many cases, the use of yields to maturity as a basis for

---

[46] Wolf, "A Model for Selecting Commercial Bank Government Security Portfolios," op. cit.

making their investment decisions. Optimality, in terms of the model, would **render** explicit recognition of future capital gains or losses when considering the entire government securities portfolio.

The recourse to computer programming solutions indicates the relatively complex nature of multiperiod stochastic programming models. These models do not allow tractable formulations of asset demands in the absence of specific applications. This would not, however, encumber the possibility of their application by portfolio managers.

These models also rely on the assumption of exogenously determined size of the government securities portfolio. Thus, they abstract from loans, mortgages, and other assets in the balance sheet.

Therefore, while these models are potentially useful tools for portfolio managers, they are not used to formulate the specifications of asset demands herein. Their contrast to actual portfolio management, and the other features noted above, make this approach inapplicable. These models do, however, indicate the importance of a multiperiod framework, stochastic future interest rates and cash flows, and risk aversion to the portfolio selection problem.

D. One-Period Portfolio Selection Models of Depository Financial Intermediaries Under Uncertainty

The one-period portfolio selection models of depository financial intermediaries examined in this section concern two related problems. First, the "pure" portfolio selection problem is examined. The important features of this model are related to actual portfolio selection behavior.

Secondly, the liquidity problem is examined in terms of the one-period models formulated by several researchers. The problems that arise when trying to integrate the liquidity problem with the "pure" portfolio selection problem are also discussed.

1. The "Pure" Portfolio Selection Problem

The "pure" portfolio selection problem, as previously defined, relates to the selection of assets or liabilities (or both) in a framework that explicitly integrates risk and return trade-offs, but excludes liquidity considerations. This definition includes Markowitz-Tobin type models of portfolio selection, as well as models such as Pringle's,[47] which maximizes the market value of equity as given by the Sharpe-Lintner capital asset pricing model.

There are several variants of the "pure" portfolio selection model that are especially relevant to the portfolio selection of depository financial intermediaries. First, it may be assumed that each individual asset category appearing in either side of the balance sheet is endoge-

---

[47] Pringle, "The Imperfect-Markets Model of Commercial Bank Financial Management," op. cit.; and John J. Pringle, "The Capital Decision in Commercial Banks," op. cit.

nous. Secondly, imperfect markets for assets and liabilities may be assumed to exist. Thirdly, either particular exogenous balance sheet items may be assumed to be stochastic, or the assets in imperfect markets may be assumed to be described by stochastic relationships. Each of these variants has important implications for the specification of the set of asset demands.

Expected utility maximization models, with either terminal wealth or portfolio rate of return as the argument of the utility function, have been used to describe the behavior of depository financial intermediaries by several researchers.[48] These researchers have also analyzed the joint determination of assets and liabilities under the assumption of perfectly competitive markets for all assets and liabilities.[49] Indeed, the primary advantage of this specification is that it stresses the dependence between assets and liabilities in the balance sheet.

The Parkin and Melton models are described by expected utility maximization problems of the form previously considered in detail in II.E.2. Their analyses assume negative exponential utility with asset rate of return distributed joint normally. The difference between these specifications arises from Parkin's use of utility of terminal wealth, whereas Melton employs utility of portfolio rate of return. These specifications have, to date, yielded the most tractable specifications for the empirical investigation of asset demands. However, the results reported

---

[48]See, for example, Hart and Jaffee, op. cit.; Parkin, op. cit.; and Pyle, "On the Theory of Financial Intermediation," op. cit.

[49]This assumption is also relaxed by Melton. Melton, op. cit.

in chapter III indicate that some of the properties of the asset demands, derived from the Parkin-Melton framework, are dependent on the utility function that they utilize. For example, this is the case for their symmetry constraint on the coefficient matrix of the vector of expected holding-period yields.

There are, however, several areas of concern in the expected utility specification with all assets and liabilities jointly determined. For example, the Hart and Jaffee, Parkin, and Pyle analyses explicitly determine the scale of the portfolio, in terms of the total value of assets or liabilities, from the properties of the utility function.[50] Thus, this method for determining the scale of a depository financial intermediary neglects cost functions and possible economies of scale.[51]

The liquidity problem implicit in these specifications can also become unwieldy. For example, in the case where deposits are exogenous and stochastic, the wealth or budget constraint has been expressed in terms of expected deposits in the maximization problem. Thus, a separate adjustment mechanism must be specified that allows the wealth constraint, involving actual values of assets, to be satisfied at all times regardless of the forecast error in deposits.[52] This seemingly unintuitive

---

[50]Melton defines scale in terms of a bank's capital, and he assumes it is exogenous. However, the utility function in his analysis still determines the total value of assets and liabilities. See Melton, op. cit.; Hart and Jaffee, op. cit.; Parkin, op. cit.; and Pyle, "On the Theory of Financial Intermediation," op. cit.

[51]See George J. Benston, "Economies of Scale in Financial Institutions," Journal of Money, Credit and Banking, IV (May, 1972), 312-341; and Pyle, "Descriptive Theories of Financial Institutions Under Uncertainty," op. cit.

[52]Melton and Pyle both formulate the general problem, and Melton

problem arises from specifying what is essentially a multiperiod problem in a one-period framework. However, at this point, this is a necessity due to the complications that are apparent in multiperiod portfolio selection models under uncertainty.

An analysis concerning imperfect asset or liability markets may be developed in the "pure" portfolio selection problem. For example, several researchers have introduced imperfect loan markets into expected utility maximization models.[53] Pringle has analyzed imperfect loan markets with the market value of a bank's equity as the object of maximization.[54]

A difficulty again arises, with respect to the wealth constraint, when imperfect markets are introduced. In particular, if the demand for loan credit is described by a stochastic relationship between the price and quantity of loans, then the wealth constraint is often in terms of expected values of assets and liabilities. Remedies for satisfying the wealth constraint in terms of actual values of assets and liabilities, are identical to those previuosly discussed for the case of exogenous and stochastic deposits.

These models based on the "pure" portfolio selection problem do not describe several potentially important factors influencing the de-

---

explicitly presents an adjustment model that satisfies the budget constraint at all times. See Melton, op. cit.; and Pyle, "Descriptive Theories of Financial Institutions Under Uncertainty," op. cit.

[53]See Klein, op. cit.; Melton, op. cit.; and Porter, op. cit.

[54]Pringle, "The Imperfect-Markets Model of Commercial Bank Financial Management," op. cit.

mand for government securities. In particular, several key areas relating to the multiperiod character of a depository financial intermediary's portfolio selection problem have not been adequately developed. For example, the liquidity problem, loan-demand-induced liquidity requirements, and potential lock-in effects have not yet been analyzed in an empirically tractable manner in this framework.[55]

2. The Liquidity Problem

The liquidity problem consists of the problem relating to stochastic future deposit flows, and the adjustment upon the realization of these flows. The liquidity problem may also be related to the corresponding problems of loans and mortgages.

Models dealing with liquidity, that are suitable for empirical estimation, have been developed by researchers including Aigner,[56] Aigner and Bryan,[57] and Bryan and Carleton.[58]

The liquidity problem is investigated using weekly data for an individual bank by Bryan and Carleton. They assume that deposits and loans

---

[55]However, several of these areas have received attention. See, for example, Edward J. Kane and Burton G. Malkiel, op. cit.; Scott, "The Availability Doctrine : Theoretical Underpinnings," op. cit.; Dudley G. Luckett, "Credit Standards and Tight Money," Journal of Money, Credit and Banking, II (November, 1970), 420-434; and Pyle, "Descriptive Theories of Financial Institutions Under Uncertainty," op. cit.

[56]Dennis J. Aigner, "On Estimation of an Econometric Model of Short-Run Bank Behavior," Journal of Econometrics, I (May, 1973), 201-228.

[57]Dennis J. Aigner and William R. Bryan, "A Model of Short-Run Bank Behavior," Quarterly Journal of Economics, LXXXV (February, 1971), 97-118.

[58]Bryan and Carleton, op. cit.

are exogenous, and their asset demand specifications are not derived from an optimization problem. They also argue that, in a weekly model, the reserve position dominates the earning assets decision. Their empirical results indicate that the borrowing position is most responsive to weekly changes in loans and deposits.

Aigner and Bryan also introduce a model that directly relates to the liquidity problem. They assume that a bank maximizes utility of liquidity in the short-run. They also introduce subjective costs into the analysis; e.g., it is assumed that the discount rate does not fully reflect the costs of a commercial bank borrowing from the Federal Reserve. These assumptions, along with additive utility for individual short-term balance sheet items, lead to a tractable empirical model.

The most desirable methodology would combine the "pure" portfolio and liquidity problems into a single optimization problem. This analysis falls naturally into a multiperiod framework, but the complexity inherent in these problems in the absence of myopic behavior does not allow tractable specifications of asset demands.[59]

Several researchers have attempted to analyze this problem in a one-period framework.[60] However, while the theoretical implications obtained by these researchers are of interest, the resulting system of asset demands do not lend themselves to direct empirical investigation.

For the specification of the demand for government securities by

---

[59]See the discussion of normative models of portfolio selection in section IV.C. The models considered therein are multiperiod models under uncertainty.

[60]Melton, op. cit.; Porter, op. cit.; Van Deventer, op. cit.

depository financial intermediaries, the "pure" portfolio and liquidity problems are both important. These approaches are reconciled in section IV.F by specifying desired levels of asset demands from a variant of the "pure" portfolio selection model, and including effects from deposit and loan flows through an adjustment model.

E. Multiperiod Behavioral Models of Depository Financial Intermediaries

As previously discussed above, a multiperiod model that jointly considers the "pure" portfolio and liquidity problems in the optimization problem would be the most desirable framework to represent the portfolio selection of depository financial intermediaries. Nevertheless, in the absence of myopic behavior, the set of asset demands resulting from this framework are overly complex in at least two respects. First, the asset demands depend on the moments of probability distributions of future random holding-period yields and assets. Secondly, the comparative statics properties are usually ambiquous in the absence of the application of specific numerical values for exogenous variables. These considerations render these models inadequate to specify asset demands in a tractable manner.

Analyses that have recognized the importance of multiperiod effects on portfolio selection have usually incorporated either of two simplifying assumptions. Either the multiperiod model is formulated under the assumption of complete certainty, or a one-period model is devised that attempts to incorporate particular multiperiod features. The former approach is taken, for example, by Goldfeld and Jaffee,[61] and Wood;[62] whereas the latter method is utilized by Van Deventer.[63] The primary advantage in using one-period approximizations to the multiperiod problem is that the risk and return trade-off remains as an important, and tractable, element in the

---

[61]Goldfeld and Jaffee, op. cit.

[62]Wood, op. cit.

[63]Van Deventer, op. cit.

analysis.

The Goldfeld and Jaffee multiperiod model of savings and loan associations demonstrates several effects that may arise from a multiperiod framework. In particular, the most interesting effects arise from the dependence of the current deposit rate on past, current, and future mortgage rates, deposit rates, and mortgage holdings. However, their analysis utilizes the assumption of perfect certainty with respect to all future interest rates and levels of assets and liabilities. In addition, mortgages are assumed to be a constant proportion of deposits.

The Goldfeld and Jaffee model also illustrates the difficulty in using even the simpliest non-myopic multiperiod models. In particular, when applying their model to a general n-period analysis, they note that "an SLA dealing with this matter in a practical context would probably have to set up a programming problem to find the solution."[64] This complexity would be increased even further by incorporating uncertainty into the model.

The model developed by Wood focuses on another important aspect of multiperiod portfolio selection. In particular, the customer relationship is investigated with respect to both the loans and deposits of commercial banks. Wood's model demonstrates the importance of the dependence of current loan policy on future loans and deposits, and therefore, on multiperiod profit maximization.

Wood also relies on the assumption of perfect certainty. This implies that his "expectations" for future loans and deposits are the actual future adjustment processes. Wood also notes the desirability of

---

[64]Goldfeld and Jaffee, op. cit., p. 626.

including uncertainty in the model, but concludes: "While a study encompassing both uncertainty and multiperiod horizons would no doubt be very useful, the resultant model and its implications would be exceedingly complex."[65]

Therefore, while the multiperiod models discussed above analyze several areas of interaction between current and future portfolio decisions, these models are not used in the empirical analysis herein. The absence of the trade-off between risk and return, which is fundamental to the portfolio selection of a depository financial intermediary, is the motivation behind this decision. The approximization that is utilized in an attempt to capture the important factors of portfolio selection for these investor groups is discussed in the next section.

---

[65]Wood, op. cit., p. 5.

F. The Specification of the Demand for U.S. Government Securities Used in the Empirical Analysis

The models that have been considered in previous sections each relate to specific determinants of the demand for U.S. Government by depository financial intermediaries. However, as the discussions indicated, each model suffers from one or more important deficiencies. These may arise from the specific assumptions utilized, or the ultimate complexity that renders the results uninterpretable.

The model presented in this section attempts to include several additional features in comparison to the previous models. This model, however, relates directly to the demand for government securities with several important areas of the balance sheet taken as exogenous.

The motivation behind the model specified herein is to include effects from both the "pure" portfolio selection problem, and from the additional factors relevant to the portfolio selection of depository financial intermediaries. Thus, financial flows relating to deposits, mortgages, and loans are included separately as possible determinants of the demand for government securities. The effects from these financial flows are also assumed to be dependent on the holding-period yields of the endogenous assets in the portfolio selection problem.

The remainder of this section presents the actual specification used in the empirical estimation, and compares it to several previous specifications estimated by other researchers.

1. The Derivation of the Demand for U.S. Government Securities

The derivation of the demand for U.S. Government securities by depository financial intermediaries proceeds under the assumption that all liabilities, along with several categories of assets, are exogenous. The endogenous assets for commercial banks are U.S. Government securities, U.S. agency securities, state and local obligations, corporate bonds, open-market paper, and excess reserves; with the exogenous items primarily consisting of loans, consumer credit, mortgages, and all categories of deposits. The endogenous assets for mutual savings banks, and savings and loan associations, are all non-mortgage financial assets.

The inclusion of the loan and mortgage markets represents a financial modeling problem well beyond the scope of this study. The exclusion of these assets could be interpreted as implying that the decisions relating to the endogenous assets are residual to the decisions concerning loans and mortgages. This is somewhat consistent with the previous discussions concerning the holdings of U.S. Government securities by these investor groups. However, in the empirical work, current flows of these assets are treated as endogenous variables. The motivation for doing so is that these variables may properly be viewed as endogenous in an implicit formulation of a larger model.

An expected utility maximization problem is utilized to determine the desired holdings of endogenous assets. In this problem, portfolio wealth is defined in terms of the total value of endogenous assets. Thus, if the investor maximizes expected utility of portfolio rate of return, represented by a negative exponential utility function, with joint normally distributed holding-period yields for the assets, then the vector of desired proportional holdings of assets may be represented as[66]

$$\underline{\alpha}^* = \frac{\underline{a}^*}{W_0} = P_{11}\underline{\mu} + \underline{p}_{12} \qquad (4.1)$$

where

$$P_{11} = (1/b)\ \Sigma^{-1} - (1/b)(\underline{1}'\Sigma^{-1}\underline{1})^{-1}\ \Sigma^{-1}\underline{1}\underline{1}'\Sigma^{-1}, \text{ and}$$

$$\underline{p}_{12} = (\underline{1}'\Sigma^{-1}\underline{1})^{-1}\ \Sigma^{-1}\underline{1}.$$

Important features relating to the exogenous items in the balance sheet, e.g., loans, mortgages, and deposits, are incorporated via the adjustment model. This is achieved by defining the new investable financial flow in terms of the net change in the total value of the endogenous assets, and then disaggregating this flow in terms of the exogenous balance sheet items. Thus, the exogenous asset and liability flows are elements of the total new investable financial flow, with the sum of these individual exogenous flows equal to the total new investable financial flow as defined above. While this is an admittedly ad hoc procedure, it circumvents many of the problems that were discussed previously.

Two portfolio adjustment models are considered below. The difference between these two models is that the first model considers the adjustment for levels of assets whereas the second deals with proportional adjustment. The model in level form is

---

[66]For a complete discussion of this framework, see II.E.
General results for mean-variance expected utility maximization problems are discussed in detail in chapter III.
The notation used in this section is introduced in chapter II.

$$\Delta a_{it} = \sum_{k}^{N} \Theta_{ik}(\alpha^*_{kt} W_{t-1} - a_{k,t-1})$$

$$+ \sum_{kj}^{NJ}\sum \phi^j_{ik}(\Delta a^j_t / W_{t-1})(\alpha^*_{kt} W_{t-1} - a_{k,t-1})$$

$$+ \sum_{j}^{J} \pi^j_i \; \Delta a^j_t \qquad , \; i=1,\dots,N \qquad (4.2)$$

where the θ_{ik} and the ϕ^j_{ik} are fixed coefficients of adjustment, and the Δa^j_t are flows of exogenous assets and liabilities such that the sum of these flows equals the flow of the total value of endogenous assets. In addition, the portfolio balance constraints are

$$\sum_{i}^{N} \theta_{ik} = \bar{\theta} \text{ , for all k,}$$

$$\sum_{i}^{N} \phi^j_{ik} = \bar{\phi}^j \text{ , for all k and j, and}$$

$$\sum_{i}^{N} \pi^j_i = 1, \text{ for all j.}$$

The model considering proportional adjustment of the portfolio is

$$\frac{a_{it}}{W_t} - \frac{a_{i,t-1}}{W_{t-1}} = \sum_{k}^{N} \theta_{ik}(\alpha^*_{kt} - \frac{a_{k,t-1}}{W_{t-1}})$$

$$+ \sum_{kj}^{NJ}\sum \phi^j_{ik}(\Delta a^j_t / W_{t-1})(\alpha^*_{kt} - \frac{a_{k,t-1}}{W_{t-1}})$$

$$i=1,\dots,N \qquad (4.3)$$

where the portfolio balance constraints imply the same adding-up properties as before.

These models incorporate several important features into the analysis.[67] First, the model appends to a simple stock adjustment model terms involving financial flows. Secondly, the new investable financial flows are disaggregated to allow for different effects from different exogenous assets and liabilities. Thirdly, these disaggregated financial flows are modeled in a manner that allows their resultant effects to be dependent on the holding-period yields of the endogenous assets.

The adjustment models in (4.2) and (4.3) do not, however, allow for asymmetric effects regarding negative and positive flows of exogenous assets and liabilities. This may be of particular importance for these investor groups. For example, the often hypothesized lock-in effect for commercial banks relates to this consideration. Thus, the models in (4.2) and (4.3) may be revised to allow for negative and positive financial flows as follows:

$$\begin{aligned}\Delta a_{it} = & \sum_{k}^{N} \theta_{ik}(\alpha^{*}_{kt}W_{t-1} - a_{k,t-1}) \\ & + \sum_{kj'}^{NJ}\sum \phi^{j'}_{ik}(\Delta a^{j'}_{t}/W_{t-1})(\alpha^{*}_{kt}W_{t-1} - a_{k,t-1}) \\ & + \sum_{kj''}^{NJ}\sum \phi^{j''}_{ik}(\Delta a^{j''}_{t}/W_{t-1})(\delta^{*}_{kt}W_{t-1} - a_{k,t-1}) \\ & + \sum_{j'}^{J} \pi^{j'}_{i}\Delta a^{j'}_{t} + \sum_{j''}^{J} \pi^{j''}_{i}\Delta a^{j''}_{t}, \qquad i=1,\ldots N \qquad (4.2')\end{aligned}$$

---

[67] The discussion that follows is in terms of (4.2). Similar considerations are relevant for (4.3) by replacing the effects on asset levels by asset proportions.

and

$$\frac{a_{it}}{W_t} - \frac{a_{i,t-1}}{W_{t-1}} = \sum_{k}^{N} \theta_{ik}\left(\alpha^*_{kt} - \frac{a_{k,t-1}}{W_{t-1}}\right)$$

$$+ \sum_{k}^{N}\sum_{j'}^{J} \phi^{j'}_{ik}(\Delta a^{j'}_t / W_{t-1})\left(\alpha^*_{kt} - \frac{a_{k,t-1}}{W_{t-1}}\right)$$

$$+ \sum_{k}^{N}\sum_{j''}^{J} \phi^{j''}_{ik}(\Delta a^{j''}_t / W_{t-1})\left(\delta^*_{kt} - \frac{a_{k,t-1}}{W_{t-1}}\right)$$

$$i=1,\ldots,N \qquad (4.3')$$

where

$$\Delta a^{j'}_t = \begin{cases} \Delta a^j_t, & \text{if } a^j_t \text{ is a liability and } \Delta a^j_t > 0, \\ -\Delta a^j_t, & \text{if } a^j_t \text{ is an asset and } \Delta a^j_t < 0, \\ 0, & \text{otherwise,} \end{cases}$$

$$\Delta a^{j''}_t = \begin{cases} \Delta a^j_t, & \text{if } a^j_t \text{ is a liability and } \Delta a^j_t < 0, \\ -\Delta a^j_t, & \text{if } a^j_t \text{ is an asset and } \Delta a^j_t > 0, \\ 0, & \text{otherwise.} \end{cases}$$

with the portfolio balance constraints implying

$$\sum_{i}^{N} \theta_{ik} = \bar{\theta}\ , \text{ for all } k,$$

$$\sum_{i}^{N} \phi^{j'}_{ik} = \bar{\phi}^{j'}\ , \text{ for all } k \text{ and } j',$$

$$\sum_{i}^{N} \phi^{j''}_{ik} = \bar{\phi}^{j''}\ , \text{ for all } k \text{ and } j'',$$

$$\sum_{i}^{N} \pi_i^{j'} = 1, \text{ for all } j', \text{ and}$$

$$\sum_{i}^{N} \pi_i^{j''} = 1, \text{ for all } j''.$$

The δ^*_{kt} differ from the α^*_{kt} in that the former explicitly represent desired short-run portfolio holdings conditional on negative financial flows.[68]

Therefore, in addition to the properties of (4.2) and (4.3), the adjustment models represented in (4.2') and (4.3') allow for asymmetric effects from negative and positive disaggregated financial flows; and these are hypothesized to be dependent on the holding-period yields of the endogenous assets. The superiority of (4.2') or (4.3') to (4.2) or (4.3), respectively, is a proper object of statistical testing.

2. Previous Empirical Studies of the Demand for U.S. Government Securities by Depository Financial Intermediaries

Three previous specifications of the demand for U.S. Government securities, each involving a disaggregation into two maturity classes, are briefly reviewed below. A comparison is made between these models and the specifications presented in the previous subsection. The particular areas examined include effects from interest rates, financial flows, financial stocks, total market supply variables, and symmetric effects from positive and negative financial flows.

---

[68]See the discussion concerning portfolio adjustment models in chapter V for the rationale in using different terms describing interest rate sensitivity for negative and positive financial flows.

The specifications considered below were devised by Goldfeld,[69] Silber,[70] and Bosworth and Duesenberry.[71] The discussion focuses primarily on their specifications for commercial banks since this investor group is the largest investor in the government securities market, and the previous specifications include several peculiar properties.

The Goldfeld model is unique, with respect to the other models surveyed in this section, from its explicit inclusion of interest rates as a determinant of the total amount of U.S. Government securities held by commercial banks. Goldfeld estimates four equations involving short-term and long-term securities for country and noncountry banks. Three of these equations include interest rates as explanatory variables. The exception involves the demand for short-term securities by noncountry banks. This, however, is the largest category of government securities.

Interest rates are determinants only for the composition of the government securities portfolio in Silber's model. The Bosworth-Duesenberry specification of the demand for long-term U.S. Government securities also excludes interest rates; and short-term holdings are treated as a residual with respect to a bank's total portfolio.

Financial flows are important in all of the models surveyed herein. They appear explicitly in the Goldfeld and Silber models. The financial flows included consist of time deposits, demand deposits, loans, and mortgages. The Bosworth-Duesenberry model may be rewritten to demonstrate

---

[69]Goldfeld, op. cit.

[70]William L. Silber, "Portfolio Substitutability, Regulations and Monetary Policy," Quarterly Journal of Economics, LXXXIII (May, 1969), 197-219.

[71]Bosworth and Duesenberry, op. cit.

the effect of the flow of total bank earning assets.

Financial flows enter into these models with the same coefficients regardless of direction (i.e., positive or negative). The flows also are not specified in a manner that allows their effects to be dependent on interest rates. In addition, tests are not performed that consider these possibilities.

Current and lagged stocks of assets and liabilities also appear in these specifications. These variables include lagged own-stocks, current demand and time deposits, lagged demand deposits, and lagged total bank earning assets. Thus, some consideration is given to a bank's allocation of existing assets, and other related effects.

The most peculiar variable included in the Goldfeld and Bosworth-Duesenberry specifications is the total non-Federal Reserve holdings of U.S. Government securities. Goldfeld includes this variable in an attempt to adjust for effects from outstanding securities changing maturity classes.[72] However, there does not appear to be a strong motivation for handling the problem in this manner. In addition, this variable becomes a very important determinant in these models.

Preliminary estimation of the demand for government securities, in conjunction with the present study, indicated the reasons for the specifications of the previous researchers. In particular, it was found that in order to adequately explain the demand for U.S. Government securities by commercial banks, without the reliance on aggregate market supply variables, the relatively complex model introduced in the previous subsection

---

[72]Bosworth and Duesenberry include this variable without explanation.

had to be utilized. The explicit effects apparent in this model, however, represent plausible behavior. For example, the dependence of the effects from financial flows on interest rates and direction (i.e., positive or negative) are potentially important in the description of the actual behavior of depository financial intermediaries. This, in fact, is demonstrated in the next chapter.

G. Summary and Conclusions

The portfolio selection behavior of depository financial intermediaries depends on a multitude of factors. The interdependency of these factors results in every aspect of their operations influencing their holdings of U.S. Government securities.

The most important determinants of the demand for U.S. Government securities, by these investor groups, were discussed in section IV.B. The sources of these determining factors include "pure" portfolio selection motives, deposit fluctuations, loan-demand-induced liquidity requirements, other interactions with assets and liabilities from multiperiod considerations, and institutional requirements.

The models reviewed in sections IV.C, IV.D, and IV.E were compared to the actual determinants of the amount and composition of the government securities portfolio. While these models, as a whole, include many of the important determining factors, an individual model does not currently exist that is sufficient to represent the actual demand for government securities.

The model introduced in section IV.F attempts to include several additional determinants into previous specifications of the demand for U.S. Government securities by depository financial intermediaries. This is achieved by applying an adjustment model to desired holdings of selected categories of endogenous assets.

The adjustment model incorporates several effects. First, the model appends to a simple stock adjustment model terms involving financial flows. Secondly, the financial flows are disaggregated to allow for different effects from different exogenous assets and liabilities. Thirdly, the disaggregated financial flows are modeled in a manner that allows their resultant effects to be dependent on the holding-period yields of the endogenous assets. Finally, the possibility of asymmetric effects from positive and negative disaggregated financial flows are included.

The next chapter utilizes the model developed in section IV.F in the empirical estimation of the demand for U.S. Government securities by these investor groups. It is demonstrated therein that the features of the model describe important determinants of their portfolio selection behavior.

CHAPTER V

EMPIRICAL RESULTS FOR THE STRUCTURAL MODEL OF THE U.S. GOVERNMENT SECURITIES MARKET

A. Introduction

The application of portfolio selection theory to the investor groups participating in the U.S. Government securities market culminates in the empirical results reported in this chapter. Relating the empirical results to models of portfolio selection allows, in most cases, the direct interpretation of certain aspects of these results. These include the behavioral implications of the determining factors of the asset demands, and the relation of the empirical results to hypotheses concerning the form of the coefficient matrix on the vector of expected holding-period yields.

The portfolio selection theory that was developed in the previous chapters is in terms of desired proportional holdings of assets. The recognition of transactions costs in portfolio adjustment motivates the introduction of adjustment models in section V.B, where actual short-run asset demands are derived.

Desired proportional holdings of assets are dependent on expected holding-period yields, variances, covariances, and parameters of the utility function. Expected holding-period yields are represented by current yields to maturity in the empirical estimation. They may alternatively be modeled in terms of rational or autoregressive expectations;

however, this area of investigation is postponed for further research.[1]

Variances of holding-period yields are explicitly introduced in the asset demand equations upon the linearization of the expressions for desired proportional holdings of assets. Thus, while these variances have been implicitly assumed to be constant throughout the sample period in previous studies, they are allowed to vary and affect the asset demands directly herein.

The estimation results are reported in section V.C. Demands for two maturity classes of U.S. Government securities are estimated for nine investor groups consisting of commercial banks, households, life insurance companies, mutual savings banks, other insurance companies, private pension funds, savings and loan associations, state and local government general funds, and state and local government retirement funds. A single demand equation for the shorter of the two maturity classes is also estimated for nonfinancial corporate businesses.

The subsections in V.C are concerned with various aspects of the estimation results. These include data sources, estimation techniques, and the properties of the asset demand equations.

In section V.D, the estimated demand equations for two maturity classes of U.S. Government securities are combined with two market-clearing identities. The resultant system of equations jointly determines the asset demands and the yields on the two maturity classes of

---

[1]For a comparison of the unitary, rational, and autoregressive expectations hypotheses in the context of a structural model of the corporate bond market, see Benjamin M. Friedman and V. Vance Roley, "Investors' Portfolio Behavior under Alternative Models of Long-Term Interest Rate Expectations: Unitary, Rational, or Autoregressive," Mimeo, Harvard University, 1977.

U.S. Government securities. This methodology is also contrasted to alternative models of interest rate determination.

The main conclusions resulting from the empirical investigation in this chapter are summarized in section V.E.

B. Portfolio Adjustment Models

The desired holdings of assets derived from portfolio theory may not fully describe the actual short-run demand for assets. The difference may result from the recognition of partial adjustment to desired holdings due to transactions costs.

Transactions costs may arise from brokerage fees and price effects resulting from asset illiquidities. There are also indirect transactions costs which could arise, for example, from the increased overhead costs within a financial institution associated with a greater level of activity in a specialized form of trading.

Two methods have been hypothesized in order to incorporate transactions costs into the portfolio selection problem. First, several researchers have included transactions costs considerations directly in an optimization framework.[2] Secondly, other researchers have included transactions costs in a portfolio adjustment framework that hypothesizes movement toward desired equilibrium levels.[3] This latter approach may differ from a simple stock adjustment model upon the recognition that new investable financial flows may be invested at lower costs than the

---

[2]See, for example, David Goldsmith, "Transactions Costs and the Theory of Portfolio Selection," Journal of Finance, XXXI (September, 1976), 1127-1139; G. A. Pogue, "An Extension of the Markowitz Portfolio Selection Model to Include Variable Transactions Costs, Short Sales, Leverage Policies, and Taxes," Journal of Finance, XXV (December, 1970), 1-23; and Donald R. Van Deventer, "Transactions Costs, Portfolio Selection, and the Existence of Financial Intermediaries," Mimeo, Harvard University, 1976.

[3]See, for example, Brainard and Tobin, "Pitfalls in Financial Model Building," op. cit.; Friedman, "A Structural Model of the Long-Term Corporate Debt Market," op. cit.; and Modigliani, "The Dynamics of Portfolio Adjustment and the Flow of Savings through Financial Intermediaries," op. cit.

corresponding adjustment of asset stocks already in the portfolio.

The methodology employed for the specification of the demand for U.S. Government securities utilizes an adjustment model to form actual asset demands from a linearization of an expression representing desired asset holdings. This linear approximization is derived from a Taylor series expansion, with respect to expected holding-period yields and variances, of previously derived expressions for desired proportional asset holdings.[4] The resultant expression may be represented as[5]

$$\underline{\alpha}_t^* = \frac{\underline{a}_t^*}{W_t} = \underline{b} + B_1\underline{\mu}_t + B_2\underline{\sigma}_t, \tag{5.1}$$

where $\underline{b}$ is a vector of constants, and B_1 and B_2 are coefficient matrices on expected holding-period yields and variances of holding-period yields, respectively. It follows that

$$\underline{i}'\underline{b} = 1,$$

$$\underline{i}'B_1 = \underline{0},$$

$$\underline{i}'B_2 = \underline{0}.$$

A major portion of chapter III is devoted to the derivation of restrictions relating to the coefficient matrix on the vector of expected holding-period yields B_1. In particular, sign restrictions, symmetry, and row and column adding-up properties are considered for the general expected utility maximization problem. These properties are empirically investigated below in section V.C.

---

[4]See chapter II for the derivation of desired proportional asset holdings from specific expected utility maximization problems.

[5]The notation used in this chapter is introduced in chapter II.

Similar considerations are not investigated for the coefficient matrix on the vector of variances of holding-period yields B_2. The properties of this coefficient matrix, in terms of symmetry and adding-up constraints, do not have economic interpretations similar to those developed for B_1 in chapter III. In addition, it may be desirable to further expand the expression in (5.1) to include affects from the co-variances of holding-period yields. Nevertheless, the empirical investigation below focuses only on the addition of variances to the usual empirical specification of asset demands. The addition of covariances is again an area that will be examined in future research.

The investor groups in this study have diverse institutional and behavioral characteristics. Thus, it is reasonable to expect that a single adjustment model may not adequately describe each investor group's short-run portfolio adjustment. This motivates the introduction of several adjustment models that incorporate various features that may be important for particular applications.

The most general adjustment model considered is that previously introduced for commercial banks in chapter IV. It includes five properties that are additional to the simple stock adjustment model:

(1) new investable financial flows have separate effects on portfolio adjustment;

(2) effects from new investable financial flows are dependent on the holding-period yields of the endogenous assets in the portfolio;

(3) new investable financial flows affect the reallocation of

existing assets in the portfolio;

(4) positive and negative new investable financial flows have asymmetric effects; and

(5) new investable financial flows are disaggregated in terms of exogenous balance sheet items.

All of the adjustment models utilized for the investor groups participating in the U.S. Government securities market may be classified by a subset of these properties. In addition, each adjustment model includes properties (1) and (2). The choice for each investor group is based on preliminary ordinary least squares estimation.

The models are presented in level form since six out of the ten investor groups are unambiguously modeled in terms of the adjustment of asset stocks. The four remaining investor groups (commercial banks, households, nonfinancial corporate businesses, and state and local government general funds) have models that are presented in level form, but similar expressions may also be derived from the adjustment of asset proportions. The proportional adjustment model is briefly discussed in the latter part of this section.

The model utilized for commercial banks, that incorporates all five of the properties listed above, may be written as[6]

---

[6]The last two terms may be replaced by

$\alpha^{*}_{it} \sum_{j'}^{J} \Delta a^{j'}_{t}$ and $\delta^{*}_{it} \sum_{j''}^{J} \Delta a^{j''}_{t}$, respectively, in order to describe

one of the adjustment models reviewed below as a special case of the general model in (5.2). In particular, as described below, the "optimal marginal adjustment" model introduced by Friedman is obtained from

$$\Delta a_{it} = \sum_{k}^{N} \theta_{ik}(\alpha^{*}_{kt}W_{t-1} - a_{k,t-1})$$

$$+ \sum_{kj'}^{NJ}\sum \phi^{j'}_{ik}(\Delta a^{j'}_{t}/W_{t-1})(\alpha^{*}_{kt}W_{t-1} - a_{k,t-1})$$

$$+ \sum_{kj''}^{NJ}\sum \phi^{j''}_{ik}(\Delta a^{j''}_{t}/W_{t-1})(\delta^{*}_{kt}W_{t-1} - a_{k,t-1})$$

$$+ \sum_{j'}^{J} \pi^{j'}_{i}\Delta a^{j'}_{t} + \sum_{j''}^{J} \pi^{j''}_{i}\Delta a^{j''}_{t}, \qquad i=1,\ldots,N. \tag{5.2}$$

where the θ_{ik}, ϕ'_{ik}, ϕ''_{ik}, $\pi^{j'}_{i}$, and $\pi^{j''}_{i}$ are fixed coefficients of adjustment, the $\Delta a^{j'}_{t}$ and $\Delta a^{j''}_{t}$ are flows of exogenous assets and liabilities such that the sum of these flows equals the flow of the total value of endogenous assets, and the α^{*}_{kt} and δ^{*}_{kt} are desired proportional holdings of assets conditional on positive and negative financial flows, respectively. In addition the positive and negative flows, with respect to the endogenous portion of the portfolio, are written as

$$\Delta a^{j'}_{t} = \begin{cases} \Delta a^{j}_{t}, \text{ if } a^{j}_{t} \text{ is a liability and } \Delta a^{j}_{t} > 0, \\ -\Delta a^{j}_{t}, \text{ if } a^{j}_{t} \text{ is an asset and } \Delta a^{j}_{t} < 0, \\ 0, \text{ otherwise,} \end{cases}$$

---

this modified version of (5.2) by setting $\phi^{j'}_{ik}$, $\phi^{j''}_{ik} = 0$ for all i, k, j', j", and $\delta^{*}_{it} = \alpha^{*}_{it}$, for all i.

The other models considered below also include the "optimal marginal adjustment" model as a special case, but, in general, they are not special cases of (5.2) because of the disaggregated financial flows in the latter.

See Friedman, "A Structural Model of the Long-Term Corporate Debt Market," op. cit.

$$\Delta a_t^{j''} = \begin{cases} \Delta a_t^j, \text{ if } a_t^j \text{ is a liability and } \Delta a_t^j < 0, \\ -\Delta a_t^j, \text{ if } a_t^j \text{ is an asset and } \Delta a_t^j > 0, \\ 0, \text{ otherwise.} \end{cases}$$

The portfolio wealth constraint implies that the parameters of the adjustment model are subject to the following constraints:

$$\sum_i^N \theta_{ik} = \bar{\theta}, \text{ for all k,}$$

$$\sum_i^N \phi_{ik}^{j'} = \bar{\phi}^{j'}, \text{ for all k and } j',$$

$$\sum_i^N \phi_{ik}^{j''} = \bar{\phi}^{j''}, \text{ for all k and } j'',$$

$$\sum_i^N \pi_i^{j'} = 1, \text{ for all } j', \text{ and}$$

$$\sum_i^N \pi_i^{j''} = 1, \text{ for all } j''.$$

The α_{kt}^* represent proportional holdings of assets that are derived directly from the portfolio selection problems in chapters II and III. They are, however, only applied to the positive financial flows (i.e., positive with respect to the endogenous portion of the portfolio) and the portfolio adjustment corresponding to the simple stock adjustment model (i.e., terms involving θ_{ik}).

The δ_{kt}^* differ from the α_{kt}^* in that the former explicitly represent desired short-run portfolio holdings conditional on negative financial flows. That is, the δ_{kt}^* are included to allow for possible asymmetric effects, regarding expected holding-period yields and variances of holding-period yields, from positive and negative financial flows. This is implicitly based on considerations such as differing transactions costs for purchasing and selling assets, and from possible effects from unrealized capital gains and losses on existing assets in the portfolio.

The advantage in introducing the δ^*_{kt} expressions may be easily seen in the simpler adjustment models considered below. In particular, if new investable financial flows are allocated according to desired asset proportions, then $\delta^*_{it} = \alpha^*_{it}$ implies that for negative investable flows, the higher the expected own-holding-period yield, the lower the amount of holdings of the asset. This may be seen from the expression for α^*_{it} in (5.1) and the terms involving marginal allocations of new investable financial flows in the adjustment models that follow.

An adjustment model incorporating properties (1) through (4) is used to describe the portfolio adjustment of nonfinancial corporate businesses. This model is similar to (5.2) except that new investable financial flows are not disaggregated. This model may be written as

$$\begin{aligned}
\Delta a_{it} = \; & \sum_{k}^{N} \theta_{ik}(\alpha^*_{kt}W_{t-1} - a_{k,t-1}) \\
& + \sum_{k}^{N} \phi'_{ik}(\Delta W'_t/W_{t-1})(\alpha^*_{kt}W_{t-1} - a_{k,t-1}) \\
& + \sum_{k}^{N} \phi''_{ik}(\Delta W''_t/W_{t-1})(\delta^*_{kt}W_{t-1} - a_{k,t-1}) \\
& + \alpha^*_{it}\Delta W'_t + \delta^*_{it}\Delta W''_t, \qquad i=1,\ldots,N, \qquad (5.3)
\end{aligned}$$

where

$$\Delta W_t' = \begin{cases} \Delta W_t, \text{ if } \Delta W_t > 0, \\ 0, \text{ otherwise,} \end{cases}$$

$$\Delta W_t'' = \begin{cases} \Delta W_t, \text{ if } \Delta W_t < 0, \\ 0, \text{ otherwise,} \end{cases}$$

with the portfolio wealth constraint implying

$$\sum_i^N \theta_{ik} = \bar{\theta}, \text{ for all k,}$$

$$\sum_i^N \phi_{ik}' = \bar{\phi}', \text{ for all k, and}$$

$$\sum_i^N \phi_{ik}'' = \bar{\phi}'', \text{ for all k.}$$

The terms in (5.3) relate to various sources of portfolio adjustment. The first term describes simple stock adjustment. The second and third terms include the effects of financial flows on the reallocation of existing assets in the portfolio dependent on the sign and magnitude of the financial flows. The final two terms involve the marginal allocation of investable financial flows according to desired proportional asset holdings, with the inclusion of asymmetric effects from positive and negative flows.

The terms in (5.3) that are additional to the simple stock adjustment model may be statistically tested for the appropriateness of their inclusion. In fact, the remaining adjustment models considered are special cases of (5.3). That is, they are formed by restricting certain parameters in this model.

The adjustment model applied to the portfolio selection problem of households and state and local government general funds includes properties (1) through (3). It may be derived from (5.3) by imposing the constraints:

$$\phi''_{ik} = \phi'_{ik}, \text{ for all i and k, and}$$

$$\delta^*_{kt} = \alpha^*_{kt}, \text{ for all k.}$$

These are straightforward constraints for these investor groups since they have strictly positive new investable financial flows throughout the sample period.

This model may be written as

$$\Delta a_{it} = \sum_{k}^{N} \theta_{ik}(\alpha^*_{kt}W_{t-1} - a_{k,t-1}) + \sum_{k}^{N} \phi_{ik}(\Delta W_t/W_{t-1})(\alpha^*_{kt}W_{t-1} - a_{k,t-1}) + \alpha^*_{it}\Delta W_t, \qquad i=1,\ldots,N, \tag{5.4}$$

where the parameters are subject to the same constraints that were introduced previously. The interpretation of this model follows from the discussion concerning (5.3).

An adjustment model including properties (1), (2), and (4) is applied to mutual savings banks and savings and loan associations. It may be derived from (5.3) by imposing the following constraint:

$$\phi''_{ik} = \phi'_{ik} = 0, \text{ for all i and k.}$$

This model may be written as

$$\Delta a_{it} = \sum_{k}^{N} \theta_{ik}(\alpha^*_{kt} W_{t-1} - a_{k,t-1})$$

$$+ \alpha^*_{it}\Delta W'_t + \delta^*_{it}\Delta W''_t, \qquad i=1,\ldots,N, \tag{5.5}$$

where the parameters are subject to the same constraints that were introduced previously.

This model also has the distinct advantage of allowing direct interpretation of the estimation results involving flow terms in any single asset demand equation. In contrast, when the adjustment model given by (5.3) is applied to a single asset demand, the coefficients on the flow terms are not directly interpretable in terms of the structural parameters of the underlying models.

Mutual savings banks and savings and loan associations have positive and negative new investable financial flows with respect to the endogenous portion of the portfolio. The application of (5.5) to these investor groups implies that there are asymmetric effects from positive and negative financial flows on the allocation of these flows. The model does not include the possibility that new investable financial flows affect the portfolio reallocation of existing assets.

The final adjustment model that is applied to the investor groups in this study is the "optimal marginal adjustment" model devised by Friedman.[7] It includes properties (1) and (2); and the model may be

---

[7] Ibid. The model is initially applied in Friedman, "Financial Flow Variables and the Short-Run Determination of Long-Term Interest Rates," op. cit.

formed by imposing the following constraints on (5.3):

$$\phi''_{ik} = \phi'_{ik} = 0, \text{ for all i and k, and}$$

$$\delta^*_{kt} = \alpha^*_{kt}, \text{ for all k.}$$

This model may be written as

$$\Delta a_{it} = \sum_{k}^{N} \theta_{ik}(\alpha^*_{kt}W_{t-1} - a_{k,t-1}) + \alpha^*_{it}\Delta W_t, \qquad i=1,\ldots,N, \tag{5.6}$$

where the parameters are subject to the same constraints that were introduced previously. It is also apparent that the "optimal marginal adjustment" model is a special case of the adjustment models in (5.4) and (5.5). Thus, the corresponding constraints are testable in each case.

The model described by (5.6) is applied to life insurance companies, other insurance companies, private pension funds, and state and local government retirement funds. All of these investor groups have strictly positive new investable financial flows throughout the sample period considered. The interpretation of this model, with respect to these investor groups, corresponds to that of (5.5) with the exclusion of negative investable financial flows.

A general portfolio adjustment model corresponding to (5.3) that involves proportions of assets to portfolio wealth may also be formed. In particular, this model may be represented as

$$\frac{a_{it}}{W_t} - \frac{a_{i,t-1}}{W_{t-1}} = \sum_{k}^{N} \theta_{ik}(\alpha^*_{kt} - \frac{a_{k,t-1}}{W_{t-1}})$$

$$+ \sum_{k}^{N} \phi'_{ik}(\frac{\Delta W'_t}{W_{t-1}})(\alpha^*_{kt} - \frac{a_{k,t-1}}{W_{t-1}})$$

$$+ \sum_{k}^{N} \phi''_{ik}(\frac{\Delta W''_t}{W_{t-1}})(\delta^*_{kt} - \frac{a_{k,t-1}}{W_{t-1}}), \qquad i=1,\ldots,N, \quad (5.3')$$

where the parameters are subject to the same constraints that were previously introduced.

In addition, a model corresponding to (5.4) may be written as

$$\frac{a_{it}}{W_t} - \frac{a_{i,t-1}}{W_{t-1}} = \sum_{k}^{N} \theta_{ik}(\alpha^*_{kt} - \frac{a_{k,t-1}}{W_{t-1}})$$

$$+ \sum_{k}^{N} \phi_{ik}(\frac{\Delta W_t}{W_{t-1}})(\alpha^*_{kt} - \frac{a_{k,t-1}}{W_{t-1}}), \qquad i=1,\ldots,N. \quad (5.4')$$

This model may be obtained from (5.3') by imposing the constraints:

$\phi'_{ik} = \phi''_{ik}$, for all i and k, and

$\delta^*_{ki} = \alpha^*_{kt}$, for all k.

Although the parameters in (5.3) and (5.4) do not correspond directly to those in (5.3') and (5.4'), except for purposes of notational convenience, the latter pair of adjustment models may be rewritten in level form such that the right-hand side variables are identical in an unconstrained reduced form sense. However, a variant of (5.3') is not directly derivable that has this same type of reduced form correspondence to the "optimal marginal adjustment" model in (5.6), and the similar model in (5.5). Thus, after preliminary experimentation, this approach was not further considered in the empirical investigation.

C. Estimation Results

Following the discussions concerning data and estimation techniques, the estimates for the structural demand equations are presented in this section. The specifications of these equations are based on the portfolio theory in chapters II and III, along with the portfolio adjustment models in the previous section.

The estimation results are discussed according to the effects that result from certain categories of variables. In particular, effects from own-yields, variances of holding-period yields, yields on competing assets, and inflation are compared within the set of investor groups. In addition, the substitution relationship between the two maturity classes of U.S. Government securities is analyzed. The discussion is organized in this manner in order to investigate the implications of economic hypotheses, rather than focus primarily on specific institutional features.

The estimation results are also directly related to the underlying portfolio selection theory in two specific instances. First, the results are interpreted according to the effects on desired asset holdings. Secondly, certain constraints on the coefficient matrix on the vector of expected holding-period yields are examined.

1. Data

The primary data source for the financial stock and flow variables is the Federal Reserve System's flow-of-funds accounts.[8] Quarterly

---

[8] Board of Governors of the Federal Reserve System, op. cit.

observations are utilized, with the sample period beginning in 1960:I and ending in 1975:IV.

The data for U.S. Government securities consist of four weighted maturity classes of federal debt that are consistent with the flow-of-funds accounts.[9] The data are defined in terms of four "definite" areas and three "borderline" areas. The definite areas include the following maturities:

(1) within 1 year (short-term),

(2) 2-4 years (short-intermediate-term),

(3) 6-8 years (long-intermediate-term), and

(4) over 12 years (long-term).

U.S. Government securities with maturities in the borderline areas are allocated to the definite classifications according to a weighting scheme. In particular, if n is the number of months in a borderline area, then the securities are allocated to the immediately preceding and successive definite maturity classes according to the following pairs of weights:

$$\left(\frac{n}{n+1}, \frac{1}{n+1}\right), \left(\frac{n-1}{n+1}, \frac{2}{n+1}\right), \ldots, \left(\frac{1}{n+1}, \frac{n}{n+1}\right),$$

where maturity is increasing from left to right.[10] The principle advantage of this procedure is that it avoids the otherwise perverse effects that occur when large debt issues cross fixed maturity boundaries.

---

[9]See Taylor and Wood, op. cit.
Selected stock and flow measures concerning these data are given in Table 1.3 in chapter I.

[10]This procedure is applied, by the Federal Reserve System, to monthly data. Quarterly observations are formed from the arithmetic means of seasonally adjusted monthly data.

Demand equations for two weighted maturity classes of U.S. Government securities are estimated. These correspond to the short-intermediate-term and long-term classifications. The two remaining maturity classifications, i.e., short-term and long-intermediate-term, will be considered in future research. The two maturity classes chosen for the empirical study serve to illustrate the determination of market yields of two unambiguously disjoint maturity classes of U.S. Government securities.

Each financial flow variable, corresponding to the individual assets of the ten investor groups, is defined in terms of seasonally adjusted net changes during the quarter.

The variables representing wealth flows are defined in terms of the endogenous portions of the investor groups' portfolios. For households, other insurance companies, state and local government general funds, and state and local government retirement funds, the wealth flow variables are defined as quarterly net acquisitions of financial assets, seasonally adjusted. For nonfinancial corporate businesses, the wealth flow is defined as the quarterly net change of liquid assets, seasonally adjusted. For life insurance companies, the wealth flow is defined as the quarterly net acquisition of financial assets, seasonally adjusted, minus the similarly defined measure for the net change in policy loans. The wealth flow variables for mutual savings banks and savings and loan associations are quarterly net acquisitions of financial assets, seasonally adjusted, minus the corresponding measures for net changes in mortgages.[11]

---

[11]For a discussion concerning the approximations utilized in the modeling of mutual savings banks and savings and loan associations, see chapter IV.

The wealth flow variable for commercial banks is disaggregated in terms of the exogenous variables that form its aggregative value.[12] The aggregative value equals the quarterly net acquisition of financial assets, seasonally adjusted, minus similarly defined measures for mortgages, bank loans, consumer credit, security credit, and required reserves.

Financial stock variables, including individual asset stocks and total portfolio wealth, are formed by decrementing seasonally adjusted quarterly flows from the value of yearend outstandings in 1975:IV. This serves to guarantee the mutual consistency of the asset stock and flow data throughout the sample period. When the asset stock data contained market valuation changes, these components were included without seasonal adjustment.

The descriptions of other variables, such as yields, variances, and inflation, are given in the summary of variable symbols in section V.C.3.

2. Estimation Techniques

Only a subset of asset demands are estimated for the investor groups; i.e., the demands for short-intermediate-term and long-term U.S. Government securities. Nevertheless, the estimated coefficients of these equations may have implications for the remaining "left-out" equations.[13]

---

[12]An exception to this procedure emerges in the demand for long-term U.S. Government securities. Evidence of structural change within the sample period led to the estimation of two separate demand equations. The equation for the earlier part of the sample period utilizes the aggregated wealth flow variable.

For a discussion of the methodology employed in the modeling of commercial banks, see chapter IV.

[13]See, for example, Brainard and Tobin, "Pitfalls in Financial Model Building," op. cit.

Ladenson[14] and Smith[15] have shown, however, that it is unnecessary to implement constrained estimation in order to satisfy the adding-up constraints in a full set of demand equations for an individual investor group. Unfortunately, the sufficient conditions for this property are often not satisfied in actual applications, necessitating the use of constrained estimation with respect to an investor group's entire portfolio. While this latter approach would be taken herein upon the complete specification of the investor groups' asset demands, this is well beyond the scope of the present study.

The individual asset demand equations, for each investor category, are formed by substituting (5.1) into the relevant adjustment model. It is impossible to estimate equations in this form, however, since both lagged wealth, and the lagged stocks of assets that comprise it, are included as right-hand side variables.

This problem may be alleviated by a prior zero constraint on at least one of the coefficients of these variables, or by substituting either for the lagged wealth variable or any lagged asset stock according to the expression for the wealth identity. Prior to either of these latter substitutions, the adjustment model parameters corresponding to the simple stock adjustment model (θ_{ik}, for all k) were identified. However, after either of these substitutions, the coefficients on lagged

---

[14]Mark L. Ladenson, "Pitfalls in Financial Model Building: Some Extensions," American Economic Review, LXI (March, 1971), 179-186.

[15]Gary Smith, "Pitfalls of Financial Model Building: A Clarification," American Economic Review, LXV (June, 1975), 510-516.

Also see Kevin Clinton, "Pitfalls in Financial Model Building: Comment," American Economic Review, LXIII (December, 1973), 1003-1004.

asset stocks are linear combinations of the parameters of the adjustment model; and, in general, these parameters are no longer identified.

As previously indicated in section V.B, the parameters in expressions for desired asset holdings (α^*_{it}) are identified, from the allocation of new investable financial flows, for six of the investor groups. The adjustment model utilized by these investor groups is either the "optimal marginal adjustment" model in (5.6), or the slightly modified version of it in (5.5). The other adjustment models do not allow the identification of the parameters for expressions of desired asset holdings.

The structure of the U.S. Government securities market model necessitates the use of simultaneous equations estimation techniques. This is the case since the yields on two maturity classes of U.S. Government securities are jointly dependent variables along with the investor groups' demands. Thus, ordinary least squares estimation would result in inconsistent estimates.

The application of an econometric technique described by Brundy and Jorgenson[16] is used to gain consistent estimates for the structural equations. In particular, a version of instrumental variables estimation is performed for the individual equations. The direct application of 2SLS is not possible herein due to the undersized sample problem; i.e., there are more predetermined variables than sample observations.

The particular instrumental variables procedure used involves re-

---

[16]James M. Brundy and Dale W. Jorgenson, "Consistent and Efficient Estimation of Systems of Simultaneous Equations by Means of Instrumental Variables," in Zarembka (ed.), Frontiers in Econometrics, (New York: Academic Press, 1974), pp. 215-244.

placing current values of dependent variables, appearing in the right-hand side of the structural equations, with fitted values obtained from a first-stage regression. In the first stage for an individual structural equation, the right-hand side variables consist of a subset of the principal components of the entire set of predetermined variables in the system of equations, augmented by the set of predetermined variables appearing in the individual structural equation. In addition, since the dependent variables being instrumented appear as products with either wealth flows or stocks, the proper procedure is to instrument the entire multiplicative term.

Due to the approximations utilized in the modeling of commercial banks, mutual savings banks, and savings and loan associations, several variables were included as exogenous whereas they may properly be viewed as endogenous in an implicit formulation of a larger model. Thus, instruments were also formed, by the procedure outlined immediately above, for terms involving contemporaneous values of assets appearing in the equations for these investor groups. For commercial banks, these consist of variables for current values of mortgages, loans, consumer credit, security credit, and wealth flows. For mutual savings banks and savings and loan associations, these consist of current wealth flows.

3. Estimation Results for the Structural Equations

The model of the U.S. Government securities market consists of nineteen demand equations for two maturity classes of government securities, and two market clearing identities. The estimation results for the individual asset demand equations, using the instrumental variables estimation procedure described above, are reported in this subsection. Again, the sample period begins in 1960:I and ends in 1975:IV.

The estimation results are discussed in detail in the subsections that follow according to their attributes. In addition, the estimated equations are combined with the two market clearing identities in section V.D to jointly determine the two endogenous yields and the individual asset demands.

The summary statistics that are reported for each equation are the coefficient of determination adjusted for degrees of freedom ($\bar{R}^2$), standard error of estimate in millions of dollars (SE), and the Durbin-Watson statistic (DW). Two measures are reported for $\bar{R}^2$; the first corresponds to the asset demands in flow form, and the number in parenthesis corresponds to the asset demands rewritten in stock form.

The numbers in parentheses below the estimated coefficients are "t-ratios"; i.e., ratios of estimated coefficients to their standard errors. By virtue of the estimation technique utilized, these statistics are asymptotically standard normal under the usual assumptions.[17]

A summary of variable symbols is provided immediately following the estimation results.

Commercial Banks

(1) $$\Delta US2_t^C = \underset{(-5.4)}{-0.1501}\, US2_{t-1}^C + \underset{(3.8)}{0.1248}\, US1_{t-1}^C + \underset{(5.2)}{0.2544}\, SL_{t-1}^C - \underset{(-4.7)}{2.258}\, CP_{t-1}^C$$

$$+ (\underset{(3.2)}{0.1107}\, \Delta DDP_t^C + \underset{(4.2)}{0.7641}\, \Delta GDP_t^C - \underset{(-2.9)}{1.182}\, \Delta LN_t^C)\cdot r_{2,t}$$

---

[17] For the assumptions underlying the instrumental variables estimation procedure, see Brundy and Jorgenson, op. cit.

$$+ (\underset{(2.8)}{9.615}\ \Delta DDN_t^C + \underset{(3.7)}{10.67}\ \Delta GDN_t^C - \underset{(-4.9)}{10.08}\ \Delta MP_t^C - \underset{(-1.9)}{2.782}\ \Delta SCP_t^C)\cdot(1/r_{2,t})$$

$$+ (\underset{(-1.8)}{-0.3469}\ \Delta GDP_t^C - \underset{(-5.3)}{0.1310}\ \Delta TDP_t^C + \underset{(3.1)}{1.563}\ \Delta LN_t^C$$

$$+ \underset{(1.4)}{0.06099}\ \Delta SCN_t^C)\cdot r_{T,t} - \underset{(-2.5)}{0.8645}\ v_{2,t-1}\cdot\Delta DDP_t^C$$

$$+ \underset{(2.0)}{1.339}\ v_{I,t-1}\cdot\Delta CDP_t^C - \underset{(-2.3)}{0.01619}\ (1/v_{I,t-1})\cdot\Delta DDN_t^C$$

$$+ \underset{(3.9)}{123.2}\ \Delta CC_t^C\cdot(US4_{t-1}^C/W_{t-1}^C) + (\underset{(-3.2)}{-7.811}\ \Delta GD_t^C + \underset{(5.0)}{29.29}\ \Delta M_t^C$$

$$- \underset{(-4.8)}{39.63}\ \Delta CC_t^C)\cdot(US3_{t-1}^C/W_{t-1}^C) + (\underset{(-2.4)}{-2.148}\ \Delta TD_t^C$$

$$+ \underset{(3.5)}{2.722}\ \Delta CD_t^C)\cdot(US1_{t-1}^C/W_{t-1}^C) + (\underset{(-3.1)}{-3.738}\ \Delta GD_t^C$$

$$- \underset{(-2.5)}{12.01}\ \Delta CC_t^C)\cdot(SL_{t-1}^C/W_{t-1}^C) + (\underset{(5.3)}{25.50}\ \Delta TD_t^C$$

$$+ \underset{(2.7)}{138.5}\ \Delta CC_t^C)\cdot(CP_{t-1}^C/W_{t-1}^C) + (\underset{(-3.3)}{-7104}\ \Delta DD_t^C$$

$$- \underset{(-3.7)}{5.291}\ \Delta CD_t^C)\cdot(USA_{t-1}^C/W_{t-1}^C)$$

$\bar{R}^2 = 0.69(0.95)$ SE = 712 DW = 2.02

(2a) Sample Period: 1960:I through 1965:I

$$\Delta US4_t^C = \underset{(3.8)}{5352} - \underset{(-4.3)}{0.6488}\ US4_{t-1}^C + \underset{(2.1)}{0.2784}\ r_{4,t}\cdot\Delta WP_t^C$$

$$+ \underset{(2.6)}{33.44}\ (1/r_{4,t})\cdot\Delta WN_t^C - \underset{(-2.3)}{0.3557}\ r_{S,t}\cdot\Delta WP_t^C$$

$$- \underset{(-2.7)}{27.56}\ (1/r_{S,t})\cdot\Delta WN_t^C - \underset{(-3.6)}{0.01265}\ r_{S,t}\cdot W_{t-1}^C$$

$\bar{R}^2 = 0.67(0.84)$ SE = 204 DW = 2.97

(2b) Sample Period: 1965:II through 1975:IV

$$\Delta US4^C_t = \underset{(-6.5)}{-0.2575}\ US4^C_{t-1} + \underset{(3.0)}{0.01107}\ US2^C_{t-1} + \underset{(2.0)}{0.0006954}\ r_{4,t} \cdot W^C_{t-1}$$

$$- \underset{(-2.9)}{0.0009651}\ r_{S,t} \cdot W^C_{t-1} + (\underset{(3.9)}{0.00387}\ \Delta DDP^C_t + \underset{(1.5)}{0.00494}\ \Delta TDP^C_t$$

$$+ \underset{(2.1)}{0.1207}\ \Delta CDP^C_t - \underset{(-1.7)}{0.01010}\ \Delta SCN^C_t) \cdot r_{4,t} - \underset{(-1.7)}{0.00898}\ r_{T,t} \cdot \Delta CDP^C_t$$

$$- \underset{(-1.7)}{4.221}\ (1/v_{48,t-1}) \cdot \Delta DDN^C_t + \underset{(2.3)}{4.555}\ \Delta SC^C_t \cdot (US4^C_{t-1}/W^C_{t-1})$$

$$- \underset{(-2.4)}{0.1117}\ \Delta L^C_t \cdot (US2^C_{t-1}/W^C_{t-1}) + (\underset{(-1.6)}{-0.7057}\ \Delta TD^C_t$$

$$+ \underset{(1.8)}{0.7986}\ \Delta M^C_t) \cdot (CP^C_{t-1}/W^C_{t-1})$$

$\bar{R}^2 = 0.64(0.90)$ SE = 79 DW = 2.22

Households[18]

(3)
$$\Delta US2^H_t = \underset{(4.7)}{4637} - \underset{(-4.0)}{0.00322}\ W^H_{t-1} - \underset{(-6.4)}{0.3377}\ US2^H_{t-1} - \underset{(-7.3)}{0.2024}\ CB^H_{t-1}$$

$$+ \underset{(4.3)}{0.4763}\ CP^H_{t-1} - \underset{(-5.0)}{0.3011}\ M^H_{t-1} + \underset{(4.3)}{0.02267}\ r_{2,t} \cdot \Delta W^H_t$$

$$- \underset{(-6.6)}{0.0002298}\ r_{P,t} \cdot W^H_{t-1} - \underset{(-5.8)}{1.339}\ v_{I,t-1} \cdot \Delta W^H_t + \underset{(6.2)}{0.02138}\ v_{I,t-1} \cdot W^H_{t-1}$$

$$+ \underset{(3.9)}{0.000002179}\ v_{48,t-1} \cdot W^H_{t-1} + \underset{(6.8)}{0.03696}\ CE_t$$

$$- \underset{(-5.5)}{46.18}\ (\Delta W^H_t / W^H_{t-1}) \cdot CP^H_{t-1}$$

$\bar{R}^2 = 0.79(0.95)$ SE = 406 DW = 2.15

---

[18] For households, equation (3) contains three dummy variables separately including unit value in 1961:I, 1970:I, and 1972:III and zero value in all other quarters; and equation (4) contains a dummy variable with unit value in 1964:III and zero value in all other quarters. See Figures 5.5 and 5.6 in section V.D.

$$(4)\quad \Delta US4^H_t = \underset{(6.5)}{6995} - \underset{(-8.1)}{0.6437}\, US4^H_{t-1} + \underset{(4.9)}{0.06874}\, US1^H_{t-1} + \underset{(5.9)}{0.2555}\, CB^H_{t-1}$$

$$+ \underset{(5.4)}{0.3171}\, CP^H_{t-1} + \underset{(3.7)}{0.1448}\, M^H_{t-1} + \underset{(3.9)}{0.04272}\, r_{4,t}\cdot\Delta W^H_t$$

$$- \underset{(-3.1)}{0.01505}\, (\%\Delta P_{t-1})\cdot\Delta W^H_t - \underset{(-2.7)}{0.01668}\, r_{P,t}\cdot\Delta W^H_t$$

$$+ \underset{(2.3)}{0.0001872}\, r_{P,t}\cdot W^H_{t-1} - \underset{(-4.1)}{0.0004488}\, r_{S,t}\cdot W^H_{t-1}$$

$$+ \underset{(4.3)}{0.0007042}\, v_{CY,t-1}\cdot W^H_{t-1} - \underset{(-6.1)}{0.03157}\, CE_t$$

$$- \underset{(-2.1)}{4.079}\, (\Delta W^H_t/W^H_{t-1})\cdot US2^H_{t-1} - \underset{(-4.0)}{13.16}\, (\Delta W^H_t/W^H_{t-1})\cdot CB^H_{t-1}$$

$$+ \underset{(6.0)}{2.402}\, (\Delta W^H_t/W^H_{t-1})\cdot TD^H_{t-1} + \underset{(2.5)}{3.349}\, (\Delta W^H_t/W^H_{t-1})\cdot DD^H_{t-1}$$

$$- \underset{(-4.5)}{19.29}\, (\Delta W^H_t/W^H_{t-1})\cdot CP^H_{t-1} - \underset{(-2.5)}{3.720}\, (\Delta W^H_t/W^H_{t-1})\cdot SL^H_{t-1}$$

$$- \underset{(-6.9)}{20.00}\, (\Delta W^H_t/W^H_{t-1})\cdot M^H_{t-1}$$

$\bar{R}^2 = 0.66(0.97)$ $\qquad$ SE = 167 $\qquad$ DW = 2.20

Life Insurance Companies[19]

$$(5)\quad \Delta US2^L_t = \underset{(-2.4)}{-0.1399}\, US2^L_{t-1} - \underset{(-3.6)}{0.00801}\, E^L_{t-1} + \underset{(2.5)}{0.00147}\, CB^L_{t-1}$$

$$+ \underset{(5.1)}{0.02988}\, r_{2,t}\cdot\Delta W^L_t - \underset{(2.2)}{0.00549}\, r_{P,t}\cdot\Delta W^L_t - \underset{(-4.3)}{0.02059}\, r_{4,t}\cdot\Delta W^L_t$$

$$+ \underset{(2.2)}{0.01744}\, v_{E,t-1}\cdot\Delta W^L_t - \underset{(-1.9)}{0.0002717}\, v_{E,t-1}\cdot W^L_{t-1}$$

---

[19] For life insurance companies, equation (5) contains a dummy variable with unit value in 1961:IV and zero value in all other quarters; and equation (6) contains two dummy variables separately including unit value in 1960:IV and 1961:III and zero value in all other quarters. See Figures 5.7 and 5.8 in section V.D.

$$- \underset{(-2.3)}{0.01661}\ v_{2,t-1}\cdot \Delta W_t^L$$

$\bar{R}^2 = 0.82(0.96)$ SE = 21 DW = 2.16

$$(6)\quad \Delta US4_t^L = \underset{(1.5)}{304.3} - \underset{(-3.8)}{0.1908}\ US4_{t-1}^L - \underset{(-5.6)}{0.2972}\ US3_{t-1}^L - \underset{(-2.5)}{0.2146}\ US2_{t-1}^L$$

$$+ \underset{(6.6)}{0.2053}\ SL_{t-1}^L - \underset{(-3.9)}{0.05142}\ CP_{t-1}^L + \underset{(4.0)}{0.01361}\ r_{4,t}\cdot \Delta W_t^L$$

$$- \underset{(-3.8)}{0.0001961}\ r_{C,t}\cdot W_{t-1}^L - \underset{(-3.7)}{0.0001791}\ v_{48,t-1}\cdot \Delta W_t^L$$

$$+ \underset{(3.0)}{0.00002125}\ v_{C,t-1}\cdot \Delta W_t^L$$

$\bar{R}^2 = 0.92(0.99)$ SE = 40 DW = 2.42

<u>Mutual Savings Banks</u>[20]

$$(7)\quad \Delta US2_t^M = \underset{(5.0)}{420.7} - \underset{(-5.4)}{0.2460}\ US2_{t-1}^M - \underset{(-1.8)}{0.09530}\ US1_{t-1}^M - \underset{(-4.9)}{0.00993}\ CB_{t-1}^M$$

$$+ \underset{(2.5)}{0.07464}\ r_{2,t}\cdot \Delta WP_t^M - \underset{(-1.4)}{0.03461}\ r_{4,t}\cdot \Delta WP_t^M - \underset{(-3.1)}{0.03769}\ r_{P,t}\cdot \Delta WP_t^M$$

$$+ \underset{(3.7)}{0.3772}\ v_{I,t-1}\cdot \Delta WP_t^M$$

$\bar{R}^2 = 0.69(0.92)$ SE = 50 DW = 1.90

$$(8)\quad \Delta US4_t^M = \underset{(4.9)}{641.4} - \underset{(-6.3)}{0.4226}\ US4_{t-1}^M + \underset{(4.9)}{0.1727}\ US3_{t-1}^M - \underset{(-2.2)}{0.1017}\ US2_{t-1}^M$$

$$- \underset{(-3.5)}{0.2259}\ E_{t-1}^M + \underset{(1.6)}{0.00388}\ r_{4,t}\cdot \Delta WP_t^M + \underset{(2.6)}{0.00226}\ r_{4,t}\cdot W_{t-1}^M$$

$$- \underset{(-1.8)}{0.1891}\ v_{I,t-1}\cdot \Delta WP_t^M$$

$\bar{R}^2 = 0.71(0.99)$ SE = 52 DW = 1.75

---

[20]For mutual savings banks, equation (7) contains two dummy variables separately including unit value in 1963:III and 1966:I and zero value in all other quarters; and equation (8) contains two dummy variables sepa-

Nonfinancial Corporate Businesses[21]

$$(9)\quad \Delta US2^N_t = \underset{(7.1)}{779.7} - \underset{(-5.6)}{1.419}\, \Delta WN^N_t - \underset{(-6.6)}{0.2548}\, US2^N_{t-1} - \underset{(-2.9)}{0.02524}\, TD^N_{t-1}$$

$$+ \underset{(4.3)}{0.1235}\, r_{2,t}\cdot\Delta WP^N_t + \underset{(5.9)}{7.746}\, (1/r_{2,t})\cdot\Delta WN^N_t$$

$$- \underset{(-1.8)}{0.0002775}\, r_{P,t}\cdot W^N_{t-1} + \underset{(3.0)}{43.83}\, (\Delta WP^N_t/W^N_{t-1})\cdot US3^N_{t-1}$$

$$- \underset{(-2.8)}{6.066}\, (\Delta WP^N_t/W^N_{t-1})\cdot US2^N_{t-1} - \underset{(-2.9)}{1.942}\, (\Delta WP^N_t/W^N_{t-1})\cdot CP^N_{t-1}$$

$$- \underset{(-4.9)}{10.46}\, (\Delta WP^N_t/W^N_{t-1})\cdot SL^N_{t-1}$$

$\bar{R}^2 = 0.80(0.96)$ $\qquad$ SE = 160 $\qquad$ DW = 1.86

Other Insurance Companies[22]

$$(10)\quad \Delta US2^O_t = \underset{(3.4)}{0.03591}\, W^O_{t-1} + \underset{(4.3)}{0.1445}\, US3^O_{t-1} - \underset{(-5.4)}{0.2012}\, US2^O_{t-1} - \underset{(-4.4)}{0.05435}\, E^O_{t-1}$$

$$- \underset{(-3.3)}{0.05353}\, SL^O_{t-1} + \underset{(4.1)}{0.1107}\, r_{2,t}\cdot\Delta W^O_t - \underset{(-3.9)}{0.09222}\, r_{C,t}\cdot\Delta W^O_t$$

$$+ \underset{(3.1)}{0.00001130}\, v_{48,t-1}\cdot W^O_{t-1}$$

$\bar{R}^2 = 0.54(0.98)$ $\qquad$ SE = 56 $\qquad$ DW = 1.86

---

rately including unit value in 1960:IV and 1961:II and zero value in all other quarters. See Figures 5.9 and 5.10 in section V.D.

[21]For nonfinancial corporate businesses, the equation contains three dummy variables separately including unit value in 1960:II, 1970:III, and 1971:I and zero value in all other quarters. See Figure 5.11 in section V.D.

[22]For other insurance companies, equation (10) contains a dummy variable with unit value in 1969:III and zero value in all other quarters; and equation (11) contains three dummy variables separately including unit value in 1965:I, 1969:II, and 1969:III and zero value in all other quarters. See Figures 5.12 and 5.13 in section V.D.

$$(11)\quad \Delta US4^{O}_{t} = \underset{(-2.4)}{-0.00277}\ W^{O}_{t-1} - \underset{(-4.7)}{0.3149}\ US4^{O}_{t-1} + \underset{(3.8)}{0.05359}\ US3^{O}_{t-1}$$

$$+ \underset{(3.6)}{0.09389}\ US2^{O}_{t-1} + \underset{(2.1)}{0.1171}\ CB^{O}_{t-1} + \underset{(2.2)}{0.01581}\ r_{4,t}\cdot \Delta W^{O}_{t}$$

$$- \underset{(-2.2)}{0.07716}\ (\overline{\%\Delta P})_{t-1}\cdot \Delta W^{O}_{t} + \underset{(2.6)}{0.00139}\ (\overline{\%\Delta P})_{t-1}\cdot W^{O}_{t-1}$$

$\bar{R}^2 = 0.65(0.96)$ SE = 24 DW = 2.35

Private Pension Funds[23]

$$(12)\quad \Delta US2^{P}_{t} = \underset{(1.9)}{0.02314}\ W^{P}_{t-1} + \underset{(2.8)}{0.2022}\ US4^{P}_{t-1} - \underset{(-1.7)}{0.1346}\ US2^{P}_{t-1} - \underset{(-1.9)}{0.02262}\ E^{P}_{t-1}$$

$$- \underset{(-2.5)}{0.04306}\ CB^{P}_{t-1} + \underset{(2.5)}{0.02387}\ r_{2,t}\cdot \Delta W^{P}_{t} - \underset{(-3.0)}{0.05770}\ r_{D,t}\cdot \Delta W^{P}_{t}$$

$$+ \underset{(3.9)}{0.00259}\ r_{D,t-1}\cdot W^{P}_{t-1} - \underset{(-3.3)}{0.0008336}\ r_{C,t}\cdot W^{P}_{t-1}$$

$$+ \underset{(2.4)}{0.0001401}\ v_{48,t-1}\cdot \Delta W^{P}_{t} + \underset{(2.7)}{0.00002291}\ v_{DK,t-1}\cdot \Delta W^{P}_{t}$$

$\bar{R}^2 = 0.75(0.96)$ SE = 47 DW = 2.21

$$(13)\quad \Delta US4^{P}_{t} = \underset{(-4.4)}{-0.3053}\ US4^{P}_{t-1} + \underset{(4.0)}{0.1673}\ US3^{P}_{t-1} + \underset{(2.4)}{0.1325}\ US2^{P}_{t-1}$$

$$+ \underset{(2.2)}{0.04905}\ US1^{P}_{t-1} + \underset{(5.2)}{0.06815}\ TD^{P}_{t-1} + \underset{(2.9)}{0.01583}\ r_{4,t}\cdot \Delta W^{P}_{t}$$

$$- \underset{(-3.5)}{0.0001717}\ r_{T,t}\cdot W^{P}_{t-1} - \underset{(-3.7)}{0.02735}\ r_{D,t-1}\cdot \Delta W^{P}_{t}$$

$\bar{R}^2 = 0.80(0.97)$ SE = 38 DW = 2.17

Savings and Loan Associations[24]

---

[23]For private pension funds, equation (13) contains a dummy variable with unit value in 1975:II and zero value in all other quarters. See Figure 5.15 in section V.D.

[24]For savings and loan associations, equation (15) contains four

$$(14)\quad \Delta US2_t^{SL} = \underset{(-2.1)}{-239.0} + \underset{(4.8)}{0.1271}\, W_{t-1}^{SL} - \underset{(-3.3)}{0.3053}\, US3_{t-1}^{SL} - \underset{(-6.2)}{0.5515}\, US2_{t-1}^{SL}$$

$$- \underset{(-4.5)}{0.2582}\, FF_{t-1}^{SL} - \underset{(-5.5)}{0.3796}\, USA_{t-1}^{SL} + \underset{(2.7)}{0.07320}\, r_{2,t}\cdot \Delta WP_t^{SL}$$

$$- \underset{(-1.4)}{0.06616}\, (\%\Delta P)_{t-1}\cdot \Delta WP_t^{SL} + \underset{(4.9)}{0.01448}\, (\%\Delta P)_{t-1}\cdot W_{t-1}^{SL}$$

$$- \underset{(-2.8)}{0.07593}\, r_{T,t}\cdot \Delta WP_t^{SL} + \underset{(1.8)}{1.030}\, v_{I,t-1}\cdot \Delta WP_t^{SL}$$

$$- \underset{(-2.0)}{0.04246}\, v_{I,t-1}\cdot W_{t-1}^{SL}$$

$\bar{R}^2 = 0.57(0.96)$ $\qquad$ SE = 161 $\qquad$ DW = 1.89

$$(15)\quad \Delta US4_t^{SL} = \underset{(6.1)}{736.9} - \underset{(-6.2)}{0.5466}\, US4_{t-1}^{SL} - \underset{(-6.7)}{0.1259}\, US2_{t-1}^{SL} + \underset{(5.1)}{0.1066}\, US1_{t-1}^{SL}$$

$$- \underset{(-6.5)}{0.1120}\, USA_{t-1}^{SL} + \underset{(1.7)}{0.00226}\, r_{4,t}\cdot \Delta WP_t^{SL} + \underset{(5.1)}{0.00286}\, r_{4,t}\cdot W_{t-1}^{SL}$$

$\bar{R}^2 = 0.67(0.99)$ $\qquad$ SE = 52 $\qquad$ DW = 2.39

<u>State and Local Government General Funds</u>[25]

$$(16)\quad \Delta US2_t^{SG} = \underset{(4.4)}{1600} - \underset{(-3.9)}{0.1886}\, US2_{t-1}^{SG} - \underset{(-4.1)}{0.5215}\, SL_{t-1}^{SG} + \underset{(4.0)}{0.05411}\, r_{2,t}\cdot \Delta W_t^{SG}$$

$$+ \underset{(2.1)}{0.0005566}\, r_{2,t}\cdot W_{t-1}^{SG} + \underset{(3.4)}{0.000004845}\, v_{S,t-1}\cdot W_{t-1}^{SG}$$

$$- \underset{(-4.6)}{1.040}\, (\Delta W_t^{SG}/W_{t-1}^{SG})\cdot TD_{t-1}^{SG}$$

$\bar{R}^2 = 0.41(0.98)$ $\qquad$ SE = 190 $\qquad$ DW = 2.02

---

dummy variables separately including unit value in 1960:I, 1963:I, 1963:III, and 1965:I and zero value in all other quarters. See Figure 5.17 in section V.D.

[25]For state and local government general funds, equation (16) contains two dummy variables separately including unit value in 1964:I and 1973:I and zero value in all other quarters; and equation (17) contains two dummy variables separately including unit value in 1963:I and 1967:I and zero value in all other quarters. See Figures 5.18 and 5.19 in section V.D.

$$(17)\quad \Delta US4_t^{SG} = \underset{(-2.3)}{-0.05456}\, US4_{t-1}^{SG} + \underset{(1.6)}{0.02421}\, r_{4,t}\cdot\Delta W_t^{SG} + \underset{(3.2)}{0.00143}\, r_{4,t}\cdot W_{t-1}^{SG}$$

$$- \underset{(-2.0)}{0.00173}\, (\%\Delta P)_{t-1}\cdot W_{t-1}^{SG} - \underset{(-2.1)}{0.0007252}\, r_{T,t}\cdot W_{t-1}^{SG}$$

$$- \underset{(-1.7)}{0.3127}\, v_{I8,t-1}\cdot\Delta W_t^{SG} + \underset{(3.1)}{0.02498}\, v_{I8,t-1}\cdot W_{t-1}^{SG}$$

$$+ \underset{(2.0)}{0.0001028}\, v_{S,t-1}\cdot\Delta W_t^{SG} - \underset{(-2.9)}{0.000005037}\, v_{S,t-1}\cdot W_{t-1}^{SG}$$

$$- \underset{(-2.1)}{2.526}\, (\Delta W_t^{SG}/W_{t-1}^{SG})\cdot US4_{t-1}^{SG} + \underset{(3.6)}{6.199}\, (\Delta W_t^{SG}/W_{t-1}^{SG})\cdot US3_{t-1}^{SG}$$

$$- \underset{(-3.4)}{0.6271}\, (\Delta W_t^{SG}/W_{t-1}^{SG})\cdot TD_{t-1}^{SG} - \underset{(-2.5)}{1.035}\, (\Delta W_t^{SG}/W_{t-1}^{SG})\cdot USA_{t-1}^{SG}$$

$\bar{R}^2 = 0.50(0.94)$ SE = 110 DW = 2.22

State and Local Government Retirement Funds[26]

$$(18)\quad \Delta US2_t^{S} = \underset{(-2.5)}{-0.06979}\, \Delta W_t^{S} + \underset{(4.1)}{0.02027}\, US4_{t-1}^{S} - \underset{(-2.0)}{0.06015}\, US3_{t-1}^{S}$$

$$- \underset{(-2.6)}{0.1056}\, US2_{t-1}^{S} + \underset{(2.6)}{0.00908}\, r_{2,t}\cdot\Delta W_t^{S} + \underset{(4.0)}{0.0001456}\, v_{K,t-1}\cdot\Delta W_t^{S}$$

$$- \underset{(-3.8)}{0.000003792}\, v_{K,t-1}\cdot W_{t-1}^{S}$$

$\bar{R}^2 = 0.40(0.96)$ SE = 25 DW = 1.76

$$(19)\quad \Delta US4_t^{S} = \underset{(3.3)}{0.05440}\, W_{t-1}^{S} - \underset{(-1.9)}{0.09346}\, US4_{t-1}^{S} - \underset{(-4.8)}{1.0306}\, US2_{t-1}^{S} - \underset{(-2.8)}{0.1010}\, E_{t-1}^{S}$$

$$- \underset{(-5.1)}{0.07464}\, CB_{t-1}^{S} + \underset{(4.2)}{0.1912}\, r_{4,t}\cdot\Delta W_t^{S} - \underset{(-3.2)}{0.1083}\, r_{2,t}\cdot\Delta W_t^{S}$$

---

[26]For state and local government retirement funds, equation (19) contains a dummy variables with unit value in 1960:III and zero value in all other quarters. See Figure 5.21 in section V.D.

$$- \underset{(-2.6)}{0.0003072}\ v_{4,t-1} \cdot \Delta W_t^S + \underset{(4.0)}{0.0001053}\ v_{C,t-1} \cdot \Delta W_t^S$$

$\bar{R}^2 = 0.63(0.99)$ SE = 108 DW = 2.02

Summary of Variable Symbols

CB = long-term corporate bonds

CC = consumer credit

CD = large negotiable certificates of deposit

CE = personal consumption expenditures

CP = open-market paper

DD = demand deposits
$\Delta DDP = \Delta DD$ if $\Delta DD > 0$; 0 otherwise
$\Delta DDN = \Delta DD$ if $\Delta DD < 0$; 0 otherwise

E = corporate equities

FF = federal funds

GD = government deposits
$\Delta GDP = \Delta GD$ if $\Delta GD > 0$; 0 otherwise
$\Delta GDN = \Delta GD$ if $\Delta GD < 0$; 0 otherwise

L = bank loans
$\Delta LN = \Delta L$ if $\Delta L < 0$; 0 otherwise

M = mortgages
$\Delta MP = \Delta M$ if $\Delta M > 0$; 0 otherwise

P = consumer price index (1967 = 100)
$\overline{\%\Delta P}$ = eight-quarter moving average of percentage change of P

TD = time deposits
$\Delta TDP = \Delta TD$ if $\Delta TD > 0$; 0 otherwise

r_C = current yield on new issues of corporate bonds (Aa utilities)

r_D = Standard and Poor's dividend/price ratio

r_P = yield on commercial paper

r_S = municipal bond yield (Moody's Aaa)

r_T = yield on Treasury bills

r_2 = yield on 3-5 year Treasury securities

r_4 = yield on 10 year and over Treasury securities

SC = security credit
$\Delta SCP = \Delta SC$ if $\Delta SC>0$; 0 otherwise

SP = Standard and Poor's composite common stock price index
$\overline{\%\Delta SP}$ = four-quarter moving average of percentage change of SP

SL = state and local government obligations

USA = U.S. Government agency issues

US1 = short-term Treasury securities (weighted maturity class data including all securities maturing within 1-year)

US2 = short-intermediate-term Treasury securities (weighted maturity class data including all securities maturing in 2-4 years)

US3 = long-intermediate-term Treasury securities (weighted maturity class data including all securities maturing in 6-8 years)

US4 = long-term Treasury securities (weighted maturity class data including all securities maturing in 12 years and over)

v_{DK} = four-quarter moving average variance of $r_D + 4\cdot(\%\Delta SP)$

v_E = four-quarter moving average variance of Standard and Poor's earnings/price ratio

v_C = four-quarter moving average variance of the holding-period yield for corporate bonds

v_{CY} = four-quarter moving average variance of r_C

v_I = four-quarter moving average variance of $\%\Delta P$

v_{I8} = eight-quarter moving average variance of $\%\Delta P$

v_K = four-quarter moving average variance of $4\cdot(\%\Delta SP)$

v_S = four-quarter moving average variance of the holding-period yield for state and local obligations

v_2 = four-quarter moving average variance of r_2

v_4 = four-quarter moving average variance of the holding-period yield for long-term Treasury securities

v_{48} = eight-quarter moving average variance of the holding-period yield for long-term Treasury securities

W = total financial assets (definition depends on the investor group)
$\Delta WP = \Delta W$ if $\Delta W>0$; 0 otherwise
$\Delta WN = \Delta W$ if $\Delta W<0$; 0 otherwise

Additional sources for evaluating the performance of the individual equations are given in section V.D. These include the measures in Table 5.7 for the root-mean-square errors of the individual equations formed by replacing the variables being instrumented with their actual values, and simulating using actual historical values in each period.

The specifications for the structural demand equations were based on preliminary ordinary least squares estimation. Since the matrix of predetermined variables is dependent on the specifications of each individual equation, further experimentation regarding the specifications was not performed after the two-stage estimation procedure was completed. Such changes in the specifications would involve the recomputation of the principal components and the first-stage regressions.

The ordinary least squares estimates of the system of equations are given in the appendix to this chapter. The signs of the estimated coefficients remain unchanged with respect to the two-stage and ordinary least squares results. The orders of magnitude of the vast majority of the coefficients also remain virtually unchanged, with the greatest differences occurring for commercial banks, mutual savings banks, and savings and loan associations. This is due, in part, to the greater number of variables being instrumented in the specifications for these investor groups.[27]

Another area concerning the final specifications is the utilization of dummy variables. The inclusion of dummy variables resulted primarily from three sources. First, while the other variables in the individual equations were capable of explaining the fundamental determinants of the demand for U.S. Government securities, there exists the possibility that certain historically unique factors were not accounted for. Secondly, the relative "smoothness" of the U.S. Government securities data is dependent on the method in which quarterly values are formed from monthly data. Finally, in comparison to other flow-of-funds data series, the weighted maturity class data are generally regarded as not being as reliable over an entire sample period. This final consideration appears to be especially prevalent in the pre-1966 sample period, where the majority of the "extreme" values occurred.[28]

The final area, in this subsection, concerning the structural equations involves the presence of structural shifts. Based on ordinary least squares estimates, this problem was evident for the demand for long-term U.S. Government securities by commercial banks. The mid-point corresponding to this apparent shift occurred during the introduction of the Federal Reserve System's Regulation F and other related regulations, which are discussed in chapter IV. As a result, two separate equations

---

[27]See section V.C.2 for the description of these variables.

[28]See, for example, Figures 5.8, 5.10, and 5.18 for illustrations concerning life insurance companies, mutual savings banks, and the state and local government general funds.

Approximately sixty percent of the dummy variables were included for observations before 1966:I.

are estimated. The first equation is estimated for 1960:I through 1965:I, and the second equation is estimated for 1965:II through 1975:IV. Chow tests were performed for each equation (i.e., (2a) and (2b)), and the null hypothesis of the Chow test was rejected at the 5% level of significance in each case.[29]

Specific areas of the estimation results are considered in the remainder of this section.

4. Own-Yield Effects

The responsiveness of the demand for U.S. Government securities, with respect to changes in own-yields, are examined in this subsection. It is useful to distinguish the effects on the equilibrium allocation of the portfolio from the effects in the short-run, and this is possible for six of the investor groups.

For six of the investor groups,[30] either the "optimal marginal adjustment" model in (5.6), or its slight variant incorporating asymmetric

---

[29]The F-statistics for (2a) and (2b) based on the ordinary least squares estimates are 13.78 and 2.44, respectively. Under the null hypothesis, the statistics have F-distributions with (7, 50) and (14, 36) degrees of freedom, respectively.

A Chow test is also performed for the demand for short-intermediate-term U.S. Government securities by commercial banks. This version of the test takes into account the inadequate degrees of freedom for the estimation during the sample period from 1960:I through 1965:I. The statistic takes the value of 0.71, and it has the F-distribution with (21, 13) degrees of freedom. Hence, the null hypothesis of the Chow test cannot be rejected at the 1% level of significance.

For a discussion of this test, see Franklin M. Fisher, "Tests of Equality between Sets of Coefficients in Two Linear Regressions: An Expository Note," Econometrica, XXXVIII (March, 1970), 361-367.

[30]i.e., life insurance companies, mutual savings banks, other insurance companies, private pension funds, savings and loan associations, and state and local government retirement funds.

effects from positive and negative investable financial flows in (5.5), are utilized in the description of portfolio adjustment. The selection of these adjustment models is based, as indicated in section V.B, on the apparent insignificance of the additional variables that are included in more general models.

The application of the adjustment models in (5.5) and (5.6) is sufficient to identify the effects on the desired equilibrium portfolio from changes in asset yields. In particular, the coefficients appearing on multiplicative terms involving yields and new investable financial flows are directly interpretable in this respect. It is not possible, in general, to identify the parameters in expressions for desired holdings of assets from applications of the other adjustment models in section V.B.

The first two columns in Table 5.1 indicate the responsiveness of the desired proportions of U.S. Government securities in the portfolio to a one percentage point increase in the respective own-yields. For the short-intermediate-term maturity class, the values for the increases in desired proportional holdings range from one percentage point for state and local government retirement funds, to eleven percentage points for other insurance companies; and all t-ratios are greater than 2.5. For the long-term maturity class, the values range from less than one percentage point for savings and loan associations, to nineteen percentage points for state and local government retirement funds; and all t-ratios are greater than 1.6. The magnitudes of these values appear to be reasonable, with the possible exception of the largest value for each maturity class.

TABLE 5.1

SELECTED MEASURES FOR THE EFFECTS RESULTING FROM A ONE PERCENTAGE POINT INCREASE IN THE OWN-YIELDS ON THE PROPORTIONS OF U.S. GOVERNMENT SECURITIES IN THE PORTFOLIO

	Desired (Long-Run)		Actual (Short-Run)	
Investor Category	Maturity Class 2	Maturity Class 4	Maturity Class 2	Maturity Class 4
Commercial Banks	-	-	.0130	.0039
Households	-	-	.0002	.0005
Life Insurance Companies	.0299	.0136	.0004	.0002
Mutual Savings Banks	.0746	.0039	.0016	.0023
Nonfinancial Corporate Businesses	-	-	.0035	-
Other Insurance Companies	.1107	.0158	.0019	.0003
Private Pension Funds	.0239	.0158	.0005	.0003
Savings and Loan Associations	.0732	.0023	.0023	.0029
State-Local General Funds	-	-	.0019	.0020
State-Local Retirement Funds	.0091	.1912	.0002	.0051

The third and fourth columns in Table 5.1 exhibit the short-run responsiveness of actual proportional holdings to changes in own-yields using the sample means of the relevant variables. Values are recorded for each investor group since this measure is independent of the particular adjustment model utilized. As expected, the short-run response is significantly smaller, with one exception,[31] in comparison to the equilibrium response. For the short-intermediate-term maturity class, the largest increase in actual proportional holdings is one and three-tenths percentage points for commercial banks, with the remaining values less than one-half of one percentage point. For the long-term maturity class, values are one-half of one percentage point or less.

5. The Substitution Relationship Between Maturity Classes of U.S. Government Securities

Various degrees of substitution between different maturity classes of otherwise similar securities have been hypothesized in models of interest rate determination. Two extreme cases, with respect to the substitutability between maturity classes, are evident in the "expectations hypothesis"[32] and the "market segmentation hypothesis".[33] It follows from the "expectations hypothesis" that "short- and long-term securities

---

[31]The exception occurs for the demand for long-term securities by savings and loan associations.

[32]See, for example, J. R. Hicks, Value and Capital (London: Oxford University Press, 1946), pp. 141-152; Friedrich A. Lutz, "The Structure of Interest Rates," Quarterly Journal of Economics, LIV (November, 1940), 36-63; and David Meiselman, The Term Structure of Interest Rates (Englewood Cliffs: Prentice-Hall, 1962).

[33]See J. M. Culbertson, "The Term Structure of Interest Rates," Quarterly Journal of Economics, LXXI (November, 1957), 485-517.

can be treated as if they were perfect substitutes and that transactors, indifferent to uncertainty and holding similar expectations, equate the forward rates in the market to the expected rates."[34] In contrast, the "market segmentation hypothesis" suggests that market participants restrict their activity to securities of a certain maturity due to institutional factors and their preferences.

Each of the above hypotheses most likely contains determining factors for long-term interest rates. Furthermore, a significant amount of research has attempted to combine the elements of these hypotheses.[35]

Two areas are investigated below that relate to the substitution relationship between maturity classes of U.S. Government securities. The first concerns the substitution between maturity classes within the individual investor groups. The second considers the possible symmetry of the cross coefficients on U.S. Government security yields. The implications of this latter consideration are developed in chapter III.

---

[34]Meiselman, op. cit., p.10.

[35]See, for example, Feldstein and Chamberlain, op. cit.; Burton G. Malkiel, "The Term Structure of Interest Rates," American Economic Review, LIV (May, 1964), 532-543; Franco Modigliani and Richard Sutch, "Innovations in Interest Rate Policy," American Economic Review, LVI (May, 1966), 178-197; and the references cited therein.

For evaluations concerning the validity of these hypotheses, see, for example, T. G. Cargill, "The Term Structure of Interest Rates: A Test of the Expectations Hypothesis," Journal of Finance, XXV (June, 1975), 761-809; Steven W. Dobson, Richard C. Sutch, and David E. Vanderford, "An Evaluation of Alternative Empirical Models of the Term Structure of Interest Rates," Journal of Finance, XXVI (September, 1976), 1035-1066; and J. W. Elliot and M. E. Echols, "Market Segmentation, Speculative Behavior, and the Term Structure of Interest Rates," Review of Economics and Statistics, LVIII (February, 1976), 40-47.

5a. A Comparison Between the Maturity Classes of the Estimated Equations

Imperfect substitution between maturity classes is implicit in the specification for the model of the U.S. Government securities market. That is, an underlying hypothesis is that individual investor groups view different maturities of securities as imperfect substitutes. This is in addition to behavioral differences between investor groups for similar maturities of securities. This latter consideration motivates the disaggregation of the demand side of the market.

It is somewhat difficult to form a strong hypothesis concerning the perfect, or near perfect, substitutability of different maturity classes of securities. There are at least two forms that this hypothesis may take. First, expressions for desired fractions of U.S. Government securities in the portfolio would include identical variables with similar coefficients on competing asset yields. The similarity of the coefficients would depend on the degree of substitutability between the maturity classes resulting from the selection of the equilibrium (long-run) portfolio. Secondly, the short-run substitutability between maturity classes also depends on portfolio adjustment, with a high degree of short-run substitutability implying similar parameters in the portfolio adjustment model.

A weaker hypothesis concerning short-run substitutability is examined herein. In particular, the demand for short-intermediate-term securities is estimated using the specification for long-term securities, and vice versa. This allows a judgemental interpretation of the appropriateness in applying the same specification, without any constraints on the coefficients, for both maturity classes within an individual investor group. Thus, in Table 5.2, the estimation results for each investor category include a pair of estimated equations for each maturity class. The pair of equations consists of the actual specification used in the model, and the respecification in terms of the actual specification utilized for the other maturity class. For each estimated equation, the coefficient of determination adjusted for degrees of freedom ($\bar{R}^2$) and the root-mean-square error of the forecasted values (RMSE) are included.[36]

The results in Table 5.2 indicate that the application of similar specifications to both maturity classes leads, in general, to a substantial loss in fit. This occurs even in the absence of further specification searches involving the deletion of statistically significant variables with inappropriate signs.

In terms of the root-mean-square errors of the forecasted values, the smallest difference between actual and respecified equations for maturity class 2 is an increase of eight percentage points for state and local government retirement funds. The largest increase for maturity class 2 is eighty-nine percentage points for households. The corresponding extreme values for maturity class 4 are eleven percentage points for commercial banks, and three-hundred-sixty-three percentage points for life insurance companies. Thus, on the basis of this subjective analysis, it appears that the perfect substitutes hypothesis can be rejected.

---

[36]The instrumental variables estimation procedure described in V.C.2 is utilized in forming the reported results. The root-mean-square errors are obtained by replacing the fitted values from the first-stage regressions by actual values, and simulating using actual historical values in each period.

TABLE 5.2

A COMPARISON OF SPECIFICATIONS BETWEEN MATURITY CLASSES

	Maturity Class 2				Maturity Class 4			
	Actual		Respecified		Actual		Respecified	
Investor Category	$\bar{R}^2$	RMSE	$\bar{R}^2$	RMSE	$\bar{R}^2$	RMSE	$\bar{R}^2$	RMSE
Commercial Banks	.69	616	.24	985	.64	61	.10	68
Households	.79	355	.35	672	.66	132	.08	260
Life Insurance Companies	.82	19	.52	30	.92	35	.05	127
Mutual Savings Banks	.69	47	.49	59	.71	47	.00	89
Other Insurance Companies	.54	53	.45	55	.65	22	.35	30
Private Pension Funds	.75	42	.64	52	.80	35	.33	63
Savings and Loan Associations	.57	146	.32	190	.67	47	.23	71
State-Local General Funds	.41	174	.00	217	.50	95	.03	142
State-Local Retirement Funds	.40	24	.28	26	.63	104	.38	133

Notes: All estimation concerning the demand for long-term securities by commercial banks is performed from 1965:II through 1975:IV.

RMSE in millions of dollars.

5b. Tests for Symmetry in the Coefficient Matrix

Several researchers[37] have imposed symmetry on the coefficient matrix that premultiplies the vector of expected holding-period yields. The usual rationale for symmetry, in financial modeling problems, has appealed to the application of negative exponential utility in mean-variance analysis.

The implications of a symmetric coefficient matrix are developed in chapter III.[38] A principle behavioral result developed therein may be restated as: the vector of asset demands has a symmetric coefficient matrix on the vector of expected holding-period yields if, and only if, an investor has constant absolute mean-variance risk aversion with respect to the mean of the argument of the utility function. Hence, the empirical verification of symmetry has a distinct behavioral implication concerning risk aversion.

Symmetry in the coefficient matrix is directly testable for the six investor groups that utilize either (5.5) or (5.6) as their adjustment model. Again, this is due to the identification of the parameters for desired fractional holdings of assets in the portfolio.

Since a complete set of asset demands is not estimated for the individual investor groups, the test for symmetry is only applied to the pair of coefficients on cross maturity class yields. When these terms are not present in the specifications listed in V.C.3, they are included

---

[37]See, for example, Melton, op. cit.; and Parkin, op. cit.

[38]In particular, see sections III.C and III.E. The correspondence between the measure of absolute mean-variance risk aversion, and the usual Pratt-Arrow measure, is also discussed therein.

for the purposes of the test.

The procedure utilized for the test involves stacking the two demand equations for each investor group, and estimating the stacked equations both with and without the symmetry constraint.[39] Under the null hypothesis of symmetry, the test statistic is asymptotically distributed as χ^2 with one degree of freedom. This is the proper framework for the test due to the two-stage technique employed for the estimation of the structural equations. However, it may be desirable, because of the small sample properties of the test statistic, to use the F-distribution.[40] Either test may be performed on the basis of the values given in Table 5.3.

At the 10% level of significance, the null hypothesis is rejected for three investor groups (life insurance companies, other insurance companies, and state and local government retirement funds); and it cannot be rejected for the remaining three investor groups.[41]

The estimated coefficients on the cross maturity class terms, with the symmetry constraint imposed, are given in the last column in Table 5.3. The t-ratios for the estimated coefficients indicate that, for the

---

[39]In addition, assumptions concerning the error terms, including zero contemporaneous correlation and identical variances for each equation, are employed to simplify the testing procedure. This contemporaneous correlation assumption is consistent with the limited information methodology employed in the estimation of the system of structural equations.

[40]For comments on a similar problem in statistical hypothesis testing, see Henri Theil, Principles of Econometrics, (New York: John Wiley & Sons, 1971), pp. 312-316, and pp. 402-403.

[41]These results hold for either the χ^2- or F-test. At the 5% level of significance, the only change occurs for other insurance companies under the F-distribution.

TABLE 5.3

A TEST FOR SYMMETRY IN THE COEFFICIENT MATRIX ON THE VECTOR OF ASSET YIELDS

Investor Category	Test Statistic	Degrees of Freedom	Estimated Coefficient with Symmetry Imposed
Life Insurance Companies	14.70	1, 105	0.008 (3.1)
Mutual Savings Banks	1.07	1, 107	-0.007 (-0.6)
Other Insurance Companies	3.87	1, 106	0.006 (0.4)
Private Pension Funds	1.06	1, 106	0.010 (1.5)
Savings and Loan Associations	0.09	1, 103	-0.004 (-0.3)
State-Local Retirement Funds	13.44	1, 110	-0.035 (-2.4)

Note: Numbers in parentheses are ratios of estimated values to standard errors (t-ratios).

three investor groups in which symmetry may not be rejected, the relevant coefficients are statistically insignificant. Thus, symmetry takes the form of zero off-diagonal elements corresponding to the yields on short-intermediate-term and long-term U.S. Government securities.

On the basis of the tests reported above, the evidence appears to favor the rejection of the symmetry hypothesis. However, tests concerning this hypothesis would benefit from the inclusion of a larger subset of an individual investor group's asset demands.

6. Yields on Competing Assets Present in the Empirical Specification of the Model

The yields on competing assets directly affect the desired holdings of U.S. Government securities. This is apparent, for example, from the expression for desired proportional holdings of assets in (5.1). However, the inclusion of yields on all potential substitutes may be impossible due to the multicollinearity present in any set of asset yields.

Interpretations may be made, regarding the estimated coefficients on competing yields, that are similar to those for the coefficients on own-yields in V.C.4. In particular, applications of the adjustment models in (5.5) and (5.6) allow the direct interpretation of coefficients on multiplicative terms involving yields and wealth flows. In these cases, the results reported below indicate the effects on desired holdings of U.S. Government securities. When other adjustment models are utilized, or when coefficients appear only on multiplicative terms involving yields and lagged wealth stocks, the interpretation is made in terms of the short-run effect on <u>actual</u> asset holdings. The results concerning the inclusion of yields on competing assets in the empirical specification of the model are summarized in Table 5.4.

The competing yields appearing in specifications for the demand for short-intermediate-term U.S. Government securities include both short- and long-term yields. For four investor groups (households, life insurance companies, mutual savings banks, and nonfinancial corporate businesses), the yield on commercial paper is included. An increase in the commercial paper yield unambiguously decreases the desired holdings of short-intermediate-term U.S. Government securities for life insurance companies and mutual savings banks. For households and nonfinancial corporate businesses, the corresponding effects are decreases in actual short-run holdings.

Another short-term yield, i.e., the yield on Treasury bills, is present in the short-intermediate-term equations for commercial banks and savings and loan associations. For these investor groups, an increase in the Treasury bill yield results in decreases in actual short-run holdings and desired holdings, respectively.

Two long-term bond yields appear in specifications for the demand for short-intermediate-term U.S. Government securities. In particular, an increase in the long-term U.S. Government securities yield results in decreases in desired holdings for life insurance companies and mutual savings banks; and an increase in the corporate bond yield results in decreases in desired holdings and actual holdings for other insurance companies and private pension funds, respectively.

The equity yield appears in the short-intermediate-term specification only for private pension funds. The equity yield is also evident in the

TABLE 5.4

YIELDS ON COMPETING ASSETS PRESENT IN THE EMPIRICAL SPECIFICATION OF THE MODEL

	r_P	r_T	r_2	r_4	r_C	r_S	r_D
Commercial Banks		S,L				L	
Households	S,L					L	
Life Insurance Companies	S			S	L		
Mutual Savings Banks	S			S			
Nonfinancial Corporate Businesses	S						
Other Insurance Companies					S		
Private Pension Funds		L			S		S,L
Savings and Loan Associations		S					
State-Local General Funds		L					
State-Local Retirement Funds			L				

Notes: The inclusion of competing yield variables in the short-intermediate-term and long-term specifications are indicated by "S" and "L", respectively.

The interpretations of the variables, in terms of desired (long-run) and actual (short-run) effects, are given in the text.

The definitions of the variables are given in the summary of variable symbols in V.C.3.

demand for long-term U.S. Government securities by private pension funds; and this is again the only appearance of this yield in equations for the long-term maturity class. In each case, an increase in the equity yield results in a decrease in desired holdings of U.S. Government securities.

In specifications for the demand for long-term U.S. Government securities, short- and long-term yields again appear with approximately equal frequency. A Treasury bill yield is included in specifications for commercial banks, private pension funds, and state and local government general funds. In each case, an increase in the Treasury bill yield results in a decrease in actual holdings of long-term U.S. Government securities. The yield on commercial paper is again included for households; however, the corresponding effect may only be interpreted as negative on the allocation of new investable financial flows. Another relatively short-term yield, i.e., the yield on short-intermediate-term U.S. Government securities, has a negative effect on the desired holdings of long-term U.S. Government securities of state and local government retirement funds.

Two competing bond yields appear in specifications for the demand for long-term U.S. Government securities. These consist of a corporate bond yield in the specification for life insurance companies; and a yield on municipal bonds in equations for commercial banks and households. In each case, an increase in the competing bond yield results in a decrease in actual holdings of long-term U.S. Government securities.

In summary, eleven of the nineteen estimated equations include yields on competing short-term assets in their specifications. In addition, competing long-term bond yields appear in seven of the equations; and an equity yield appears in two equations (i.e., the two equations for private pension funds). Hence, on the basis of asset yields, U.S. Government securities emerge as better substitutes for other credit market securities than for equities.

7. Non-Yield Variables Present in the Empirical Specification of the Model

Certain non-yield variables are included in the specifications for the demand for U.S. Government securities on the basis of the portfolio theory developed in previous chapters. These variables include past levels of inflation, variances of asset holding-period yields, the variance of inflation, and a variable for personal consumption expenditures in the two household equations.[42] The results concerning the inclusion of non-yield variables in the empirical specification of the model are summarized in Table 5.5.

The interpretations of the effects from these variables are given utilizing the methodology of the previous subsection. That is, an interpretation is given in terms of the effects on desired asset holdings when possible; and when this is not possible, the interpretation is in terms of actual short-run holdings.

Levels of inflation may affect asset demands in at least two ways.[43]

---

[42]For the definitions of these variables, see the summary of variable symbols in V.C.3.

[43]See the discussions concerning the effects of inflation on portfolio selection in chapters II and III. In particular, see II.B.6 and III.C.

TABLE 5.5

NON-YIELD VARIABLES PRESENT IN THE EMPIRICAL SPECIFICATION OF THE MODEL

	$\%\Delta P, \overline{\%\Delta P}$	v_I, v_{I8}	v_2	v_4, v_{48}	v_C, v_{CY}	v_S	v_{DK}, v_E, v_K
Commercial Banks		S	S	L			
Households	L	S		S	L		
Life Insurance Companies			S	L	L		S
Mutual Savings Banks		S,L					
Nonfinancial Corporate Businesses							
Other Insurance Companies	L						
Private Pension Funds				S			S
Savings and Loan Associations	S	S					
State-Local General Funds	L	L				S,L	
State-Local Retirement Funds				L	L		S

Notes: The inclusion of non-yield variables in the short-intermediate-term and long-term specifications are indicated by "S" and "L", respectively.

The interpretations of the variables, in terms of desired (long-run) and actual (short-run) effects, are given in the text.

The definitions of the variables are given in the summary of variable symbols in V.C.3.

First, investors may form expectations concerning real holding-period yields by subtracting the expected level of inflation from their nominal expectations. Secondly, investors may base their investment decisions on nominal expected holding-period yields; and expectations concerning inflation may be utilized in forming these nominal expectations.

For the short-intermediate-term specifications, variables used to examine the effects of inflation, consisting of either actual values lagged one period or a four-quarter moving average of actual values lagged one period, appear only for savings and loan associations. In this case, an increase in inflation results in a decrease in desired holdings of short-intermediate-term U.S. Government securities.

Variances of holding-period yields may also enter into the specifications based on the linearization of expressions for desired asset holdings in (5.1). For specifications of the demand for short-intermediate-term U.S. Government securities, these holding-period variances consist of the relevant measures for the own-yield, the long-term U.S. Government security yield, the yield on municipal bonds, and equity yields.

The variance of the own-yield, in the demand for short-intermediate-term securities, appears in specifications for commercial banks and life insurance companies. For these investor groups, an increase in this variance results in decreases in actual short-run holdings and desired holdings, respectively.

The variances of the holding-period yields on bonds have positive effects on the demand for short-intermediate-term securities. In particular, an increase in the variance of the holding-period yield on long-term U.S. Government securities results in increases in actual short-run holdings and desired holdings for households and private pension funds, respectively. In addition, an increase in the variance of the holding-period yield on municipal bonds results in an increase in actual short-run holdings for state and local government general funds.

Variances of equity yields appear in three equations for the demand for short-intermediate-term U.S. Government securities. The corresponding investor groups are life insurance companies, private pension funds, and state and local government retirement funds. In each case, an increase in this variance results in an increase in desired holdings of short-intermediate-term U.S. Government securities.

Similar to the rationale concerning the effects from changes in the level of inflation, the variance of inflation may also be important in portfolio selection. The variance of inflation is included in the final specifications for four investor groups (commercial banks, households, mutual savings banks, and savings and loan associations) in the short-intermediate-term maturity class. For mutual savings banks and savings and loan associations, an increase in this variance results in increases in the relevant desired asset holdings. For households, an increase in this variance reduces the proportional allocation of the new investable financial flow to short-intermediate-term securities. For commercial banks, the corresponding short-run effect is negative for certain inflows into the endogenous portion of the portfolio, and positive for certain outflows.

A similar set of non-yield variables also appears in specifications for the demand for long-term U.S. Government securities. In particular, the level of inflation appears in equations for households, other insurance companies, and state and local government general funds. An increase in this measure results in decreases of actual short-run holdings for households and state and local government general funds, and a decrease in desired holdings for other insurance companies.

An increase in the variance of the own-holding-period yield, for the long-term maturity class, results in a decrease in actual short-run holdings for commercial banks, and decreases in desired holdings for life insurance companies and state and local government retirement funds.

Variances on the holding-period yields of competing categories of bonds have positive effects on the demand for long-term U.S. Government securities. For corporate bonds, an increase in the corresponding variance increases actual short-run holdings for households, and increases desired holdings for life insurance companies and state and local government retirement funds. For municipal bonds, an increase in the corresponding variance increases the allocation of the new investable financial flow to long-term U.S. Government securities for state and local government general funds.

The variance of inflation also affects the demand for long-term U.S. Government securities for two investor groups. In particular, an increase in this variance results in a decrease in desired holdings for mutual savings banks, and a decrease in the allocation of the new investable financial flow to long-term U.S. Government securities for state and local government general funds.

An additional non-yield variable appears in both of the estimated household equations. This variable is personal consumption expenditures. As described in chapter II, the demands for financial assets by households are modeled to include the effects from both transactions and portfolio motives. The personal consumption expenditures variable is used to determine the size of the liquid asset holdings of households due to the transactions motive. Thus, as expected, the personal consumption expenditure variable has a highly statistically significant positive coefficient for the short-intermediate-term maturity class equation, and a highly statistically significant negative coefficient for the long-term maturity class equation.

In conclusion, the principle category of statistically significant non-yield variables consist of the variances of asset holding-period yields, and the variance of inflation. Thus, as the mean-variance portfolio selection theory indicates, one should consider more than the means in empirical investigations of the demand for financial assets.

8. Portfolio Own-Stock Adjustment Speeds

The estimates of the own-stock adjustment parameter are given in Table 5.6. These include estimated values for the simple stock adjustment parameter (θ_{ii}), and the average total own-stock adjustment when a flexible adjustment component is included ($\theta_{ii} + \phi_{ii}(\overline{\Delta W_t/W_{t-1}})$).

For the short-intermediate-term maturity class, estimated values for total average own-stock adjustment range from .1056 for state and local government retirement funds, to .5515 for savings and loan associations; with all t-ratios greater than 1.7, and median equal to 5.4. For the long-term maturity class, these values range from .0935 for the state

TABLE 5.6

ESTIMATES OF THE OWN-STOCK ADJUSTMENT PARAMETER

	Simple Stock Adjustment Component (θ_{ii})		Total Average Stock Adjustment $[\theta_{ii} + \phi_{ii}\overline{(\Delta W_t/W_{t-1})}]$	
Investor Category	Maturity Class 2	Maturity Class 4	Maturity Class 2	Maturity Class 4
Commercial Banks	.1501	.2575	-	.2520
Households	.3377	.6437	-	-
Life Insurance Companies	.1399	.1908	-	-
Mutual Savings Banks	.2460	.4226	-	-
Nonfinancial Corporate Businesses	.2548	-	.3571	-
Other Insurance Companies	.2012	.3149	-	-
Private Pension Funds	.1346	.3053	-	-
Savings and Loan Associations	.5515	.5466	-	-
State-Local General Funds	.1886	.0546	-	.1162
State-Local Retirement Funds	.1056	.0935	-	-

and local government retirement funds, to .6437 for households; with all t-ratios greater than 1.9, and median equal to 4.7. This latter adjustment parameter for households is most likely too high in comparison to the other investor groups. The other estimated values may be considered reasonable for a quarterly model.

D. The Short-Run Determination of Yields on U.S. Government Securities

This section examines the short-run determination of the yields on short-intermediate-term and long-term U.S. Government securities. These yields are determined in a market-clearing framework that utilizes the estimated structural equations in V.C.3. In particular, the set of estimated asset demands, taken with two market-clearing identities that place aggregate demands equal to the exogenous supplies of U.S. Government securities in the two maturity classes, determines the two endogenous yields. That is, the nineteen estimated demand equations and the two market-clearing identities determine nineteen endogenous demands and the two endogenous U.S. Government security yields.

The reduced form term structure approach may be contrasted to the structural model of the U.S. Government securities market by noting that the difference, at the methodological level, is essentially that of unrestricted versus restricted estimation. That is, the structural model developed herein has implicit reduced form equations for the endogenous yields, but these reduced forms are constrained by the underlying structural demand equations.

There are at least two assumptions that are implicitly accepted in the reduced form term structure methodology.[44] First, it is assumed that short-term interest rates and the determinants of interest rate spreads are exogenous with respect to the investors in the long-term financial capital markets. Secondly, it is assumed that quantities of long-term

---

[44]For a discussion concerning the assumptions involved in the reduced form term structure theory, see Friedman, "A Structural Model of the Long-Term Corporate Debt Market," op. cit.

securities transacted in a given period, either by individual investor groups or in the aggregate, do not affect the ex post outcome of long-term interest rates. The structural model of the U.S. Government securities market explicitly drops this latter assumption by directly representing the portfolio behavior of the investors participating in this market. In addition, because of the disaggregated maturity classes, short-term and long-term yields become jointly determined endogenous variables in the model.

Selected simulation results are reported in Table 5.7. In particular, the summary measures listed therein are for the one-period forecasts, the separate dynamic simulations for each maturity class, and the joint dynamic simulation that includes the two maturity classes contemporaneously. Parallel results are given in the appendix that concern the ordinary least squares estimation of the model. This appendix is included primarily because of the forecast bias present in both equations for commercial banks. In each case, the bias results from the relatively large number of instrumented variables appearing in the second stage of the simultaneous equations estimation procedure.

The results from the independent dynamic simulations of the sets of equations for the two maturity classes are reported in the third and fourth columns of Table 5.7. For the yields on short-intermediate-term and long-term U.S. Government securities, the root-mean-square errors are thirty-three and twenty basis points, respectively. Thus, as expected, this measure is higher for the yield on short-intermediate-term securities due to the greater volatility of short-term yields. However, the

TABLE 5.7

SIMULATION RESULTS FOR 1960:I-1975:IV

Variable	Forecast		Separate Dynamic		Joint Dynamic	
	M.E.	R.M.S.E.	M.E.	R.M.S.E.	M.E.	R.M.S.E.
r_2	-	-	0.01	0.33	-0.01	0.34
r_4	-	-	-0.01	0.20	-0.02	0.20
$\Delta US2^C$	-30.5	616	-1.7	334	-0.4	337
$\Delta US4^C$	31.4	116	0.4	120	0.8	123
$\Delta US2^H$	0.0	355	3.4	348	3.0	348
$\Delta US4^H$	0.0	132	-0.3	190	0.5	196
$\Delta US2^L$	-0.1	19	-0.1	29	-0.4	31
$\Delta US4^L$	0.0	35	0.0	37	-0.1	39
$\Delta US2^M$	0.0	47	-0.2	50	-0.4	50
$\Delta US4^M$	0.0	47	0.4	49	0.4	48
$\Delta US2^N$	0.0	148	-0.2	205	-0.6	206
$\Delta US2^O$	0.2	53	-0.1	55	-0.2	55
$\Delta US4^O$	0.0	22	-0.1	24	0.0	25
$\Delta US2^P$	-0.2	42	-0.2	46	0.2	43
$\Delta US4^P$	-0.1	35	-0.1	37	0.2	37
$\Delta US2^{SL}$	0.0	146	-4.2	164	-4.3	164
$\Delta US4^{SL}$	0.0	50	-0.7	56	-1.1	63
$\Delta US2^{SG}$	0.0	174	3.5	165	3.4	164
$\Delta US4^{SG}$	-0.6	95	-0.2	94	0.4	96
$\Delta US2^S$	0.0	24	-0.1	25	-0.3	26
$\Delta US4^S$	-0.4	104	0.5	94	-0.9	119

Notes: r_i in percent, ΔUSi in millions of dollars.
M.E. is the mean error.
R.M.S.E. is the root-mean-square error.

magnitudes of both of these values indicate that the structural modeling methodology is capable of a high degree of accuracy.

The results for the separate dynamic simulations also show no evidence of any bias in the individual equations. This is true even for the equations for commercial banks. In addition, irregularities in the root-mean-square errors are not apparent in these results.

The joint determination of the asset demands and the two endogenous yields is the ultimate outcome of the estimated structural model. The results for the corresponding dynamic simulation are given in the last two columns of Table 5.7. These results are also illustrated in Figures 5.1 through 5.21, where plots of actual and simulation values are given. For each endogenous variable, the results are similar to those of the separate dynamic simulations. For the yields, the root-mean-square errors are thirty-four basis points and twenty basis points for the short-intermediate-term maturity class and the long-term maturity class, respectively. Again, the yields are explained with an unexpectedly high degree of accuracy.

Table 5.8 exhibits additional characteristics of the simulation results for the yields. In particular, the sample period is divided at 1965:I, and separate summary measures for the joint dynamic simulation are shown. This particular break point corresponds to the partitioned sample period utilized in the estimation of the demand for long-term U.S. Government securities by commercial banks. In addition, it also corresponds to one of the most drastic partitions possible in terms of differing values for the corresponding root-mean-square errors. These

TABLE 5.8

DYNAMIC SIMULATION RESULTS FOR U.S. GOVERNMENT SECURITY YIELDS

	r_2		r_4	
	M.E.	R.M.S.E.	M.E.	R.M.S.E.
1960:I-1975:IV	-0.01	0.34	-0.02	0.20
1960:I-1965:I	-0.08	0.40	-0.03	0.27
1965:II-1975:IV	0.02	0.30	-0.01	0.14

Notes: r_i in percent.

M.E. is the mean error.

R.M.S.E. is the root-mean-square error.

results indicate, along with Figures 5.1 and 5.2, that the model performs somewhat better in more recent periods despite the greater volatility in actual market yields.

A final issue concerning the joint determination of the two endogenous yields deals with the effects from relative asset supplies. While this area is potentially very interesting, it will be examined in future research involving further applications of the U.S. Government securities market model. One experiment was performed, however, to determine the extent of the dependence between maturity classes. In particular, the stock of outstanding short-intermediate-term U.S. Government securities was increased by $2.5 billion in 1959:IV.[45] That is, in each period, the value of outstanding short-intermediate-term securities was greater by $2.5 billion than previously. This resulted in an average increase, over the sample period, of twenty-one basis points for the yield on short-intermediate-term U.S. Government securities, and an increase of three basis points for the yield on long-term U.S. Government securities. Based on this experiment, the corresponding elasticities of the yields with respect to the supply of short-intermediate-term U.S. Government securities are 0.64 and 0.09, respectively. Thus, the cross-maturity effects implicit in the model include elements from both of the extreme reduced form term structure theories; i.e., the "expectations hypothesis" and the "market segmentation hypothesis".

---

[45]In terms of the average value of outstandings held during the sample period by the ten investor groups in the model, this is approximately a six percentage point increase.

FIGURE 5.1

DYNAMIC SIMULATION RESULTS FOR THE YIELD ON SHORT-INTERMEDIATE-TERM

U.S.GOVERNMENT SECURITIES

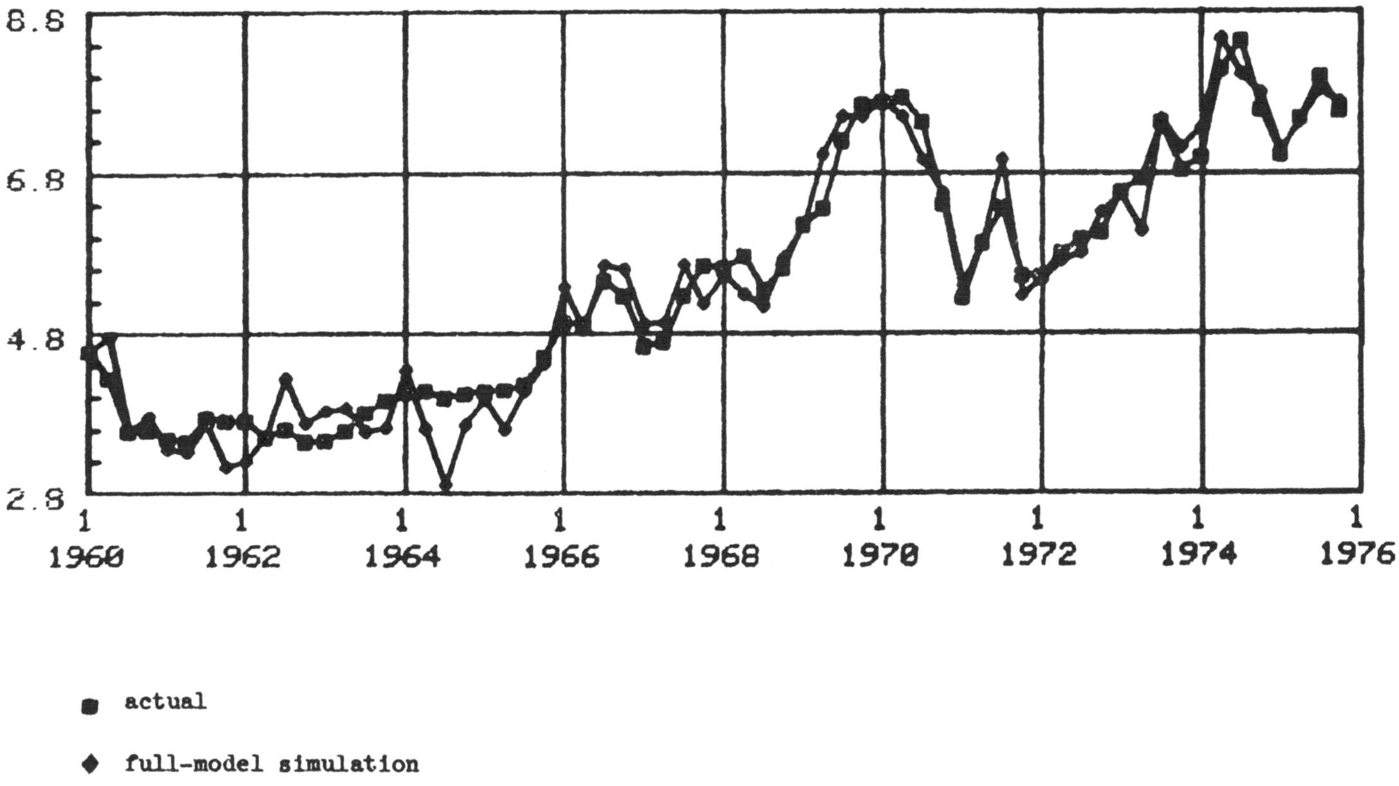

FIGURE 5.2

DYNAMIC SIMULATION RESULTS FOR THE YIELD ON LONG-TERM U.S. GOVERNMENT SECURITIES

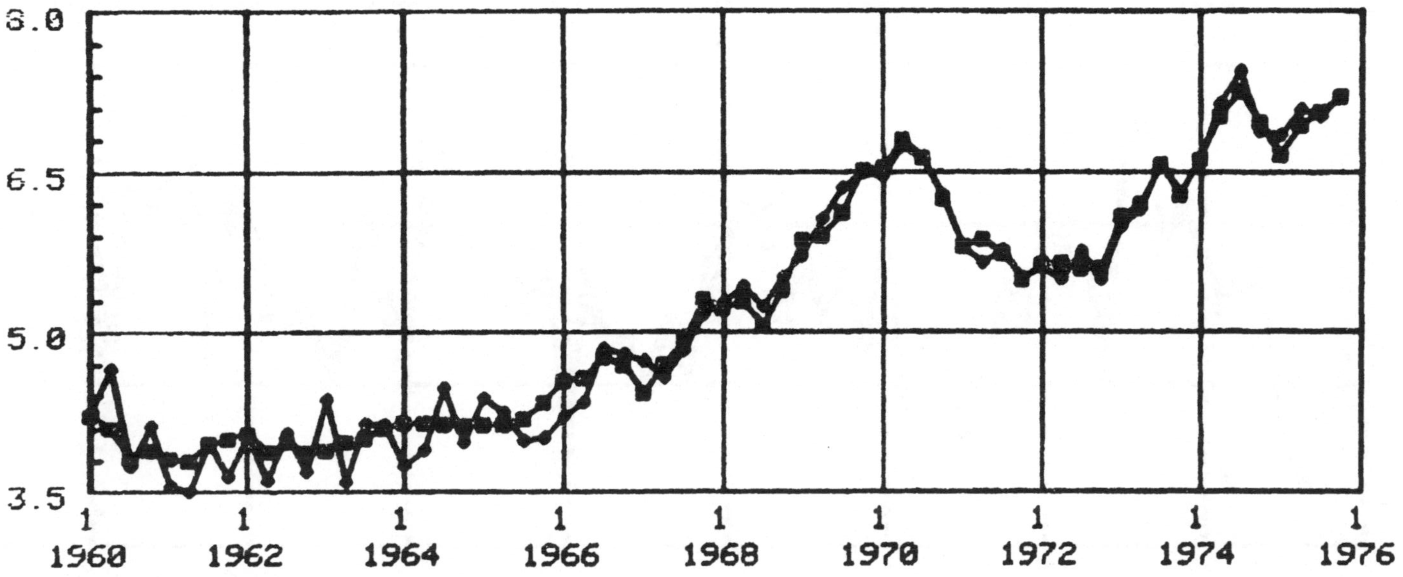

■ actual

♦ full-model simulation

FIGURE 5.3

DYNAMIC SIMULATION RESULTS FOR NET PURCHASES OF SHORT-INTERMEDIATE-TERM

U.S. GOVERNMENT SECURITIES BY COMMERCIAL BANKS

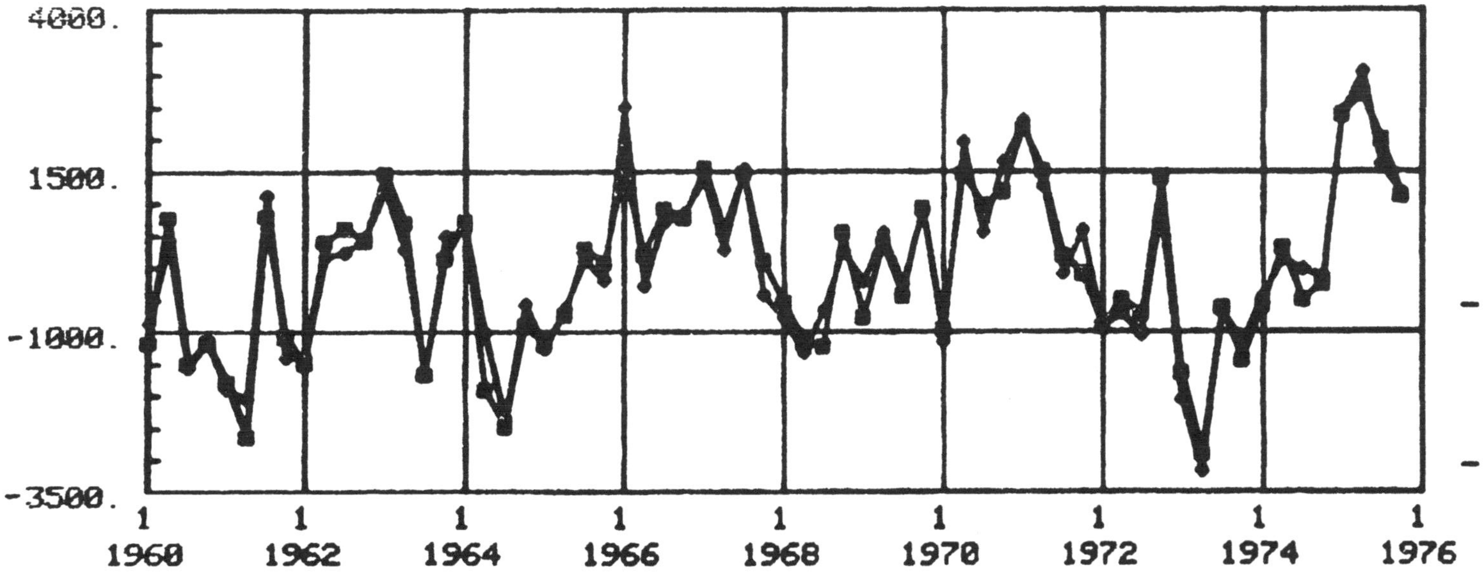

■ actual

♦ full-model simulation

FIGURE 5.4

DYNAMIC SIMULATION RESULTS FOR NET PURCHASES OF LONG-TERM U.S. GOVERNMENT SECURITIES BY COMMERCIAL BANKS

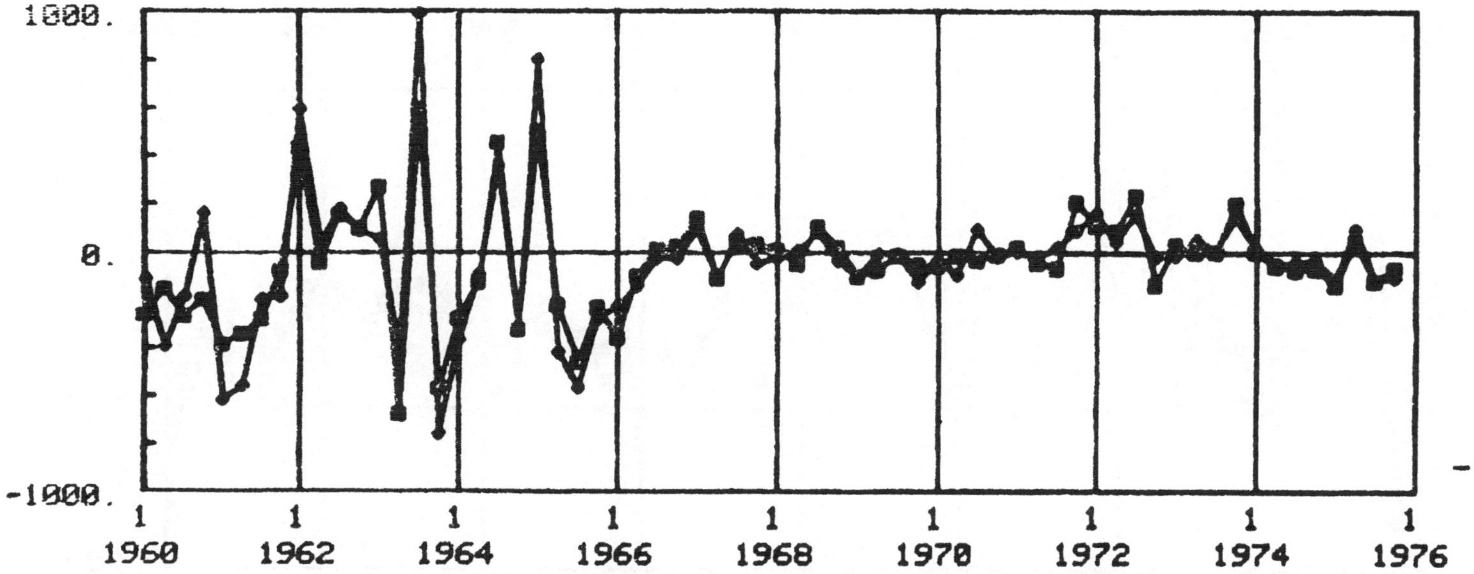

■ actual

◆ full-model simulation

FIGURE 5.5

DYNAMIC SIMULATION RESULTS FOR NET PURCHASES OF SHORT-INTERMEDIATE-TERM U.S. GOVERNMENT SECURITIES BY HOUSEHOLDS

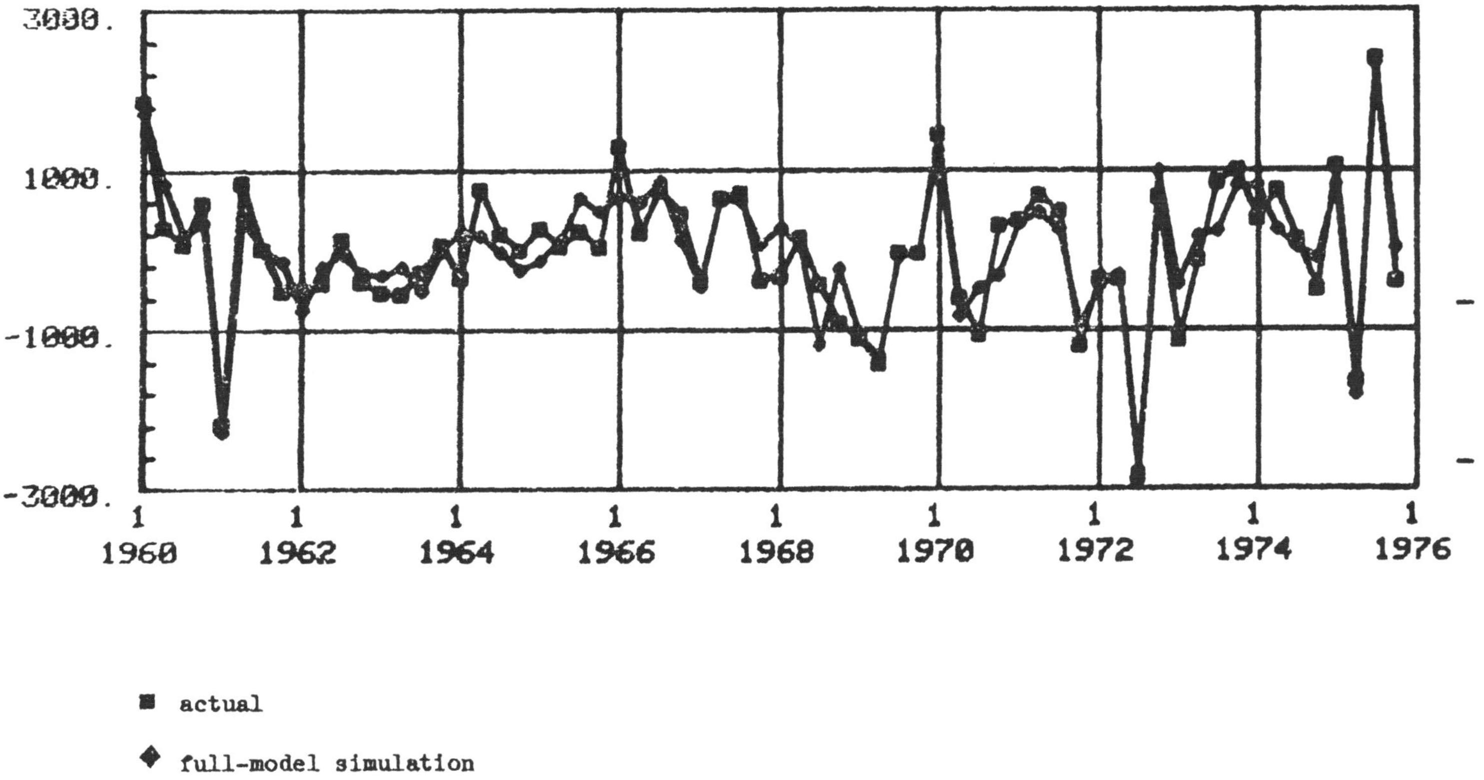

FIGURE 5.6

DYNAMIC SIMULATION RESULTS FOR NET PURCHASES OF LONG-TERM

U.S. GOVERNMENT SECURITIES BY HOUSEHOLDS

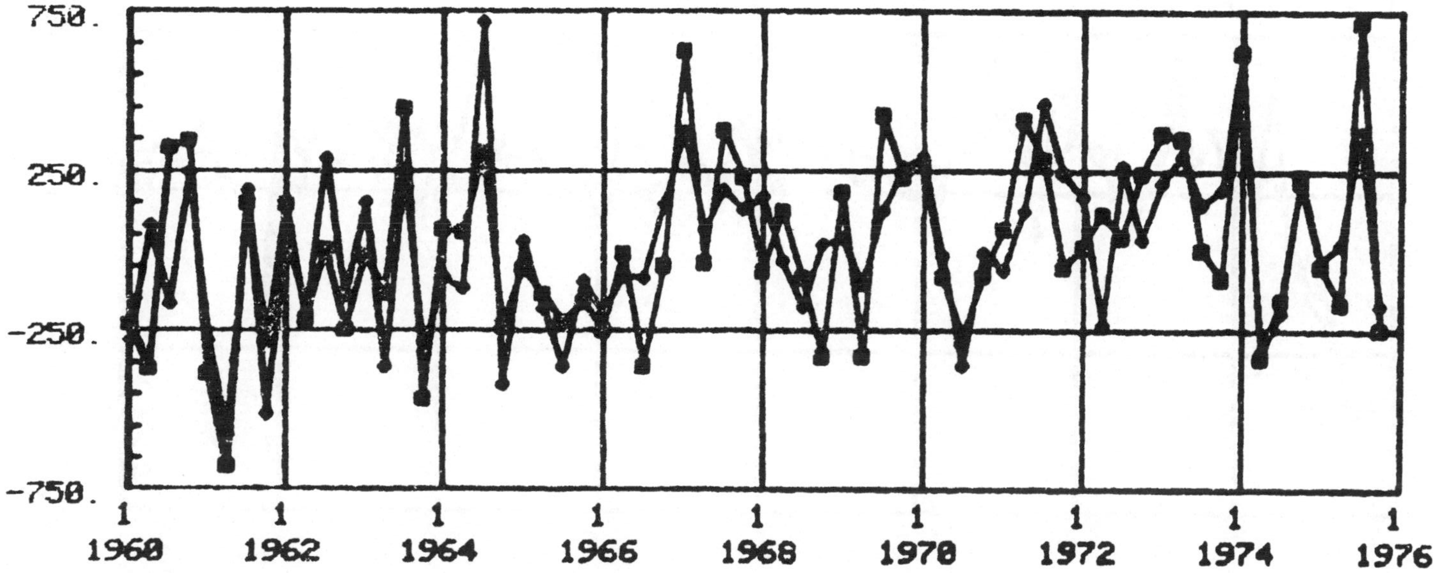

■ actual

◆ full-model simulation

FIGURE 5.7

DYNAMIC SIMULATION RESULTS FOR NET PURCHASES OF SHORT-INTERMEDIATE-TERM

U.S. GOVERNMENT SECURITIES BY LIFE INSURANCE COMPANIES

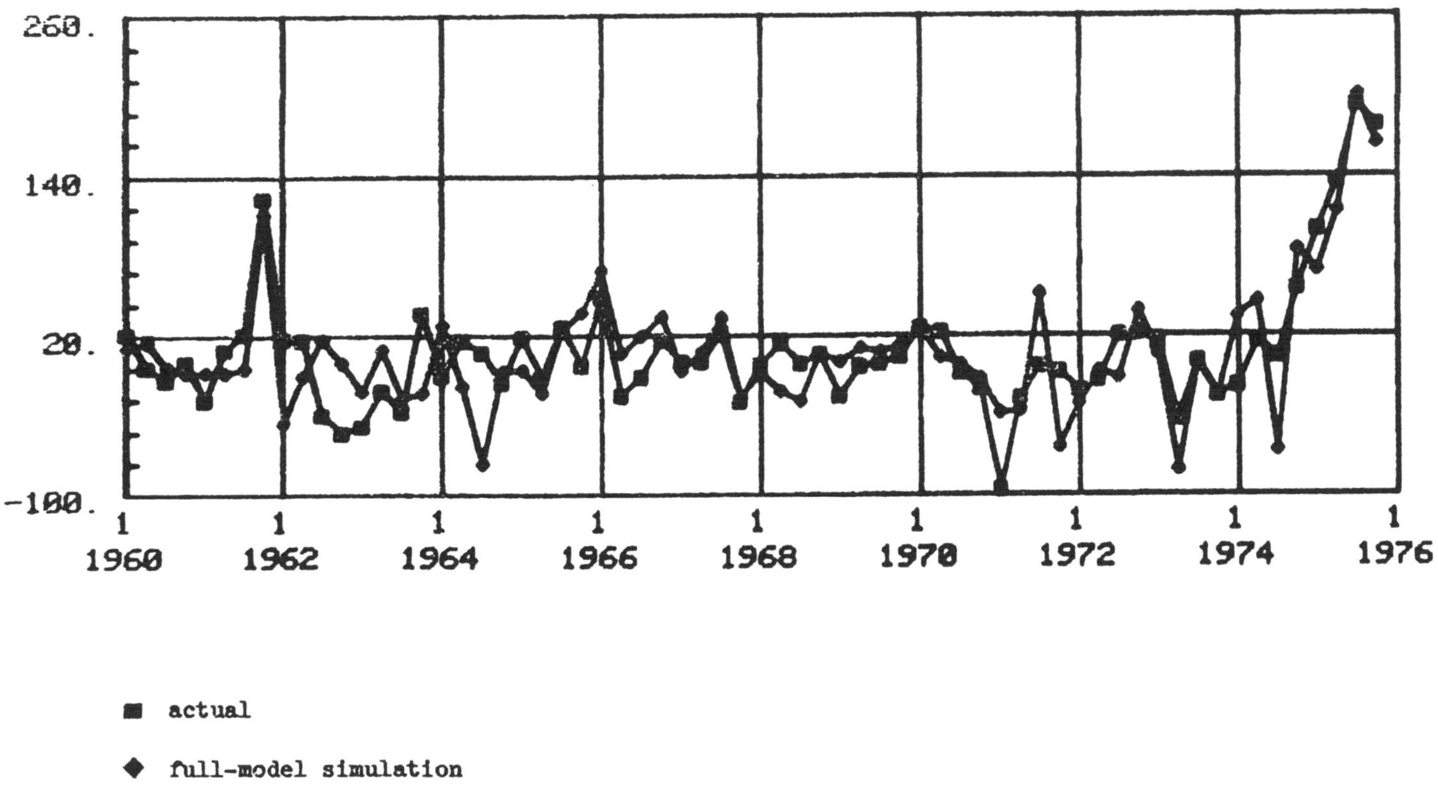

FIGURE 5.8

DYNAMIC SIMULATION RESULTS FOR NET PURCHASES OF LONG-TERM

U.S. GOVERNMENT SECURITIES BY LIFE INSURANCE COMPANIES

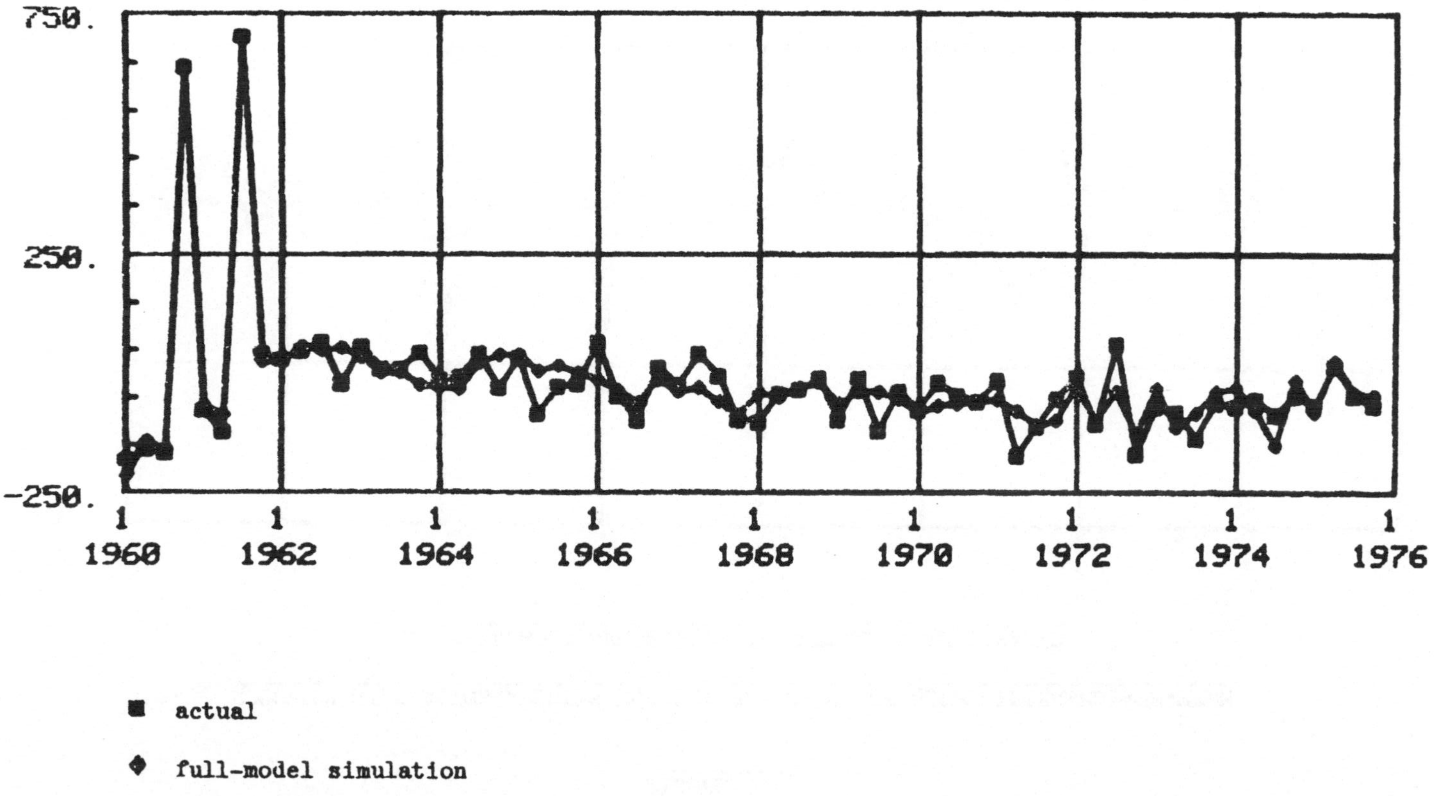

FIGURE 5.9

DYNAMIC SIMULATION RESULTS FOR NET PURCHASES OF SHORT-INTERMEDIATE-TERM

U.S. GOVERNMENT SECURITIES BY MUTUAL SAVINGS BANKS

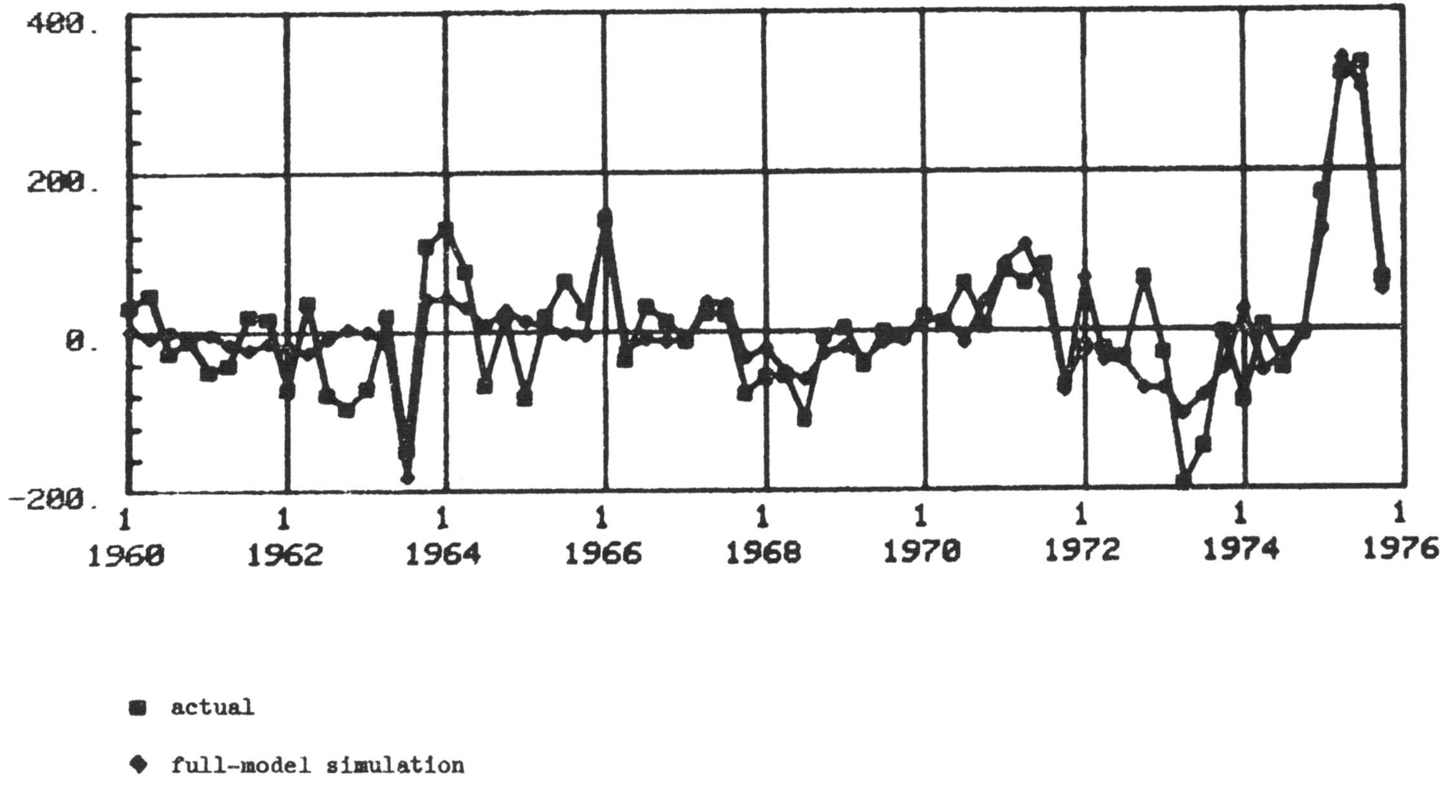

FIGURE 5.10

DYNAMIC SIMULATION RESULTS FOR NET PURCHASES OF LONG-TERM

U.S. GOVERNMENT SECURITIES BY MUTUAL SAVINGS BANKS

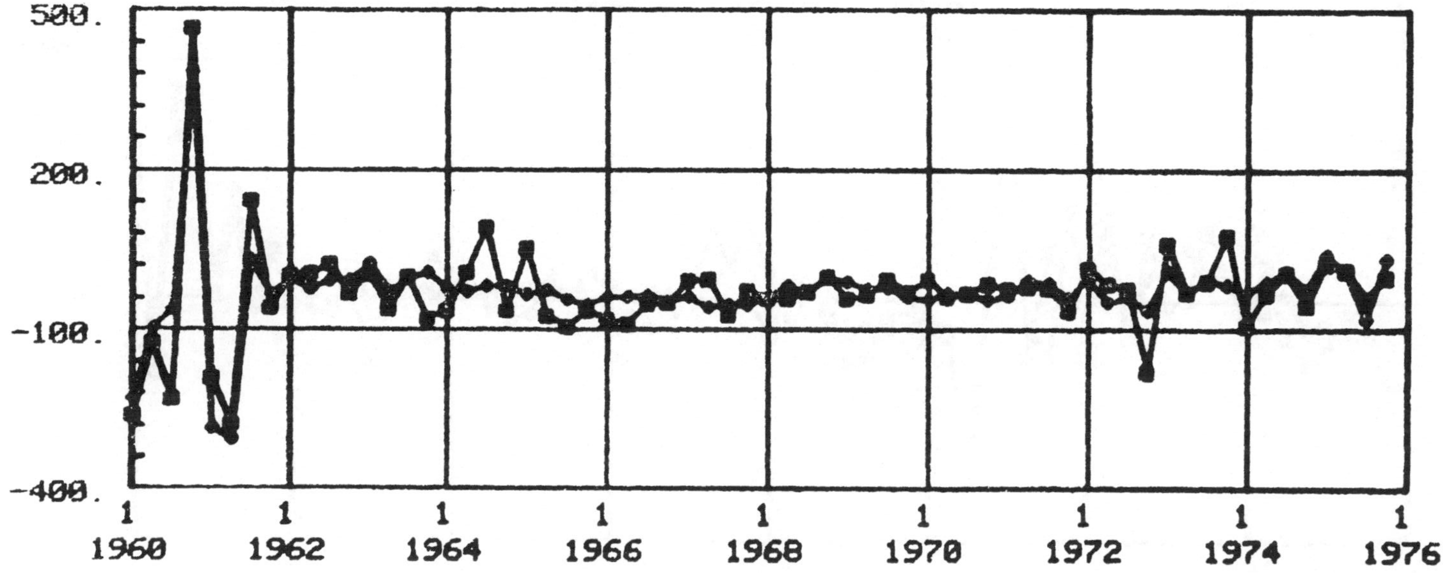

■ actual

◆ full-model simulation

FIGURE 5.11

DYNAMIC SIMULATION RESULTS FOR NET PURCHASES OF SHORT-INTERMEDIATE-TERM U.S. GOVERNMENT SECURITIES BY NONFINANCIAL CORPORATE BUSINESSES

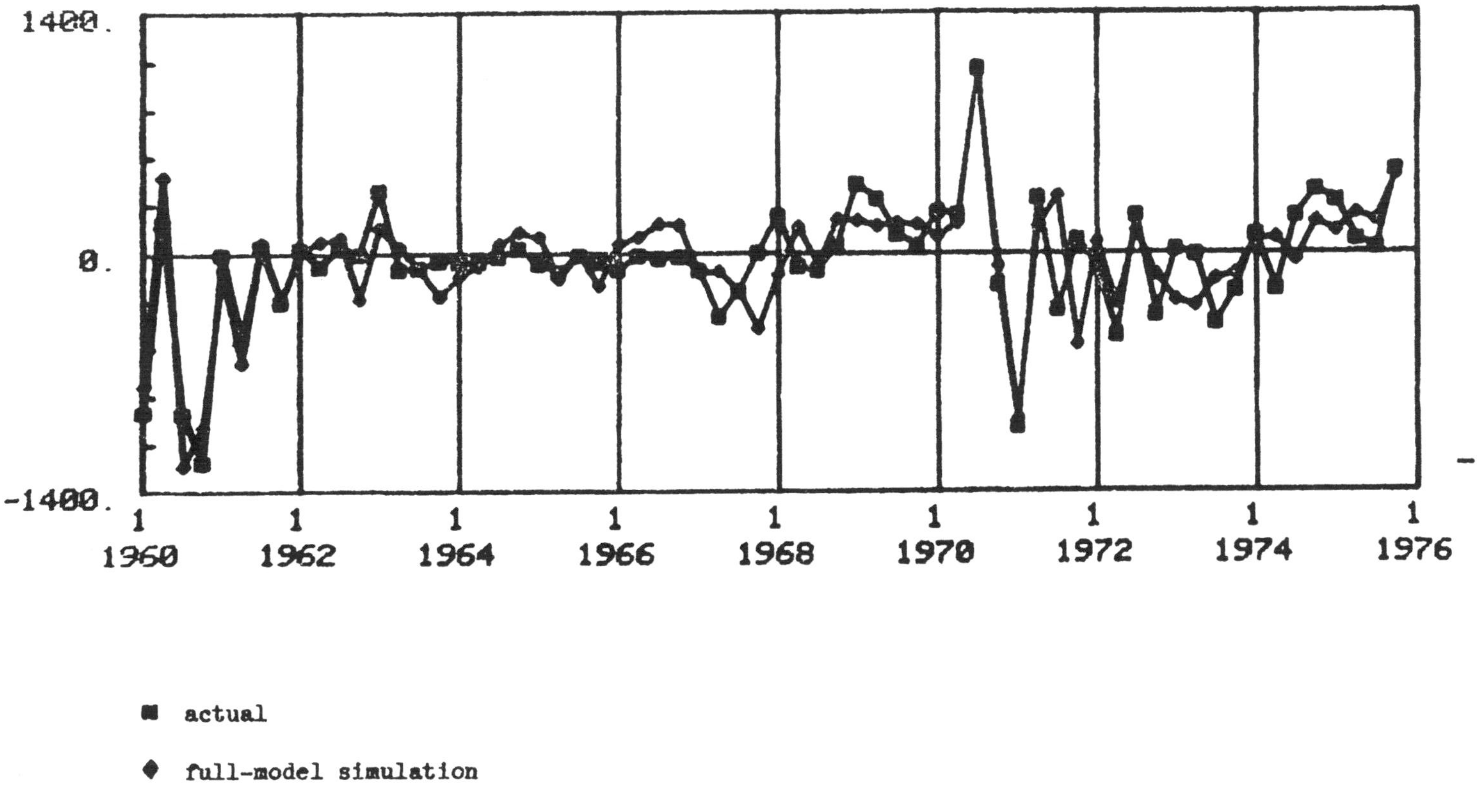

FIGURE 5.12

DYNAMIC SIMULATION RESULTS FOR NET PURCHASES OF SHORT-INTERMEDIATE-TERM

U.S. GOVERNMENT SECURITIES BY OTHER INSURANCE COMPANIES

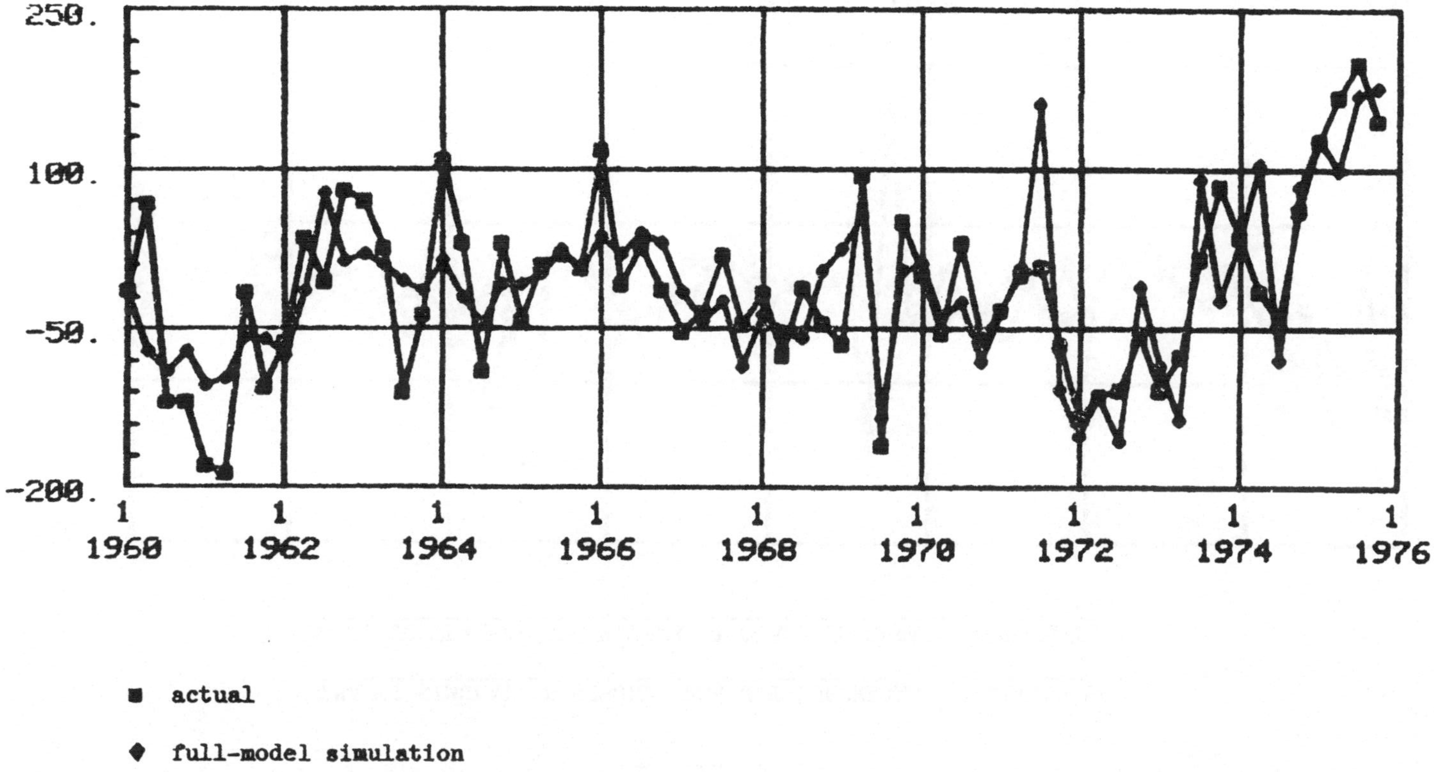

FIGURE 5.13

DYNAMIC SIMULATION RESULTS FOR NET PURCHASES OF LONG-TERM

U.S. GOVERNMENT SECURITIES BY OTHER INSURANCE COMPANIES

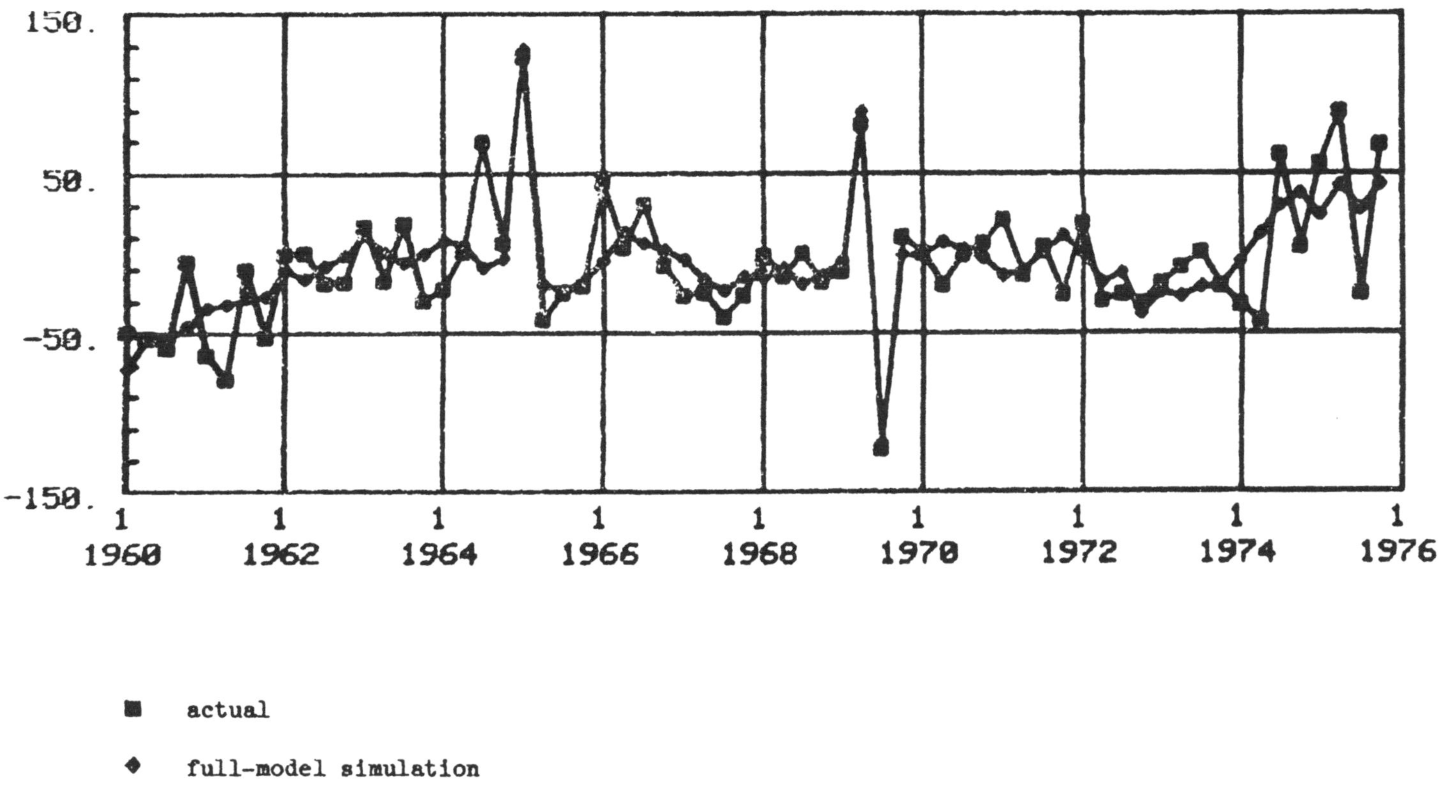

FIGURE 5.14

DYNAMIC SIMULATION RESULTS FOR NET PURCHASES OF SHORT-INTERMEDIATE-TERM

U.S. GOVERNMENT SECURITIES BY PRIVATE PENSION FUNDS

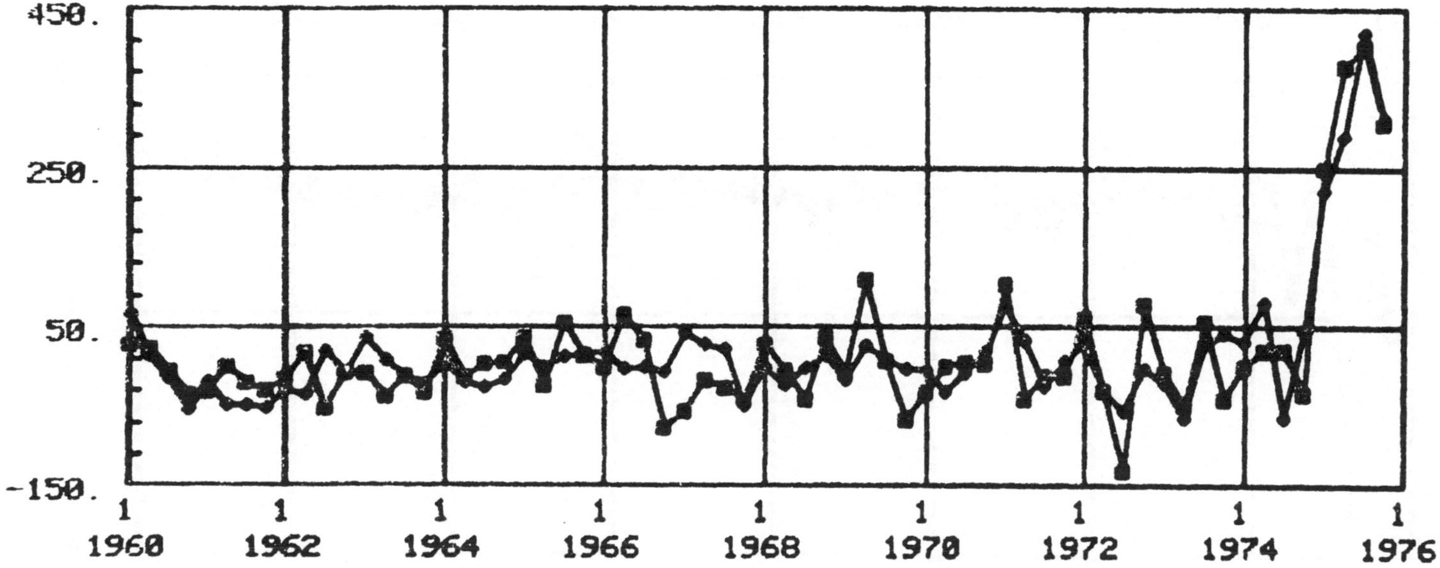

■ actual

♦ full-model simulation

FIGURE 5.15

DYNAMIC SIMULATION RESULTS FOR NET PURCHASES OF LONG-TERM

U.S. GOVERNMENT SECURITIES BY PRIVATE PENSION FUNDS

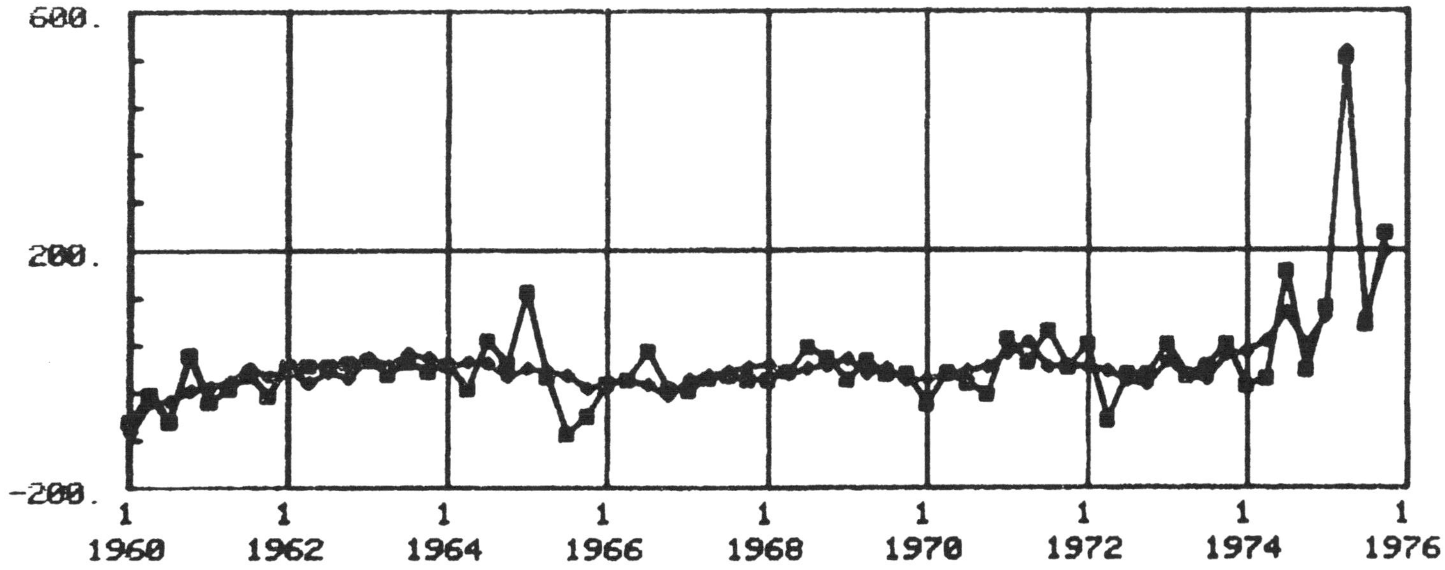

■ actual

◆ full-model simulation

FIGURE 5.16

DYNAMIC SIMULATION RESULTS FOR NET PURCHASES OF SHORT-INTERMEDIATE-TERM U.S. GOVERNMENT SECURITIES BY SAVINGS AND LOAN ASSOCIATIONS

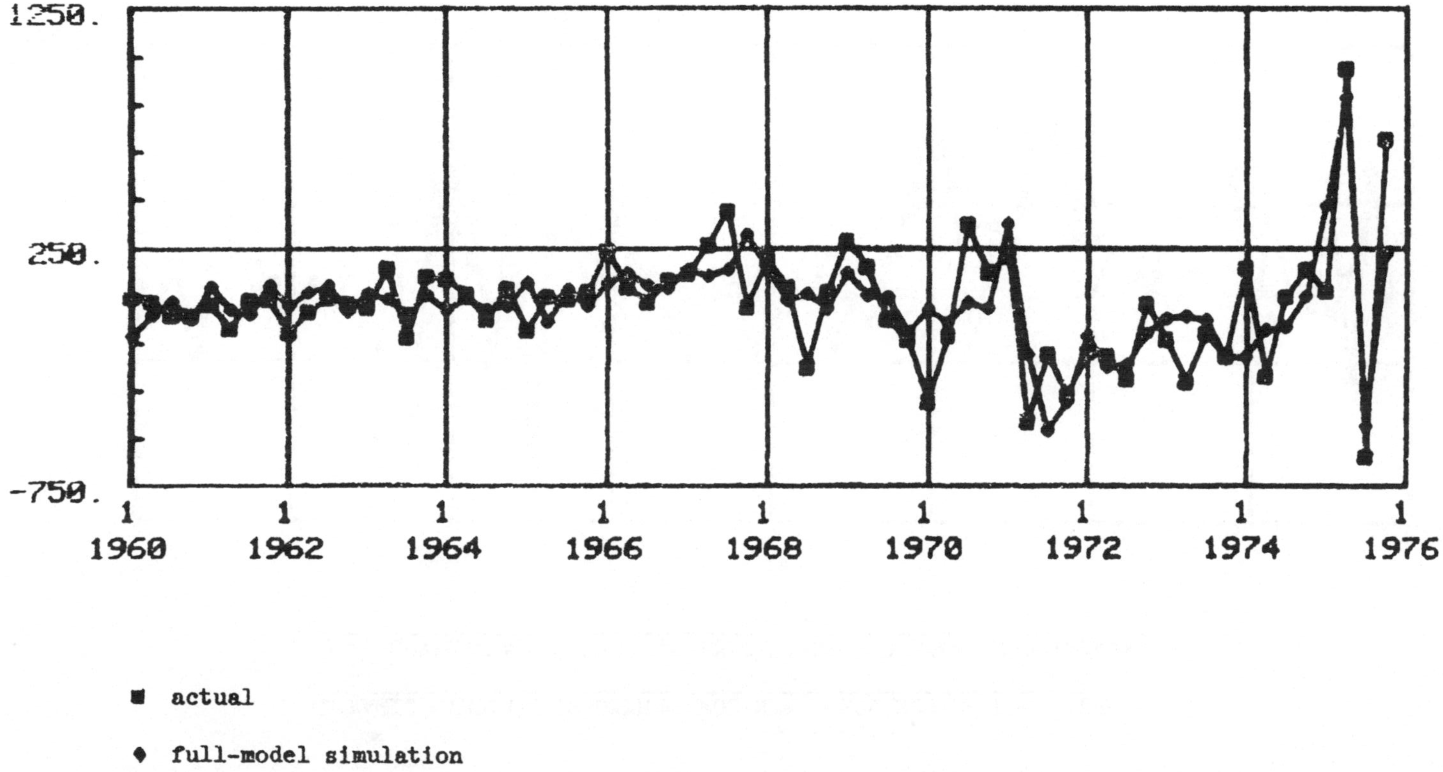

FIGURE 5.17

DYNAMIC SIMULATION RESULTS FOR NET PURCHASES OF LONG-TERM U.S. GOVERNMENT SECURITIES BY SAVINGS AND LOAN ASSOCIATIONS

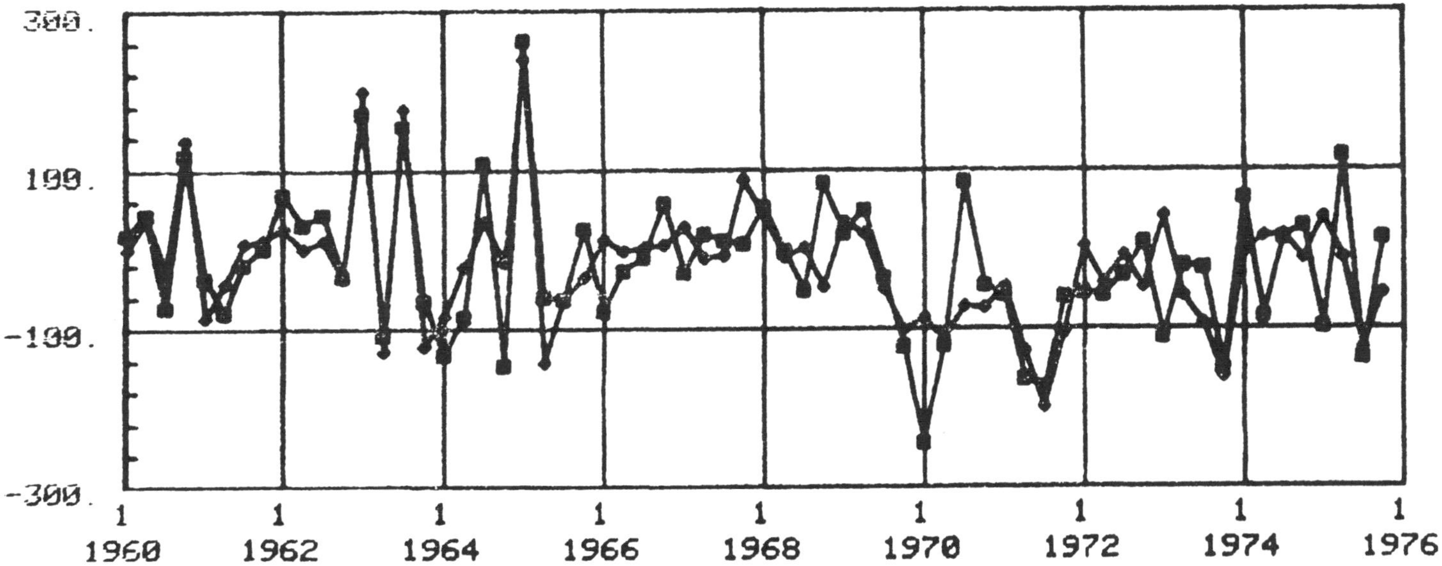

■ actual

♦ full-model simulation

FIGURE 5.18

DYNAMIC SIMULATION RESULTS FOR NET PURCHASES OF SHORT-INTERMEDIATE-TERM U.S. GOVERNMENT SECURITIES BY STATE AND LOCAL GOVERNMENT GENERAL FUNDS

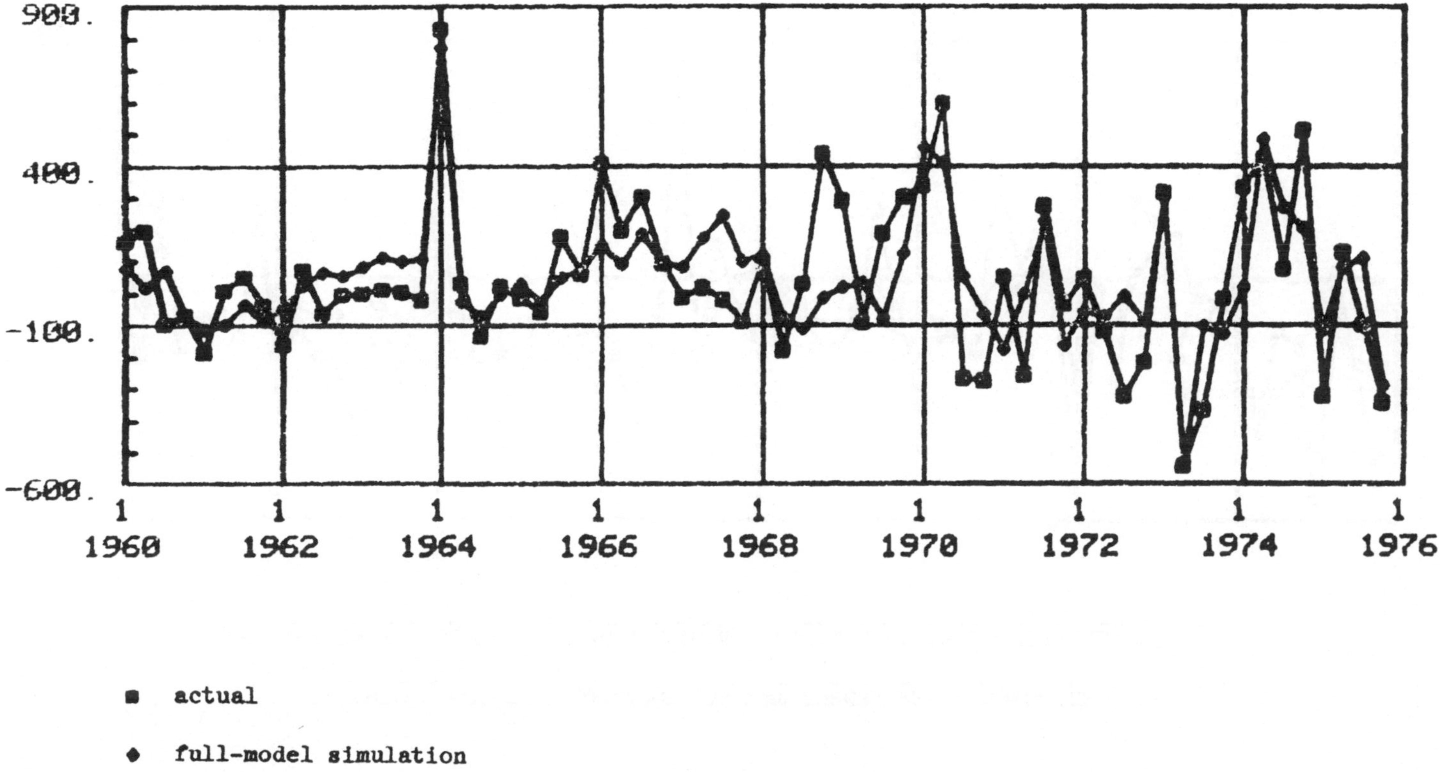

FIGURE 5.19

DYNAMIC SIMULATION RESULTS FOR NET PURCHASES OF LONG-TERM

U.S. GOVERNMENT SECURITIES BY STATE AND LOCAL GOVERNMENT GENERAL FUNDS

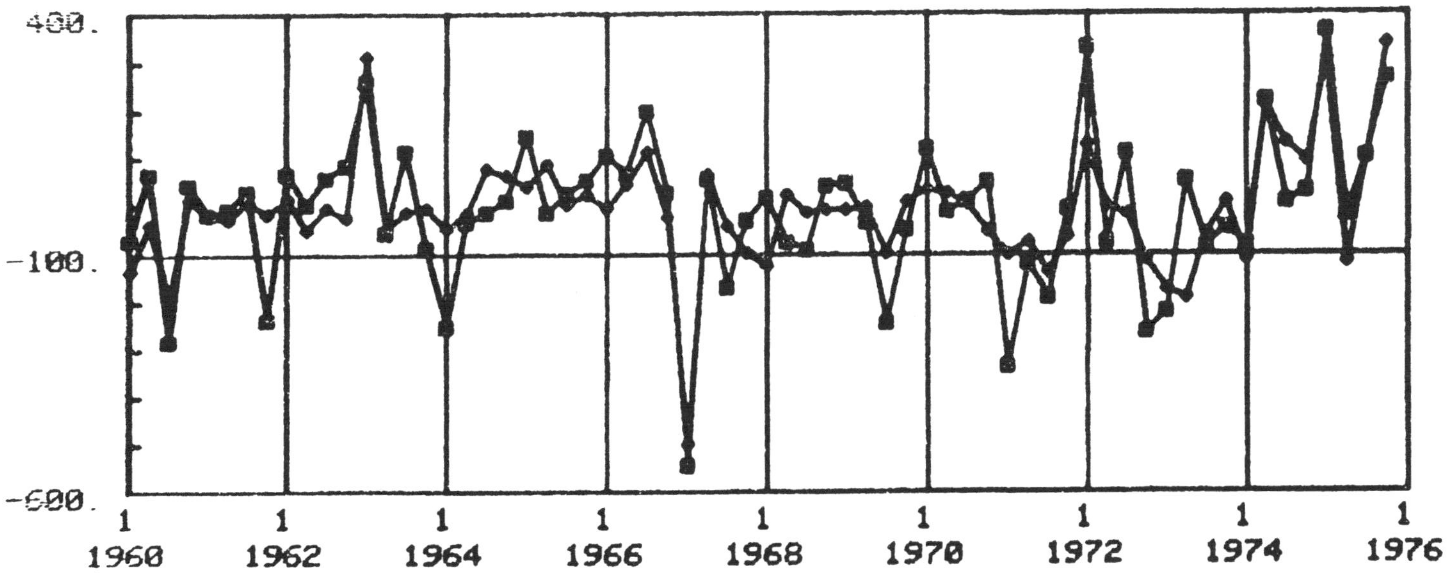

■ actual

◆ full-model simulation

FIGURE 5.20

DYNAMIC SIMULATION RESULTS FOR NET PURCHASES OF SHORT-INTERMEDIATE-TERM U.S. GOVERNMENT SECURITIES BY STATE AND LOCAL GOVERNMENT RETIREMENT FUNDS

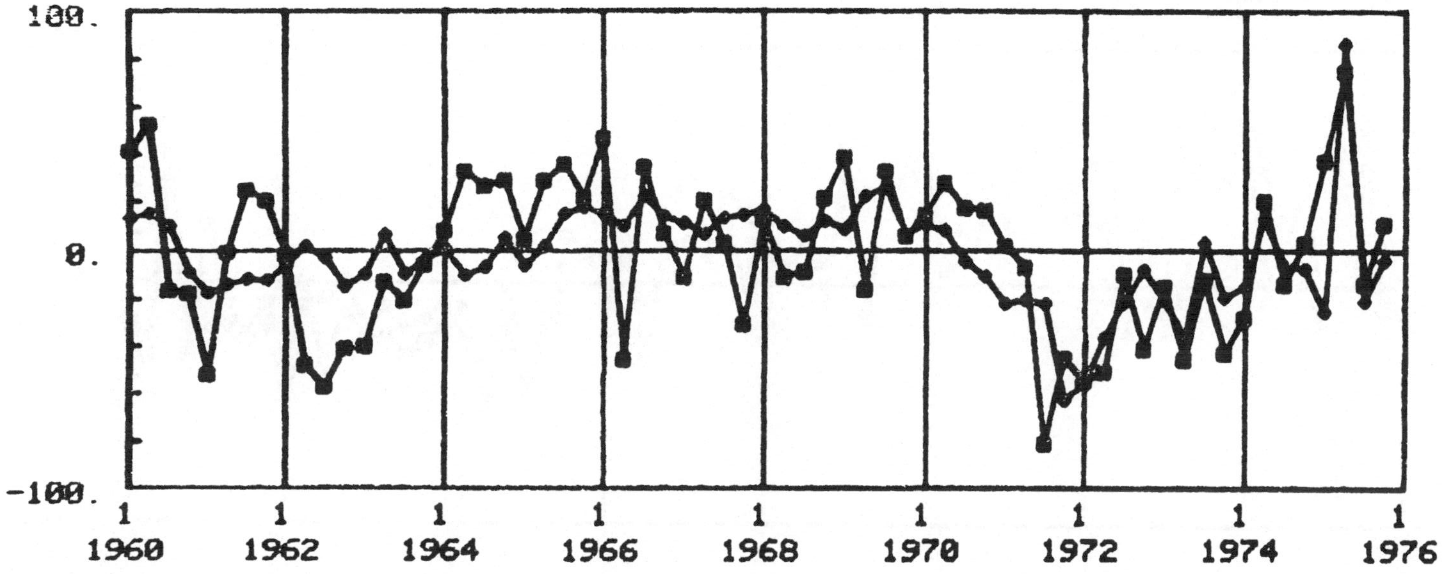

■ actual

◆ full-model simulation

FIGURE 5.21

DYNAMIC SIMULATION RESULTS FOR NET PURCHASES OF LONG-TERM

U.S. GOVERNMENT SECURITIES BY STATE AND LOCAL GOVERNMENT RETIREMENT FUNDS

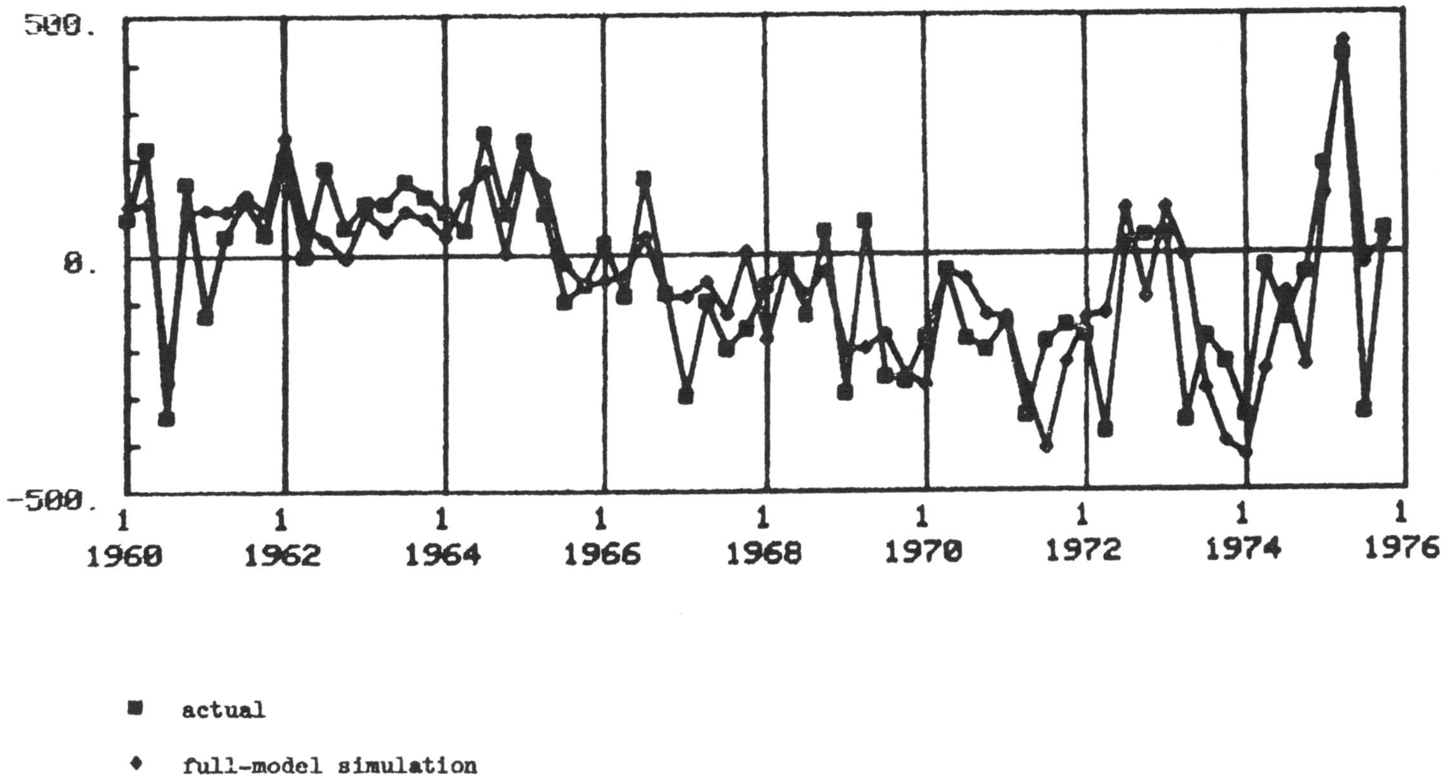

E. Summary and Conclusions

The sections in this chapter have presented the specifications of the actual demands for U.S. Government securities, and their estimation. In addition, the structural model consisting of the estimated equations, and two market-clearing identities, is used to jointly determine the yields on short-intermediate-term and long-term U.S. Government securities.

Several adjustment models, that translate desired proportional asset holdings into actual demands, are presented in section V.B. Each of these adjustment models contain a subset of the following properties: (1) new investable financial flows have separate effects on portfolio adjustment; (2) effects from new investable financial flows are dependent on the holding-period yields of the endogenous assets in the portfolio; (3) new investable financial flows affect the reallocation of existing assets in the portfolio; (4) positive and negative new investable financial flows have asymmetric effects; and (5) new investable financial flows are disaggregated in terms of exogenous balance sheet items. In the application to each investor group, the choice of the proper adjustment model is based on the ordinary least squares estimation results reported in the appendix.

The estimation procedures and results for the structural model of the U.S. Government securities market are presented in section V.C. On the basis of a subjective analysis, the two maturity classes of U.S. Government securities appear to be far from perfect substitutes. Additional analysis concerning the symmetry of the coefficient matrix on the vector of holding-period yields is considered therein. This symmetry constraint can not be rejected for half of the investor groups considered in the test. However, for these investor groups, the relevant coefficient on the cross-maturity yield is statistically insignificant. Thus, in order to conclusively reject symmetry, further tests should be performed on a larger subset of the assets in each investor group's portfolio.

The effects from additional yield and non-yield variables are also discussed in section V.C. Based on the corresponding results, it appears that U.S. Government securities are better substitutes for other credit market securities than for equities. In addition, the importance of including variances of holding-period yields in specifications of the demand for financial assets is empirically established.

The joint determination of the nineteen endogenous demands for U.S. Government securities, and the two endogenous yields, is presented in section V.D. In the full-model dynamic simulation results, the yields on short-intermediate-term and long-term U.S. Government securities have root-mean-square errors of thirty-four and twenty basis points, respectively. The magnitudes of these values indicate the plausibility of utilizing the structural modeling methodology in the determination of market yields on financial assets. In addition, based on a simulation experiment, there are less than perfect cross-maturity effects in the joint determination of the yields on short-intermediate-term and long-term U.S. Government securities. The cross-maturity effects are greater, however, than those implied from an extreme interpretation of the "market segmentation hypothesis".

APPENDIX TO CHAPTER V

THE ORDINARY LEAST SQUARES ESTIMATES OF THE STRUCTURAL EQUATIONS

The ordinary least squares estimates of the structural equations are included for several reasons. First, the final form of the model is based on specifications searches using ordinary least squares estimation. Secondly, the estimates given in V.C.3 are dependent on the particular simultaneous equations estimation technique utilized. Finally, the specific instrumental variables estimation procedure, employed in the final estimation, resulted in a non-trivial forecast bias in each equation for commercial banks.[46] This is primarily due to the relatively large number of variables being instrumented in these equations.

The ordinary least squares estimates are given immediately below. In addition, simulation results parallel to those in Table 5.7 are reported below in Table 5.9. In comparison to the estimated equations in V.C.3, the ordinary least squares estimates have the same signs, but, in a few instances, the magnitudes and statistical significance differ to some extent.

Commercial Banks

(1) $$\Delta US2^C_t = \underset{(-7.5)}{-0.1977}\ US2^C_{t-1} + \underset{(4.1)}{0.1441}\ US1^C_{t-1} + \underset{(6.2)}{0.2887}\ SL^C_{t-1} - \underset{(-5.5)}{2.545}\ CP^C_{t-1}$$

---

[46] See Table 5.7.

$$+ (\underset{(3.3)}{0.1065}\ \Delta DDP_t^C + \underset{(4.9)}{0.8258}\ \Delta GDP_t^C - \underset{(-2.8)}{0.9795}\ \Delta LN_t^C)\cdot r_{2,t}$$

$$+ (\underset{(2.6)}{7.410}\ \Delta DDN_t^C + \underset{(4.1)}{10.86}\ \Delta GDN_t^C - \underset{(-5.6)}{14.54}\ \Delta MP_t^C$$

$$- \underset{(-2.1)}{2.897}\ \Delta SCP_t^C)\cdot(1/r_{2,t}) + (\underset{(-2.3)}{-0.4143}\ \Delta GDP_t^C - \underset{(-5.6)}{0.1280}\ \Delta TDP_t^C$$

$$+ \underset{(2.9)}{1.319}\ \Delta LN_t^C + \underset{(2.2)}{0.09348}\ \Delta SCN_t^C)\cdot r_{T,t} - \underset{(-3.4)}{1.080}\ v_{2,t-1}\cdot\Delta DDP_t^C$$

$$+ \underset{(2.5)}{1.508}\ v_{I,t-1}\cdot\Delta CDP_t^C - \underset{(-2.1)}{0.01234}\ (1/v_{I,t-1})\cdot\Delta DDN_t^C$$

$$+ \underset{(6.9)}{233.5}\ \Delta CC_t^C\cdot(US4_{t-1}^C/W_{t-1}^C) + (\underset{(-3.5)}{-7.645}\ \Delta GD_t^C + \underset{(6.2)}{55.06}\ \Delta M_t^C$$

$$- \underset{(-6.8)}{74.61}\ \Delta CC_t^C)\cdot(US3_{t-1}^C/W_{t-1}^C) + (\underset{(-3.0)}{-2.562}\ \Delta TD_t^C$$

$$+ \underset{(4.5)}{3.317}\ \Delta CD_t^C)\cdot(US1_{t-1}^C/W_{t-1}^C) + (\underset{(-3.3)}{-3.769}\ \Delta GD_t^C$$

$$- \underset{(-4.4)}{18.97}\ \Delta CC_t^C)\cdot(SL_{t-1}^C/W_{t-1}^C) + (\underset{(5.8)}{25.83}\ \Delta TD_t^C$$

$$+ \underset{(4.7)}{228.0}\ \Delta CC_t^C)\cdot(CP_{t-1}^C/W_{t-1}^C) + (\underset{(-3.2)}{-6.438}\ \Delta DD_t^C$$

$$- \underset{(-4.8)}{6.458}\ \Delta CD_t^C)\cdot(USA_{t-1}^C/W_{t-1}^C)$$

$\bar{R}^2 = 0.73(0.96)$ SE = 665 DW = 1.91

(2a) Sample Period: 1960:I through 1965:I

$$\Delta US4_t^C = \underset{(4.2)}{5389} - \underset{(-4.6)}{0.6460}\ US4_{t-1}^C + \underset{(2.5)}{0.2976}\ r_{4,t}\cdot\Delta WP_t^C$$

$$+ \underset{(3.0)}{34.85}\ (1/r_{4,t})\cdot\Delta WN_t^C - \underset{(-2.7)}{0.3796}\ r_{S,t}\cdot WP_t^C$$

$$- \underset{(-3.1)}{28.69}\ (1/r_{S,t})\cdot\Delta WN_t^C - \underset{(-4.0)}{0.01280}\ r_{S,t}\cdot W_{t-1}^C$$

$\bar{R}^2 = 0.72(0.89)$ SE = 186 DW = 2.90

(2b) Sample Period: 1965:II through 1975:IV

$$\Delta US4^C_t = \underset{(-7.0)}{-0.2585}\ US4^C_{t-1} + \underset{(3.3)}{0.01105}\ US2^C_{t-1} + \underset{(2.5)}{0.0007921}\ r_{4,t}\cdot W^C_{t-1}$$

$$- \underset{(-3.4)}{0.00107}\ r_{S,t}\cdot W^C_{t-1} + (\underset{(4.2)}{0.00377}\ \Delta DDP^C_t + \underset{(1.8)}{0.00495}\ \Delta TDP^C_t$$

$$+ \underset{(2.4)}{0.01338}\ \Delta CDP^C_t - \underset{(-1.9)}{0.01089})\cdot r_{4,t} - \underset{(-2.0)}{0.01012}\ r_{T,t}\cdot \Delta CDP^C_t$$

$$- \underset{(-1.7)}{3.940}\ (1/v_{48,t-1})\cdot \Delta DDN^C_t + \underset{(2.6)}{4.984}\ \Delta SC^C_t\cdot (US4^C_{t-1}/W^C_{t-1})$$

$$+ (\underset{(-1.8)}{-0.7144}\ \Delta TD^C_t + \underset{(1.9)}{0.8216})\cdot (CP^C_{t-1}/W^C_{t-1})$$

$\bar{R}^2 = 0.68(0.95)$ SE = 74 DW = 2.26

Households[47]

(3) $$\Delta US2^H_t = \underset{(4.6)}{4513} - \underset{(-3.8)}{0.00301}\ W^H_{t-1} - \underset{(-6.3)}{0.3337}\ US2^H_{t-1} - \underset{(-7.2)}{0.1925}\ CB^H_{t-1}$$

$$+ \underset{(4.1)}{0.4419}\ CP^H_{t-1} - \underset{(-5.0)}{0.3024}\ M^H_{t-1} + \underset{(4.3)}{0.01854}\ r_{2,t}\cdot \Delta W^H_t$$

$$- \underset{(-6.5)}{0.0002145}\ r_{P,t}\cdot W^H_{t-1} - \underset{(-5.7)}{1.260}\ v_{I,t-1}\cdot \Delta W^H_t$$

$$+ \underset{(6.0)}{0.02041}\ v_{I,t-1}\cdot W^H_{t-1} + \underset{(3.7)}{0.000001990}\ v_{48,t-1}\cdot W^H_{t-1}$$

$$+ \underset{(6.8)}{0.03686}\ CE_t - \underset{(-5.3)}{43.03}\ (\Delta W^H_t/W^H_{t-1})\cdot CP^H_{t-1}$$

$\bar{R}^2 = 0.79(0.95)$ SE = 406 DW = 2.12

(4) $$\Delta US4^H_t = \underset{(6.7)}{6908} - \underset{(-8.4)}{0.6428}\ US4^H_{t-1} + \underset{(5.1)}{0.06883}\ US1^H_{t-1} + \underset{(6.1)}{0.2521}\ CB^H_{t-1}$$

---

[47] See footnote 19.

$$+ \underset{(5.6)}{0.3138}\, CP^H_{t-1} + \underset{(3.8)}{0.1465}\, M^H_{t-1} + \underset{(4.5)}{0.03955}\, r_{4,t}\cdot\Delta W^H_t$$

$$- \underset{(-3.3)}{0.01525}(\%\Delta P)_{t-1} \cdot\Delta W^H_t - \underset{(-2.8)}{0.01578}\, r_{P,t}\cdot\Delta W^H_t$$

$$+ \underset{(2.3)}{0.0001779}\, r_{P,t}\cdot W^H_{t-1} - \underset{(-4.4)}{0.0004232}\, r_{S,t}\cdot W^H_{t-1}$$

$$+ \underset{(4.6)}{0.0006714}\, v_{CY,t-1}\cdot W^H_{t-1} - \underset{(-6.4)}{0.03163}\, CE_t$$

$$- \underset{(-2.1)}{3.972}\, (\Delta W^H_t/W^H_{t-1})\cdot US2^H_{t-1} - \underset{(-4.1)}{13.03}\, (\Delta W^H_t/W^H_{t-1})\cdot CB^H_{t-1}$$

$$+ \underset{(6.3)}{2.419}\, (\Delta W^H_t/W^H_{t-1})\cdot TD^H_{t-1} + \underset{(2.8)}{3.529}\, (\Delta W^H_t/W^H_{t-1})\cdot DD^H_{t-1}$$

$$- \underset{(-4.7)}{19.03}\, (\Delta W^H_t/W^H_{t-1})\cdot CP^H_{t-1} - \underset{(-2.6)}{3.798}\, (\Delta W^H_t/W^H_{t-1})\cdot SL^H_{t-1}$$

$$- \underset{(-7.2)}{20.07}\, (\Delta W^H_t/W^H_{t-1})\cdot M^H_{t-1}$$

$\bar{R}^2 = 0.69(0.97)$ SE = 161 DW = 2.15

Life Insurance Companies[48]

(5) $$\Delta US2^L_t = \underset{(-2.4)}{-0.1434}\, US2^L_{t-1} - \underset{(-3.6)}{0.00755}\, E^L_{t-1} + \underset{(2.6)}{0.00150}\, CB^L_{t-1}$$

$$+ \underset{(5.0)}{0.02572}\, r_{2,t}\cdot\Delta W^L_t - \underset{(-3.1)}{0.00455}\, r_{P,t}\cdot\Delta W^L_t - \underset{(-4.1)}{0.01777}\, r_{4,t}\cdot\Delta W^L_t$$

$$+ \underset{(2.7)}{0.02081}\, v_{E,t-1}\cdot\Delta W^L_t - \underset{(-2.3)}{0.0003260}\, v_{E,t-1}\cdot W^L_{t-1}$$

$$- \underset{(-2.2)}{0.01550}\, v_{2,t-1}\cdot\Delta W^L_t$$

$\bar{R}^2 = 0.81(0.96)$ SE = 21 DW = 2.23

(6) $$\Delta US4^L_t = \underset{(1.6)}{306.8} - \underset{(-4.0)}{0.1913}\, US4^L_{t-1} - \underset{(-5.9)}{0.2978}\, US3^L_{t-1} - \underset{(-2.6)}{0.2152}\, US2^L_{t-1}$$

---

[48] See footnote 20.

$$+ \underset{(6.8)}{0.2053}\ SL^{L}_{t-1} - \underset{(-4.2)}{0.05165}\ CP^{L}_{t-1} + \underset{(4.6)}{0.01370}\ r_{4,t} \cdot \Delta W^{L}_{t}$$

$$- \underset{(-4.2)}{0.0001970}\ r_{C,t} \cdot W^{L}_{t-1} - \underset{(-3.9)}{0.0001795}\ v_{48,t-1} \cdot \Delta W^{L}_{t}$$

$$+ \underset{(3.1)}{0.00002125}\ v_{C,t-1} \cdot \Delta W^{L}_{t}$$

$\bar{R}^2 = 0.92(0.99)$ SE = 39 DW = 2.31

Mutual Savings Banks[49]

(7) $$\Delta US2^{M}_{t} = \underset{(4.8)}{403.7} - \underset{(-5.1)}{0.2338}\ US2^{M}_{t-1} - \underset{(-1.9)}{0.09429}\ US1^{M}_{t-1} - \underset{(-4.9)}{0.00967}\ CB^{M}_{t-1}$$

$$+ \underset{(3.1)}{0.08671}\ r_{2,t} \cdot \Delta WP^{M}_{t} - \underset{(-2.2)}{0.05014}\ r_{4,t} \cdot \Delta WP^{M}_{t}$$

$$- \underset{(-3.0)}{0.03450}\ r_{P,t} \cdot \Delta WP^{M}_{t} + \underset{(3.6)}{0.3500}\ v_{I,t-1} \cdot \Delta WP^{M}_{t}$$

$\bar{R}^2 = 0.69(0.92)$ SE = 51 DW = 1.78

(8) $$\Delta US4^{M}_{t} = \underset{(5.1)}{643.8} - \underset{(-6.5)}{0.4239}\ US4^{M}_{t-1} + \underset{(5.1)}{0.1738}\ US3^{M}_{t-1} - \underset{(-2.2)}{0.1027}\ US2^{M}_{t-1}$$

$$- \underset{(-3.9)}{0.2277}\ E^{M}_{t-1} + \underset{(1.9)}{0.00424}\ r_{4,t} \cdot \Delta WP^{M}_{t} + \underset{(2.9)}{0.00228}\ r_{4,t} \cdot W^{M}_{t-1}$$

$$- \underset{(-2.0)}{0.1941}\ v_{I,t-1} \cdot \Delta WP^{M}_{t}$$

$\bar{R}^2 = 0.72(0.99)$ SE = 51 DW = 1.77

Nonfinancial Corporate Businesses[50]

(9) $$\Delta US2^{N}_{t} = \underset{(6.6)}{738.2} - \underset{(-5.6)}{1.397}\ \Delta WN^{N}_{t} - \underset{(-6.3)}{0.2464}\ US2^{N}_{t-1} - \underset{(-2.7)}{0.02450}\ TD^{N}_{t-1}$$

---

[49]See footnote 21.

[50]See footnote 22.

$$+ \underset{(3.5)}{0.09284}\ r_{2,t} \cdot \Delta WP^N_t + \underset{(5.9)}{7.609}\ (1/r_{2,t}) \cdot \Delta WN^N_t$$

$$- \underset{(-1.6)}{0.0002463}\ r_{P,t} \cdot W^N_{t-1} + \underset{(2.4)}{34.06}\ (\Delta WP^N_t / W^N_{t-1}) \cdot US3^N_{t-1}$$

$$- \underset{(-2.5)}{5.495}\ (\Delta WP^N_t / W^N_{t-1}) \cdot US2^N_{t-1} - \underset{(-2.0)}{1.253}\ (\Delta WP^N_t / W^N_{t-1}) \cdot CP^N_{t-1}$$

$$- \underset{(-4.2)}{8.460}\ (\Delta WP^N_t / W^N_{t-1}) \cdot SL^N_{t-1}$$

$\bar{R}^2 = 0.78(0.98)$ SE = 165 DW = 1.89

Other Insurance Companies[51]

$$(10)\quad \Delta US2^O_t = \underset{(3.0)}{0.03082}\ W^O_{t-1} + \underset{(4.3)}{0.1449}\ US3^O_{t-1} - \underset{(-5.1)}{0.1887}\ US2^O_{t-1} - \underset{(-4.2)}{0.04767}\ E^O_{t-1}$$

$$- \underset{(-3.0)}{0.04589}\ SL^O_{t-1} + \underset{(3.9)}{0.08800}\ r_{2,t} \cdot \Delta W^O_t - \underset{(-3.7)}{0.07301}\ r_{C,t} \cdot \Delta W^O_t$$

$$+ \underset{(3.7)}{0.00001097}\ v_{48,t-1} \cdot W^O_{t-1}$$

$\bar{R}^2 = 0.53(0.95)$ SE = 56 DW = 1.93

$$(11)\quad \Delta US4^O_t = \underset{(-2.3)}{-0.00263}\ W^O_{t-1} - \underset{(-4.7)}{0.3123}\ US4^O_{t-1} + \underset{(3.7)}{0.05221}\ US3^O_{t-1}$$

$$+ \underset{(3.6)}{0.09272}\ US2^O_{t-1} + \underset{(2.1)}{0.01155}\ CB^O_{t-1} + \underset{(2.1)}{0.01476}\ r_{4,t} \cdot \Delta W^O_t$$

$$- \underset{(-2.1)}{0.07270}\ (\overline{\%\Delta P})_{t-1} \cdot \Delta W^O_t + \underset{(2.6)}{0.00132}\ (\overline{\%\Delta P})_{t-1} \cdot W^O_{t-1}$$

$\bar{R}^2 = 0.65(0.96)$ SE = 24 DW = 2.40

Private Pension Funds[52]

$$(12)\quad \Delta US2^P_t = \underset{(1.9)}{0.02291}\ W^P_{t-1} + \underset{(2.8)}{0.2008}\ US4^P_{t-1} - \underset{(-1.7)}{0.1327}\ US2^P_{t-1} - \underset{(-1.9)}{0.02237}\ E^P_{t-1}$$

---

[51] See footnote 23.

[52] See footnote 24.

$$- \underset{(-2.6)}{0.04287}\ CB^P_{t-1} + \underset{(2.9)}{0.02471}\ r_{2,t} \cdot \Delta W^P_t - \underset{(-3.8)}{0.0008531}\ r_{C,t} \cdot W^P_{t-1}$$

$$- \underset{(-3.5)}{0.05930}\ r_{D,t-1} \cdot \Delta W^P_t + \underset{(4.4)}{0.00264}\ r_{D,t-1} \cdot W^P_{t-1}$$

$$+ \underset{(2.5)}{0.0001423}\ v_{48,t-1} \cdot \Delta W^P_t + \underset{(2.7)}{0.00002278}\ v_{DK,t-1} \cdot \Delta^P_t$$

$\bar{R}^2 = 0.76(0.96)$ SE = 46 DW = 2.14

(13) $$\Delta US4^P_t = \underset{(-4.4)}{0.3051}\ US4^P_{t-1} + \underset{(4.0)}{0.1672}\ US3^P_{t-1} + \underset{(2.4)}{0.1323}\ US2^P_{t-1} + \underset{(2.2)}{0.04911}\ US1^P_{t-1}$$

$$+ \underset{(5.3)}{0.06812}\ TD^P_{t-1} + \underset{(3.3)}{0.01591}\ r_{4,t} \cdot \Delta W^P_t - \underset{(-3.7)}{0.0001722}\ r_{T,t} \cdot W^P_{t-1}$$

$$- \underset{(-4.1)}{0.02745}\ r_{D,t-1} \cdot \Delta W^P_t$$

$\bar{R}^2 = 0.81(0.97)$ SE = 37 DW = 2.16

Savings and Loan Associations[53]

(14) $$\Delta US2^{SL}_t = \underset{(-2.4)}{-263.1} + \underset{(5.4)}{0.1365}\ W^{SL}_{t-1} - \underset{(-3.9)}{0.3367}\ US3^{SL}_{t-1} - \underset{(-6.8)}{0.5817}\ US2^{SL}_{t-1}$$

$$- \underset{(-4.8)}{0.2659}\ FF^{SL}_{t-1} - \underset{(-6.1)}{0.4057}\ USA^{SL}_{t-1} + \underset{(2.6)}{0.05596}\ r_{2,t} \cdot \Delta WP^{SL}_t$$

$$- \underset{(-2.4)}{0.09732}\ (\%\Delta P)_{t-1} \cdot \Delta WP^{SL}_t + \underset{(5.6)}{0.01531}\ (\%\Delta P)_{t-1} \cdot W^{SL}_{t-1}$$

$$- \underset{(-2.1)}{0.04827}\ r_{T,t} \cdot \Delta WP^{SL}_t + \underset{(3.0)}{1.376}\ v_{I,t-1} \cdot \Delta WP^{SL}_t$$

$$- \underset{(-3.2)}{0.05652}\ v_{I,t-1} \cdot W^{SL}_{t-1}$$

$\bar{R}^2 = 0.59(0.96)$ SE = 157 DW = 1.72

---

[53]See footnote 25.

$$(15)\quad \Delta US4_t^{SL} = \underset{(6.2)}{724.4} - \underset{(-6.4)}{0.5368}\ US4_{t-1}^{SL} - \underset{(-6.7)}{0.1241}\ US2_{t-1}^{SL} + \underset{(5.1)}{0.1066}\ US1_{t-1}^{SL}$$

$$- \underset{(-6.8)}{0.1090}\ USA_{t-1}^{SL} + \underset{(1.8)}{0.00226}\ r_{4,t}\cdot\Delta WP_t^{SL} + \underset{(5.3)}{0.00276}\ r_{4,t}\cdot W_{t-1}^{SL}$$

$\bar{R}^2 = 0.67(0.99)$ SE = 52 DW = 2.27

<u>State and Local Government General Funds</u>[54]

$$(16)\quad \Delta US2_t^{SG} = \underset{(4.3)}{1523} - \underset{(-3.8)}{0.1779}\ US2_{t-1}^{SG} - \underset{(-4.0)}{0.4958}\ SL_{t-1}^{SG} + \underset{(4.3)}{0.04984}\ r_{2,t}\cdot\Delta W_t^{SG}$$

$$+ \underset{(2.1)}{0.0005254}\ r_{2,t}\cdot W_{t-1}^{SG} + \underset{(3.3)}{0.000004531}\ v_{S,t-1}\cdot W_{t-1}^{SG}$$

$$- \underset{(-4.8)}{0.9611}\ (\Delta W_t^{SG}/W_{t-1}^{SG})\cdot TD_{t-1}^{SG}$$

$\bar{R}^2 = 0.43(0.98)$ SE = 187 DW = 1.76

$$(17)\quad \Delta US4_t^{SG} = \underset{(-2.4)}{-0.0550} + \underset{(1.7)}{0.02540}\ r_{4,t}\cdot\Delta W_t^{SG} + \underset{(3.4)}{0.00145}\ r_{4,t}\cdot W_{t-1}^{SG}$$

$$- \underset{(-2.1)}{0.00177}\ (\%\Delta P)_{t-1}\cdot W_{t-1}^{SG} - \underset{(-2.2)}{0.0007463}\ r_{T,t}\cdot W_{t-1}^{SG}$$

$$- \underset{(-1.8)}{0.3139}\ v_{I8,t-1}\cdot\Delta W_t^{SG} + \underset{(3.2)}{0.02527}\ v_{I8,t-1}\cdot W_{t-1}^{SG}$$

$$+ \underset{(2.0)}{0.0001017}\ v_{S,t-1}\cdot\Delta W_t^{SG} - \underset{(-3.0)}{0.000005041}\ v_{S,t-1}\cdot W_{t-1}^{SG}$$

$$- \underset{(-2.2)}{2.569}\ (\Delta W_t^{SG}/W_{t-1}^{SG})\cdot US4_{t-1}^{SG} + \underset{(3.6)}{6.233}\ (\Delta W_t^{SG}/W_{t-1}^{SG})\cdot US3_{t-1}^{SG}$$

$$- \underset{(-3.6)}{0.6414}\ (\Delta W_t^{SG}/W_{t-1}^{SG})\cdot TD_{t-1}^{SG} - \underset{(-2.7)}{1.067}\ (\Delta W_t^{SG}/W_{t-1}^{SG})\cdot USA_{t-1}^{SG}$$

$\bar{R}^2 = 0.51(0.94)$ SE = 108 DW = 2.19

---

[54]See footnote 26.

State and Local Government Retirement Funds[55]

(18) $$\Delta US2^S_t = \underset{(-2.2)}{-0.05651}\ \Delta W^S_t + \underset{(4.2)}{0.02086}\ US4^S_{t-1} - \underset{(-2.2)}{0.06781}\ US3^S_{t-1}$$

$$- \underset{(-2.8)}{0.1145}\ US2^S_{t-1} + \underset{(2.3)}{0.00740}\ r_{2,t}\cdot\Delta W^S_t + \underset{(3.8)}{0.0001404}\ v_{K,t-1}\cdot\Delta W^S_t$$

$$- \underset{(-3.7)}{0.000003641}\ v_{K,t-1}\cdot W^S_{t-1}$$

$\bar{R}^2 = 0.39(0.95)$ SE = 25 DW = 1.66

(19) $$\Delta US4^S_t = \underset{(3.5)}{0.05985}\ W^S_{t-1} - \underset{(-2.1)}{0.1079}\ US4^S_{t-1} - \underset{(-4.7)}{1.029}\ US2^S_{t-1} - \underset{(-2.8)}{0.1060}\ E^S_{t-1}$$

$$- \underset{(-5.1)}{0.07766}\ CB^S_{t-1} + \underset{(3.3)}{0.1399}\ r_{4,t}\cdot\Delta W^S_t - \underset{(-2.3)}{0.07305}\ r_{2,t}\cdot\Delta W^S_t$$

$$- \underset{(-2.6)}{0.0003085}\ v_{4,t-1}\cdot\Delta W^S_t + \underset{(4.0)}{0.0001087}\ v_{C,t-1}\cdot\Delta W^S_t$$

$\bar{R}^2 = 0.61(0.99)$ SE = 112 DW = 2.11

---

[55]See footnote 27.

TABLE 5.9

SIMULATION RESULTS FOR 1960:I-1975:IV

Variable	Forecast		Separate Dynamic		Joint Dynamic	
	M.E.	R.M.S.E.	M.E.	R.M.S.E.	M.E.	R.M.S.E.
r_2	-	-	0.01	0.30	-0.01	0.31
r_4	-	-	0.00	0.22	0.00	0.21
$\Delta US2^C$	-2.0	485	3.4	303	5.4	312
$\Delta US4^C$	0.3	101	0.5	125	0.8	127
$\Delta US2^H$	0.0	351	3.3	339	2.7	341
$\Delta US4^H$	0.0	132	-0.3	193	0.1	195
$\Delta US2^L$	-0.1	19	-0.4	24	-0.7	26
$\Delta US4^L$	0.0	35	0.0	37	0.0	38
$\Delta US2^M$	0.0	46	-0.4	49	-0.8	48
$\Delta US4^M$	0.0	47	0.4	49	0.4	48
$\Delta US2^N$	0.0	146	-2.4	187	-3.0	187
$\Delta US2^O$	0.2	52	-0.4	54	-0.5	54
$\Delta US4^O$	0.0	22	-0.1	24	-0.1	24
$\Delta US2^P$	-0.2	42	-0.4	45	0.0	42
$\Delta US4^P$	-0.1	35	-0.1	36	0.2	36
$\Delta US2^{SL}$	0.0	142	-5.1	161	-5.2	161
$\Delta US4^{SL}$	0.0	47	-0.7	56	-1.2	62
$\Delta US2^{SG}$	0.0	174	2.7	168	2.6	168
$\Delta US4^{SG}$	-0.6	95	-0.2	94	0.2	96
$\Delta US2^S$	0.0	24	-0.2	25	-0.5	26
$\Delta US4^S$	-0.4	103	0.4	96	-0.6	109

Notes: r_i in percent, ΔUSi in millions of dollars.
M.E. is the mean error.
R.M.S.E. is the root-mean-square error.

CHAPTER VI

SUMMARY AND CONCLUSIONS

This study has developed a disaggregated structural model of the U.S. Government securities market. The model is disaggregated both in terms of the individual investor groups participating in the U.S. Government securities market, and different maturity classes of U.S. Government securities. The disaggregation of U.S. Government securities into separate maturity classes is in accordance with a scheme devised by the Federal Reserve System. In particular, the total amount of outstanding Treasury issues is divided into four weighted maturity classes.[1] However, this study focuses on only two of these classifications; i.e., short-intermediate-term (2-4 years) and long-term (over 12 years) U.S. Government securities.

The demand side of the U.S. Government securities market is disaggregated into ten investor categories. These consist of commercial banks, households, life insurance companies, mutual savings banks, nonfinancial corporate businesses, other insurance companies, private pension funds, savings and loan associations, state and local government general funds, and state and local government retirement funds. This disaggregation allows the separate influences from the individual investor groups on the determination of the asset yields to become apparent. The total net

---

[1]See Taylor and Wood, <u>op. cit</u>.

supply corresponding to the holdings of these investor groups is taken as exogenous.

The individual asset demand equations are specified in terms of explicit short-run portfolio selection models. These models are formed from the derivations of desired holdings of assets by the individual investor groups, and the applications of portfolio adjustment models that translate desired holdings into actual demands.

The conclusions corresponding to the main areas of this study are summarized below. These areas involve the specifications of the asset demands, models of portfolio adjustment, and the relationship between the two different maturity classes of U.S. Government securities. The final section of this chapter considers areas for future research.

A. The Specification of Asset Demands from the Application of Portfolio Selection Theory

Similar portfolio selection frameworks are applied to all of the investor groups. However, the resultant models differ with respect to the portion of the balance sheet taken as endogenous. For the categories of investors exclusive of depository financial intermediaries, the approximation utilized in the development of the specification for asset demands is similar to those prevalent in the literature.[2] That is, the portfolio selection problem deals with the allocation of a fixed amount of portfolio wealth among financial assets. In addition, a one-period expected utility maximization model is selected to describe the desired holdings of assets for these investor groups.

It is shown, in chapter II, that the expected utility maximization framework incorporates many of the important features of portfolio selection for all of the investor groups considered in the model of the U.S. Government securities market. In particular, in the mean-variance version of the expected utility maximization model, the trade-off between risk and return is explicitly introduced. In addition, this framework is flexible enough to model diverse attitudes toward the risk and return trade-off by varying the parameters and form of the utility function.

Since the portfolio selection theory is ultimately related to specifications of asset demands for empirical analysis, various simplifying assumptions are employed in order to formulate tractable specifications. The mean-variance model is especially important in this respect. Never-

---

[2] e.g., Tobin, "Liquidity Preference as Behavior Toward Risk," op. cit.

theless, it incorporates at least some additional variables, i.e., variances and covariances of asset holding-period yields, into the usual empirical specifications of asset demands. Thus, the primary focus is on the mean-variance expected utility maximization model of portfolio selection.

The properties of asset demands derived from mean-variance expected utility maximization have not been thoroughly investigated in previous research. The exception to this occurs for certain specific utility functions and distributions of asset holding-period yields.[3] Thus, the asset demands derived from mean-variance expected utility maximization are considered for the general case in chapter III.

As the analysis in chapter III indicates, the characteristics of the framework in terms of the functional form of utility, the argument of the utility function, and the assumption concerning the existence of a riskless asset are all important in determining the resultant comparative statics properties of asset demands. In particular, it is shown that commonly used specifications of expected utility of end-of-period wealth imply that a bliss exists in the all-risky assets case. This bliss point is defined in terms of the highest level of expected utility conditional on the union of the sets of attainable portfolios obtained by varying the level initial wealth. This bliss point may be generally avoided by specifying the argument of the utility function in terms of portfolio rate of return, or by including the property of con-

---

[3]For the case of negative exponential utility and joint normally distributed asset holding-period yields, see Melton, op. cit.; and Parkin, op. cit.

stant relative risk aversion for the end-of-period wealth case.

A necessary and sufficient condition for a symmetric coefficient matrix on the vector of expected holding-period yields is also introduced in chapter III. Furthermore, this result is related to risk aversion, with the following result derived therein: the vector of asset demands has a symmetric coefficient matrix on the vector of expected holding-period yields if, and only if, the investor has constant absolute mean-variance risk aversion with respect to the mean and variance of the argument of the utility function.

The hypothesis corresponding to the symmetry property is empirically investigated in chapter V. It is found, for the investor groups subjected to this test, that in only one-half of the cases the null hypothesis concerning the imposition of the symmetry constraint could not be rejected at the 10% level of significance.[4]

The modeling of the depository financial intermediaries, with primary focus on commercial banks, is considered separately in chapter IV. This is primarily due to the special importance of both sides of the balance sheet in their portfolio selection problems. The specifications for desired asset holdings are based on expected utility maximization frameworks similar to those in chapters II and III. However, for these investor groups, additional assumptions concerning the endogeneity of certain categories of assets are utilized. The effects of exogenous categories of assets and liabilities are included in the portfolio adjustment model by

[4]See section V.C.5 for the details of this test.

disaggregating the portfolio wealth flow in terms of the exogenous balance sheet items. This approach is necessitated due to the complexity of the portfolio selection problem of depository financial intermediairies. This approach results in empirical specifications that appear to be much more reasonable than previous attempts at the empirical modeling of these investor groups.[5]

---

[5]See, for example, Bosworth and Duesenberry, op. cit.; Goldfeld, op. cit.; and Silber, "Portfolio Substitutability, Regulations, and Monetary Policy," op. cit.; and compare their empirical results to those in section V.C.

Also see the discussion in section IV.F.

B. Portfolio Adjustment Models

The portfolio selection theory in chapters II and III is in terms of desired holdings of assets. However, there may not be instantaneous adjustment to desired holdings of assets because of transactions costs. Thus, models of portfolio adjustment are introduced in chapter V that transform desired holdings of assets into actual asset demands.

Furthermore, a linearization is performed on expressions of desired asset holdings for purposes of empirical implementation. This linearization is done with respect to expected holding-period yields and variances of holding-period yields. The resultant expression, presented in chapter V, is used in the applications of the portfolio adjustment models.

The most general portfolio adjustment model is formulated for the short-run portfolio selection problem of commercial banks. It includes the following properties that are additional to the simple stock adjustment model:

(1) new investable financial flows have separate effects on portfolio adjustment;

(2) effects from new investable financial flows are dependent on the holding-period yields of the endogenous assets in the portfolio;

(3) new investable financial flows affect the reallocation of existing assets in the portfolio;

(4) positive and negative new investable financial flows have asymmetric effects; and

(5) new investable financial flows are disaggregated in terms of

exogenous balance sheet items.

The portfolio adjustment models that are applied to the remaining investor groups contain subsets of these properties.

The "optimal marginal adjustment" model,[6] which includes properties (1) and (2), is applied to four investor groups. In addition, a slight modification of this model that incorporates asymmetric effects from positive and negative new investable financial flows (property (4)) is used for two other investor groups. These models are especially advantageous in that the parameters from expressions of desired asset holdings are identified in the specifications used for empirical analysis.

The particular adjustment model selected for each individual investor group is based on preliminary experimentation using ordinary least squares estimation.

---

[6]This model is introduced in Friedman, "A Structural Model of the Long-Term Corporate Debt Market," op. cit.

C. The Relationship between the Two Maturity Classes of U.S. Government Securities

The relationship between the two maturity classes of U.S. Government securities is investigated in two specific areas in chapter V. First, a comparison is made between the estimated structural equations within individual investor categories. Secondly, the relationship between the respective yields is investigated on the basis of their joint determination in the structural market-clearing framework.

The results in chapter V indicate that the two maturity classes of U.S. Government securities appear to be far from perfect substitutes. In particular, when identical right-hand side variables were included in the two demand equations within each investor category, the statistical fits of the resultant estimated equations were substantially less than those for the independent specifications. The inclusion of similar sets of right-hand side variables, along with comparable coefficient estimates, would indicate a relatively high degree of substitutability between the maturity classes.

The short-run determination of the yields on short-intermediate-term and long-term U.S. Government securities is also considered in chapter V. These yields are determined in a framework that utilizes the estimated structural demand equations, along with two market-clearing identities. This approach may be contrasted to the reduced form term structure approach by noting that the difference, at the methodological level, is essentially that of restricted versus unrestricted estimation. That is, the structural model of the U.S. Government securities market has implicit reduced form equations for the endogenous yields, but these reduced form equations are constrained by the underlying structural demand equations.

The joint determination of the endogenous asset demands and the two endogenous yields is accomplished by the dynamic simulation of the structural model. The simulation is performed for the period beginning in 1960:I and ending in 1975:IV. For the yields, the root-mean-square errors are thirty-four basis points and twenty basis points for the short-intermediate-term and long-term maturity classes, respectively. Thus, as expected, this measure is higher for the yield on short-intermediate-term securities due to the greater volatility of short-term yields. However, the magnitudes of these values indicate that the structural modeling methodology is capable of a high degree of accuracy.

The issue concerning the effects of relative asset supplies is also briefly examined in the context of the joint determination of the two endogenous yields. The particular simulation experiment performed, in chapter V, involves an increase in the total supply of short-intermediate-term U.S. Government securities throughout the sample period. This resulted in an increase of both yields, with the increase of the long-term yield being approximately one-seventh as large. Thus, it appears that cross-maturity effects are influential in the joint determination of market yields. However, the resultant effects are not sufficiently large to conform with the term structure theory described by the "expectations hypothesis".

D. Areas for Future Research

Several areas related to this study are appropriate topics for future research. A primary area for future investigation involves the modeling of the markets for short-term (within 1 year) and long-intermediate-term (6-8 years) U.S. Government securities. The inclusion of these maturity classes would directly facilitate the analysis of possible relative asset supply effects on different maturity classes of U.S. Government securities.

Additional experimentation may also be desirable in the modeling of expected holding-period yields. This study has implicitly assumed unitary expectations, whereas approaches involving rational or autoregressive expectations may be more appropriate.[7]

Finally, with the inclusion of the two remaining maturity classes, the model may be further exploited in simulation experiments. In particular, partial equilibrium analyses of alternative debt management policies, and structural shifts involving reform or behavioral changes, may be further investigated in this framework.

---

[7]For a comparison of these alternative approaches in the context of a structural model of the long-term corporate debt market, see Friedman and Roley, "Investors' Portfolio Behavior under Alternative Models of Long-Term Interest Rate Expectations: Unitary, Rational, or Autoregressive," op. cit.

BIBLIOGRAPHY

Adler, Michael, "On the Risk-Return Trade-Off in the Valuation of Assets," Journal of Financial and Quantitiative Analysis, IV (December, 1969), 493-512.

Aigner, Dennis J., "On Estimation of an Econometric Model of Short-Run Bank Behavior," Journal of Econometrics, I (May, 1973), 201-228.

____________ and William R. Bryan, "A Model of Short-Run Bank Behavior," Quarterly Journal of Economics, LXXXV (February, 1971), 97-118.

Anderson, Leonall C. and Albert E. Burger, "Asset Management and Commercial Bank Portfolio Behavior: Theory and Practice," Journal of Finance, XXIV (May, 1969), 207-222.

Arrow, Kenneth J., Aspects of the Theory of Risk-Bearing (Helsinki: The Yrjö Jahsson Foundation, 1965).

____________, Essays in the Theory of Risk-Bearing (Chicago: Markham Publishing Company, 1971).

____________, "Unbounded Utility Functions in Expected Utility Maximization: Response," Quarterly Journal of Economics, LXXXVIII (February, 1974), 136-138.

Auerbach, Irving, "United States Treasury Cash Balances and the Control of Member Bank Reserves," in Commission on Money and Credit, Fiscal and Debt Management Policies (Englewood Cliffs: Prentice-Hall, Inc., 1963), pp. 311-398.

Benston, George J., "Economies of Scale in Financial Institutions," Journal of Money, Credit and Banking, IV (May, 1972), 312-341.

Bierderman, Kenneth R. and John A. Tuccillo, Taxation and Regulation of the Savings and Loan Industry (Lexington: D. C. Heath and Company, 1976).

Bierwag, G. O. and M. A. Grove, "Indifference Curves in Asset Analysis," Economic Journal, LXXVI (June, 1966), 337-343.

__________________________, "Slutsky Equations for Assets," Journal of Political Economy, LXXVI (January/February, 1968), 114-127.

Board of Governors of the Federal Reserve System, Flow of Funds Accounts 1946-1975 (Washington, 1976).

Borch, K. "A Note on Uncertainty and Indifference Curves," Review of Economic Studies, XXXVI (January, 1969), 1-4.

Bosworth, Barry, and James S. Duesenberry, "A Flow of Funds Model and its Implications," in Federal Reserve Bank of Boston, Issues in Federal Debt Management (Boston: Federal Reserve Bank of Boston, 1973), pp. 39-149.

Bradley, Stephen P., and Dwight B. Crane, "A Dynamic Model for Bond Portfolio Management," Management Science, XIX (October, 1972, 139-151.

Brainard, William C., and James Tobin, "Pitfalls in Financial Model-Building," American Economic Review, LXVIII (May, 1968), 99-122.

Brundy, James M., and Dale W. Jorgenson, "Consistent and Efficient Estimation of Systems of Simultaneous Equations by Means of Instrumental Variables," in Zarembka (ed.), Frontiers in Econometrics (New York: Academic Press, 1974), pp. 215-244.

Bryan, William R., and Willard T. Carleton, "Short-Run Adjustments of an Individual Bank," Econometrica, XXXV (April, 1967), 321-347.

Cargill, T. F., "The Term-Structure of Interest Rates: A Test of the Expectations Hypothesis," Journal of Finance, XXV (June, 1975), 761-809.

Carson, Deane, and Ira O. Scott, "Commercial Bank Attributes and Aversion to Risk," in Carson (ed.), Banking and Monetary Studies (Homewood: Irwin, 1963), pp. 420-433.

Chambers, D., and A. Charnes, "Inter-Temporal Analysis and Optimization of Bank Portfolios," Management Science, VII (July, 1961), 393-410.

Chase, Sam B., "Bank Reactions to Securities Losses," in Cawthorne, et al., (eds.), Essays on Commercial Banking (Kansas City: Federal Reserve Bank of Kansas City, 1962), pp. 87-98.

Christ, Carl F., "A Simple Macroeconomic Model with a Government Budget Constraint," Journal of Political Economy, LXXVI (January/ February, 1968), 53-67.

Clinton, Kevin, "Pitfalls in Financial Model Building: Comment," American Economic Review, LXIII (December, 1973), 1003-1004.

Cohen, Kalman J., and Frederick S. Hammer, "Linear Programming and Optimal Bank Asset Management Decisions," Journal of Finance, XXII (May, 1967), 147-165.

Crane, Dwight B., "A Stochastic Programming Model for Commercial Bank Bond Portfolio Portfolio Management," Journal of Financial and Quantitative Analysis, VI (June, 1971), 955-976.

Culbertson, J. M., "The Term Structure of Interest Rates," Quarterly Journal of Economics, LXXI (November, 1957), 485-517.

DeGroot, Morris, Optimal Statistical Decisions (New York: McGraw-Hill, 1970).

Diamond, Peter A., and Joseph E. Stiglitz, "Increases in Risk and Risk Aversion," Journal of Economic Theory, VIII (July, 1974), 337-360.

Dobson, Steven W., Richard C. Sutch, and David E. Vanderford, "An Evaluation of Alternative Empirical Models of the Term Structure of Interest Rates, Journal of Finance, XXVI (September, 1976), 1035-1066.

Duesenberry, James S., "The Portfolio Approach to the Demand for Money and Other Assets," Review of Economics and Statistics, XLV (February, 1963), 9-31.

Elliott, J. W., and M. E. Echols, "Market Segmentation, Speculative Behavior, and the Term Structure of Interest Rates," Review of Economics and Statistics, LVIII (February, 1976), 40-47.

Fama, Eugene F., "Multiperiod Consumption-Investment Decisions," American Economic Review, LX (March, 1970), 163-174.

Feldstein, Martin S., "Mean-Variance Analysis in the Theory of Liquidity Preference and Portfolio Selection," Review of Economic Studies, XXXVI (January, 1969), 5-12.

____________, and Gary Chamberlain, "Multimarket Expectations and the Rate of Interest," Journal of Money, Credit and Banking, V (November, 1973), 873-902.

____________, and Otto Eckstein, "The Fundamental Determinants of the Interest Rate," Review of Economics and Statistics, LII (November, 1970), 363-375.

Fisher, Franklin M., "Tests of Equality Between Sets of Coefficients in Two Linear Regressions: An Expository Note," Econometrica, XXXVIII (March, 1970), 361-367.

Fortune, Peter, A Constrained Econometric Analysis of Household Sector Liquid Asset Allocation (Boston: Federal Reserve Bank of Boston, 1972).

Friedman, Benjamin M., "Credit Rationing: A Review", Mimeo, Board of Governors of the Federal Reserve System, 1972.

____________, "A Structural Model of the Long-Term Corporate Debt Market," Mimeo, Harvard University, 1974.

___________, "Financial Flow Variables and the Short-Run Determination of Long-Term Interest Rates," Mimeo, Harvard University, 1975.

___________, and V. Vance Roley, "Investors' Portfolio Behavior under Alternative Models of Long-Term Interest Rate Expectations: Unitary Rational, or Autoregressive," Mimeo, Harvard University, 1977.

Goldfeld, Stephen M., Commercial Bank Behavior and Economic Activity (Amsterdam: North-Holland Publishing Company, 1966).

___________, and Dwight M. Jaffee, "The Determinants of Deposit-Rate Setting by Savings and Loan Associations," Journal of Finance, XXV (June, 1970), 615-632.

Goldsmith, David, "Transactions Costs and the Theory of Portfolio Selection," Journal of Finance, XXXI (September, 1976), 1127-1139.

Gramley, Lyle E., "Interest Rates and Credit Availability at Commercial Banks," in Cawthorne, et al., (eds.), Essays on Commercial Banking (Kansas City: Federal Reserve Bank of Kansas City, 1962), pp. 77-86.

Gressis, Nicolas, and William A. Remaley, "Comment: 'Safety First-An Expected Utility Principle," Journal of Financial and Quantitative Analysis, IX (December, 1974), 1057-1061.

Hakansson, Nils H., "Multiperiod Mean-Variance Analysis: Toward a General Theory of Portfolio Choice," Journal of Finance, XXVI (September, 1971), 857-884.

Hamburger, Michael J., "The Demand for Money by Households, Money Substitutes, and Monetary Policy," Journal of Political Economy, LXXIV (December, 1966), 600-623.

___________, "Household Demand for Financial Assets," Econometrica, XXXVI (January, 1968), 97-118.

Hart, Oliver D., and Dwight M. Jaffee, "On the Application of Portfolio Theory to Depository Financial Intermediaries," Review of Economic Studies, XLI (January, 1974), 129-147.

Henderson, James M., and Richard E. Quandt, Microeconomic Theory: A Mathematical Approach (New York: McGraw-Hill, 1971).

Hestor, Donald D., and James L. Pierce, Bank Management and Portfolio Behavior (New Haven: Yale University Press, 1975).

Hicks, J. R., Value and Capital (London: Oxford University Press, 1946).

Hodgman, Donald R., "The Deposit Relationship and Commercial Bank Investment Behavior," Review of Economics and Statistics, XLII (August, 1961), 257-268.

Jones-Lee, M. W., "Some Portfolio Adjustment Theorems for the Case of Non-Negativity Constraints on Security Holdings," Journal of Finance, XXVI (June, 1971), 763-775.

Kane, Edward J., "Is there a Predilected Lock-in Effect?," National Tax Journal, XXI (December, 1968), 365-385.

____________, and Burton G. Malkiel, "Bank Portfolio Allocation, Deposit Variability, and the Availability Doctrine," Quarterly Journal of Economics, LXXIX (May, 1965), 113-134.

Kataoka, Shinji, "A Stochastic Programming Model," Econometrica, XXXI (January/April, 1963), 181-196.

Klein, Michael A., "Imperfect Asset Elasticity and Portfolio Theory," American Economic Review, LX (June, 1970), 491-494.

Ladenson, Mark L., "Pitfalls in Financial Model Building: Some Extensions," American Economic Review, LXI (March, 1971), 179-186.

Leijonhufvud, Axel, On Keynesian Economics and the Economics of Keynes (New York: Oxford University Press, 1968).

Levy, Haim, and Marshall Sarnat, "Safety First -- An Expected Utility Principle," Journal of Financial and Quantitative Analysis, VII (June, 1972), 1827-1834.

____________________, "Reply: 'Safety First - An Expected Utility Principle," Journal of Financial and Quantitative Analysis, IX (December, 1974), 1063-1064.

Lintner, John, "The Valuation of Risk Assets and the Selection of Risky Investments in Stock Portfolios and Capital Budgets," Review of Economics and Statistics, XLVII (February, 1965), 13-37.

__________, "The Aggregation of Investors' Diverse Judgments and Preferences in Purely Competitive Security Markets," Journal of Financial and Quantitative Analysis, IV (December, 1969), 347-400.

__________, "The Impact of Uncertainty on the 'Traditional' Theory of the Firm," in J. W. Markham and G. F. Papanek (eds.), Industrial Organization and Economic Development: In Honor of E. S. Mason (Boston: Houghton Mifflin, 1970), pp. 238-265.

__________, "The Effect of Short Selling and Margin Requirements in Perfect Capital Markets," Journal of Financial and Quantitative Analysis, VI (December, 1971), 1173-1195.

__________, "The Lognormality of Security Returns, Portfolio Selection and Market Equilibrium," Mimeo, Harvard University, undated.

Luckett, Dudley G., "Compensatory Cyclical Bank Asset Adjustments," Journal of Finance, XVII (March, 1962), 53-62.

__________, "Credit Standards and Tight Money," Journal of Money, Credit and Banking, II (November, 1970), 420-434.

Lutz, Frederich A., "The Structure of Interest Rates," Quarterly Journal of Economics, LIV (November, 1940), 36-63.

McGouldrick, Paul F., and John E. Petersen, "Monetary Restraint and Borrowing and Capital Spending by State and Local Governments in 1966," in Gibson and Kaufman (eds.), Monetary Economics: Readings on Current Issues (New York: McGraw-Hill, 1971), 474-482.

Maddala, G. S., and Robert C. Vogel, "Estimating Lagged Relationships in Corporate Demand for Liquid Assets," Review of Economics and Statistics, LI (February, 1969), 53-61.

Malkiel, Burton G., "The Term Structure of Interest Rates," American Economic Review, LIV (May, 1964), 532-543.

Markowitz, Harry, "Portfolio Selection," Journal of Finance, VII (March, 1952), 77-91.

Meiselman, David, The Term Structure of Interest Rates (Englewood Cliffs: Prentice-Hall, 1962).

Melton, William C., Simultaneous Restricted Estimation of a New Model of Commercial Bank Portfolio Behavior: Estimates for Swedish Commercial Banks, unpublished Ph.D. dissertation, Harvard University, 1976.

Menezes, C. F. and D. L. Hanson, "On the Theory of Risk Aversion," International Economic Review, II (October, 1970), 481-487.

Merton, Robert C., and Paul A. Samuelson, "Fallacy of the Log-Normal Approximation to Optimal Portfolio Decision Making Over Many Periods," Journal of Financial Economics, I (May, 1974), 67-94.

Michaelson, Jacob B., and Robert C. Goshay, "Portfolio Selection in Financial Intermediaries: A New Approach," Journal of Financial and Quantitative Analysis, II (June, 1967), 166-199.

Miller, Stephen M., "Measures of Risk Aversion: Some Clarifying Comments," Journal of Financial and Quantitative Analysis, X (June, 1975), 299-309.

Modigliani, Franco, "The Dynamics of Portfolio Adjustment and the Flow of Savings through Financial Intermediaries," in Gramlich and Jaffee (eds.), Savings Deposits, Mortgages, and Housing (Lexington: D.C. Heath and Company, 1972), pp. 63-102.

___________, and Robert J. Shiller, "Inflation, Rational Expectations, and the Term Structure of Interest Rates," Economica, XL (February, 1973), 12-43.

___________, and Richard Sutch, "Innovations in Interest Rate Policy," American Economic Review, LVI (May, 1966), 178-197.

Mossin, Jan, "Optimal Multiperiod Portfolio Policies," Journal of Business, XLI (April, 1968), 215-229.

Neumann, J. von, and O. Morgenstern, Theory of Games and Economic Behavior (Princeton: Princeton University Press, 1947).

Parkin, Michael, "Discount House Portfolio and Debt Selection," Review of Economic Studies, XXXVII (October, 1970), 469-497.

Pierce, James L., "The Monetary Mechanism: Some Partial Relationships," American Economic Review, LIV (May, 1964), 523-531.

Pogue, G. A., "An Extension of the Markowitz Portfolio Selection Model to Include Variable Transactions Costs, Short Sales, Leverage Policies, and Taxes," Journal of Finance, XXV (December, 1970), 1-23.

Porter, Richard C., "A Model of Bank Portfolio Selection," in Donald D. Hestor, and James Tobin, (eds.), Financial Markets and Economic Activity (New Haven: Yale University Press, 1967), pp. 12-54.

Pratt, John W., "Risk Aversion in the Small and in the Large," Econometrica, XXXII (January/April, 1964), 122-136.

Pringle, John J., "The Imperfect-Markets Model of Commercial Bank Financial Management," Journal of Financial and Quantitative Analysis, IX (January, 1974), 69-87.

___________, "The Capital Decision in Commercial Banks," Journal of Finance, XXIV (June, 1974), 779-795.

Pyle, David H., "On the Theory of Financial Intermediation," Journal of Finance, XXVI (June, 1971), 737-746.

___________, "Descriptive Theories of Financial Institutions Under Uncertainty," Journal of Financial and Quantitative Analysis, VII (December, 1972), 2009-2029.

___________, and Stephen J. Turnovsky, "Safety-First and Expected Utility

Maximization in Mean-Standard Deviation Portfolio Analysis," Review of Economics and Statistics, LII (February, 1970), 75-81.

__________, "Risk Aversion in Chance Constrained Portfolio Selection," Management Science, XXVIII (November, 1971), 218-225.

Roosa, Robert V., "Interest Rates and the Central Bank," in Money, Trade, and Economic Growth. Essays in Honor of John H. Williams (New York: The Macmillan Company, 1951), pp. 270-295.

Roy, A. D., "Safety First and the Holding of Assets," Econometrica, XX (July, 1952), 431-449.

Rubenstein, M. E., "The Fundamental Theorem of Parameter-Preference Security Valuation,"Journal of Financial and Quantative Analysis, VIII (January, 1973), 61-69.

__________, "A Comparative Statics Analysis of Risk Premiums," Journal of Business, XLVI (October, 1973), 605-615.

Russell, William R., "Commercial Bank Portfolio Adjustments," American Economic Review, LIV (May, 1964), 544-553.

Ryan, Terence M., "Unbounded Utility Functions in Expected Utility Maximization: Comment," Quarterly Journal of Economics, LXXXVIII (February, 1974), 133-135.

Saito, Mitsuo, "Household Flow-of-Fund Equations: Specification and Estimation," Journal of Money, Credit and Banking, IX (February, 1977), 1-20.

Samuelson, Paul A., Foundations of Economic Analysis (New York: Atheneum, 1972).

__________, "Lifetime Portfolio Selection by Dynamic Stochastic Programming," Review of Economics and Statistics, LI (August, 1969), 239-246.

__________, "The Fundamental Approximation Theorem of Portfolio Analysis in Terms of Means, Variances, and Higher Moments," Review of Economic Studies, XXXVII (October, 1970), 537-542.

Scott, Ira O., "The Availability Doctrine: Theoretical Underpinnings," Review of Economic Studies, XXV (October, 1957), 41-48.

__________, The Government Securities Market (New York: McGraw-Hill, 1965).

Sharpe, William F., "Capital Asset Prices: A Theory of Market Equilibrium under Conditions of Risk," Journal of Finance, XIX (September, 1964), 425-442.

Silber, William L., "Portfolio Substitutability, Regulations, and Monetary Policy," Quarterly Journal of Economics, LXXXIII (May, 1969) 197-219.

__________, "Fiscal Policy in IS-LM Analysis: A Correction," Journal of Money, Credit and Banking, II (November, 1970), 461-472.

Smith, Gary, "Pitfalls in Financial Model Building: A Clarification," American Economic Review, LXV (June, 1975), 510-516.

Stiglitz, Joseph E., "The Effects of Income, Wealth, and Capital Gains Taxation on Risk-Taking," Quarterly Journal of Economics, LXXXIII (May, 1969), 263-283.

Taylor, Stephen P., and John Wood, "Federal Debt by Weighted Maturity Classes for Use in Flow-of-Funds Accounts," Mimeo, Board of Governors of the Federal Reserve System, 1963.

Telser, Lester G., "Safety-First and Hedging," Review of Economic Studies, XXIII (1955-1956), 1-16.

Theil, Henri, Principles of Econometrics (New York: John Wiley & Sons, 1971).

Tobin, James, "Liquidity Preference as Behavior Toward Risk," Review of Economic Studies, XXV (February, 1958), 65-86.

__________, "Comment on Borch and Feldstein," Review of Economic Studies, XXXVI (January, 1969), 13-14.

Van Deventer, Donald R., "Transactions Costs, Portfolio Selection, and the Existence of Financial Intermediaries," Mimeo, Harvard University, 1976.

__________, "Optimal Commercial Bank Liquidity and Portfolio Policy," Mimeo, Harvard University, 1977.

Wolf, Charles R., "A Model for Selecting Commercial Bank Government Security Portfolios," Review of Economics and Statistics, LI (February, 1969), 40-52.

__________, "Regulation F and the Yield Structure of the U.S. Government Securities Market," Journal of Money, Credit and Banking, II (February, 1970), 112-122.

__________, "Bank Preferences and Government Security Yields," Quarterly Journal of Economics, LXXXV (May, 1971), 283-303.

Wood, John H., Commercial Bank Loan and Investment Behavior (New York: John Wiley & Sons, 1975).

Zeckhauser, Richard R., and Emmett E. Keeler, "Another Type of Risk Aversion," Econometrica, XXXVIII (September, 1970), 661-665.